I0828427

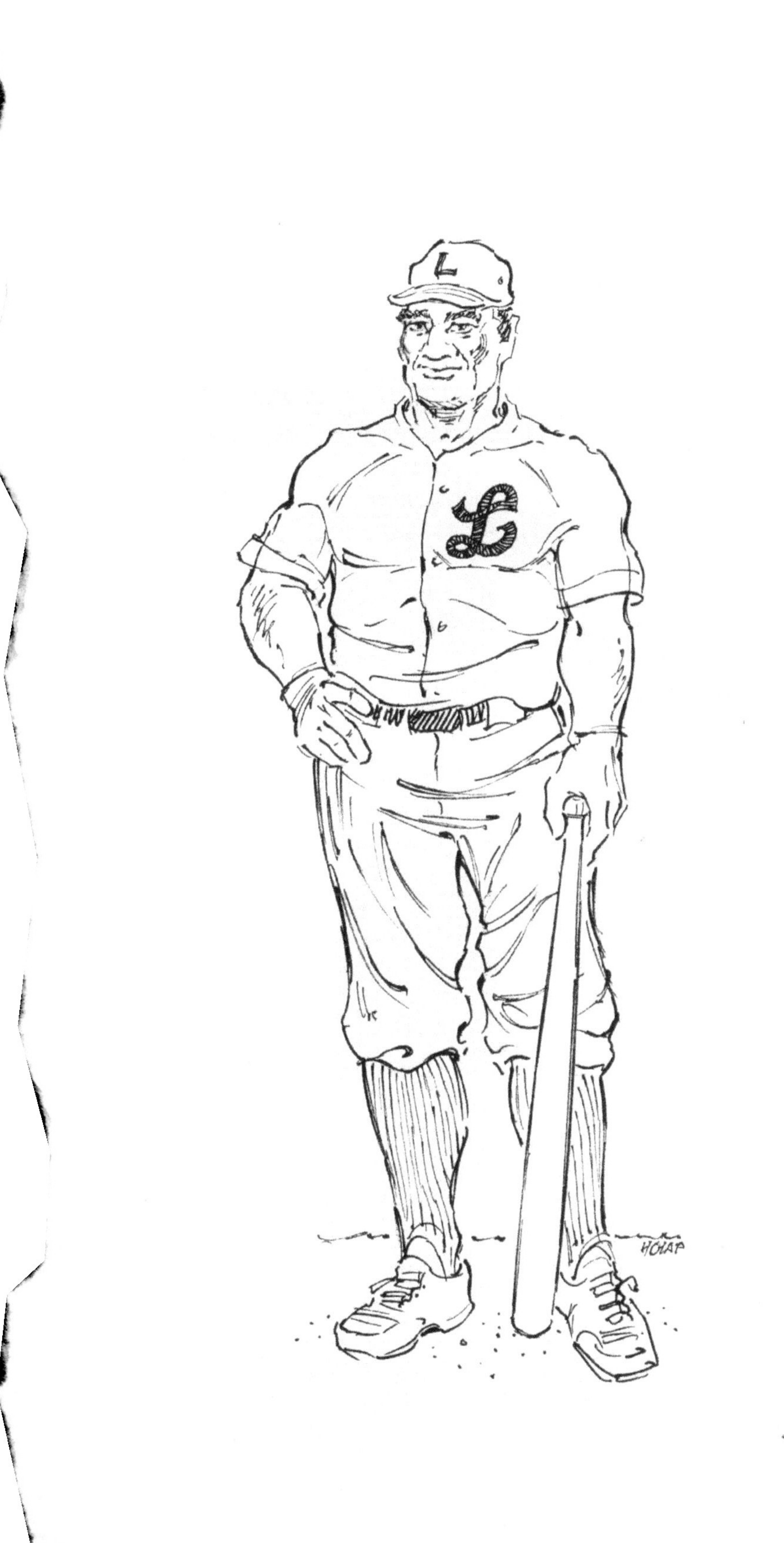
L
L

PHILIP VON BORRIES

Published by The History Press
Charleston, SC 29403
www.historypress.net



*Front cover*: *Top, left to right*: Guy Hecker, Red Ehret, William Wolf, Gus Weyhing. *Bottom*: 1916 Louisville American Association Colonels. *Overlapping*: Tony Mullane. *All pictures courtesy of the National Baseball Hall of Fame Library, Cooperstown New York.*

*Back cover*: *Top*: Earle Combs (left), Carl Mays (right). *Courtesy of the National Baseball Hall of Fame Library, Cooperstown, New York. Bottom, left*: Carlton Fisk. *Courtesy of the Boston Red Sox. Bottom, right*: Pete Browning. *Courtesy of the National Baseball Hall of Fame Library, Cooperstown, New York.*

*First page*: Sketch of an old-time Louisville minor-leaguer based on 1920s Louisville Colonels star Joe Guyon. *Eclipse BBHR.*

First published 2010

ISBN 978-1-5402-0485-1

Library of Congress Cataloging-in-Publication Data

Von Borries, Philip, 1947-
The Louisville baseball almanac / Philip Von Borries.
p. cm.
Includes bibliographical references and index.
ISBN 978-1-5402-0485-1
1. Baseball--Kentucky--Louisville--History. I. Title.
GV863.K46L 68 2010
796.35709769'44--dc22
2010019894

*Notice*: The information in this book is true and complete to the best of our knowledge. It is offered without guarantee on the part of the author or The History Press. The author and The History Press disclaim all liability in connection with the use of this book.

# Contents

# YESTERYEAR

*Most of the* [Pittsburgh] *Pirates were busy yesterday morning selecting "wagon tongues" at Hillerich's bat factory thirty minutes after the team stepped from the Illinois Central train.*

—Louisville Courier-Journal, *Tuesday, April 3, 1900*

*Second-baseman Homer C. Hausen's recent fight on the diamond here with Catcher Bill Wilson of Omaha cost him his position on the Sioux City* [Iowa] *nine, but won him a wife. It was in defense of his sweetheart's reputation that he struck Wilson a terrific blow over the head with a baseball bat. His friends sympathized with him, but agreed that the time and place for action were ill chosen. President Hickey, of the Western League, was so sure of it that he blacklisted him.*

*Mrs. Jessie Pierce, of Kansas City, didn't take this view of the case. She only knew that the blow had been struck in her defense, and respected her athletic lover the more for his ardor. Last morning, she arrived here, and not many minutes later, Rev. Robert Bagnell, of the First Methodist Church, had pronounced them husband and wife.*

—Louisville Courier-Journal, *Tuesday, July 24, 1900*

*A few years ago at Maysville, Ky., the Reds lost an exhibition game under remarkable circumstances. The local team was at bat in the ninth inning, with one man on base and two runs needed to win.*

*There were two out when the batsman tore off a swat that would ordinarily have been good for two bases, but the ball, rolled into a peach can in left field and stuck there. Being unable to extricate the ball, the left fielder relayed the can and contents to the shortstop, who passed it to the third baseman.*

*Meanwhile, a run had scored from second base, and the batsman, seeing the can headed his way, kept on coming. He was half way between third and home when the third baseman threw the canned ball to the catcher, and that player tagged the runner twenty feet from the plate.*

*The Reds naturally contended that the man was out, while the umpire held that he was simply touched with the tin can and not with the ball. Therefore, the run counted.*

—Louisville Courier-Journal, *Friday, September 14, 1900*

*"Louisville seems to me the most demoralizing city in the major league, and in that belief, I am sustained by certain players who have been on Louisville contracts off and on the past ten years," says* [Nap] *Lajoie.*

*"It's Kentucky hospitality, with the latchstring nodding in the wind on the outside, and the decanter ever ready for the invitation on the sideboard.*

*"McGee* [Bill Magee], *Pitcher Pete Dowling and old Gus Weyhing are among the players on the Louisville teams of past seasons, who fell for Kentucky hospitality, in their effort to retain their membership in the Kentucky order of good fellowship. Barney Dreyfuss was glad to transfer some of his most promising players from Louisville to Pittsburgh, especially Rube Waddell, who is inclined to be a deucedly sporty boy, a devil of a fellow, as Bertie says in the play."*

—Louisville Courier-Journal, *Wednesday, February 21, 1900*

*Heavyweight champion James J. Jeffries umpired a match between the Nicelys and the Porzigs on Sunday, June 10, 1900 in Louisville. The Porzigs won 11–4, with the* Courier-Journal *commenting the next day that "Jeffries Is A Good Umpire."*

*Some 2,000 fans attended the game held at League Park* [the city's third major-league park, also known as Eclipse Park II, located at Twenty-eighth and Broadway].

*James Jackson Jeffries* [1875–1953] *was this country's heavyweight champion from 1899 to 1905, when he retired undefeated. He made an unsuccessful comeback against Jack Johnson in 1910.*

—Louisville Courier-Journal, *Monday, June 11, 1900*

*The* Louisville Courier-Journal *carries this fascinating "pickup" from the neighboring* Shelbyville Sentinel*: that on August 14, 1867, one of the first baseball games ever played in Kentucky saw a Lawrenceburg club best the Shelby Baseball Club of Hardsinville* [Kentucky] *140–41.*

*The score is no typo, and neither are the following stats. Lawrenceburg had 14 home runs (the Shelbys had three). There were also 31 passed balls in the game, 19 of them by the Shelbys. A scorekeeper's nightmare all the way to say the least.*

—Louisville Courier-Journal, *Sunday, August 5, 1900*

*While on their way to St. Paul yesterday afternoon, the train on which the Colonels were traveling was wrecked near Lafayette, Ind. The engineer and fireman of the train were killed and six passengers were severely injured. None of the Louisville players was hurt, but received a severe shaking-up. The wreck was caused by an open switch, and the train was running at a high rate of speed.*

*The mail and baggage cars were completely wrecked and four passenger coaches were thrown from their trucks and dashed 100 feet ahead of the engine, which buckled. The parlor car at the rear of the train did not leave the track. Almost every passenger was either cut by flying glass or bruised. Several narrowly escaped death.*

*Immediately after being able to leave their car, the players rushed into the work of getting the unfortunate passengers out of the wreck. Outfielder* [Dan] *Kerwin, shortstop* [Larry] *Quinlan and Pitcher* [Ed] *Kenna did heroic work, and greatly aided the rescuers in alleviating the suffering of the injured passengers.*

—Louisville Evening Post, *Tuesday, May 16, 1905*

NOTE: This was not their season. In late August, a Kansas City, Missouri trolley accident injured seven players and the team secretary. The most seriously injured was one of the train wreck heroes, Ed Kenna, whose career ended prematurely because of the Kansas City accident.

*August Weyhing, whose home is at 1207 Rufer Avenue, but who, last season, pitched for the Athletic baseball club, of Philadelphia* [American Association], *and has lately signed with the Philadelphias* [Phillies of the National League] *for the coming season, was arrested last evening, charged with the theft of two valuable pigeons from the exhibit at the pigeon show of A.A. Heroux, of Toronto. He was locked up in the county jail, where the charge of grand larceny was preferred against him, under the name of William Joyce.*

*Weyhing is a pigeon fancier as well as a mighty ball-tosser, and while at his home here devotes a great deal of his time to the breeding and rearing of pigeons of the fancy varieties. He entered eight of his birds for competition at the exhibit of the Louisville and American Columbian Associations. Last night closed the pigeon show, and Weyhing placed his pigeons in a covered basket made for their transportation.*

*He did not at once leave Liederkrantz Hall, where the show had been held. When A.A. Heroux had taken all his birds from the compartments in which his stock had been shown, two very fine Blondinettes, valued at $50 each, were missing. Another count of the birds was made, as it was feared the pair might have been missed in the checking up made, as the birds are placed in the baskets. They were again missing, and a search of the cages and the room was at once made, as the owner of the birds supposed the birds had been stolen by some of the other exhibiters.*

*Weyhing, just about this time, started from the place.*

*As each owner takes his feathered stock away, his baskets are examined, and the pigeons are checked off on the entry book, as their numbers are called from the tags on their legs. When this was done in Weyhing's case, two extra birds were found. He was asked for an explanation, which he could not give, saying he did not know in what manner the pair of Blondinettes happened to be in his basket.*

*When it came to the knowledge of Heroux that his birds had been found in Weyhing's basket, he at once charged him with their theft. Patrol wagon No. 2 was called and Wagon Guards Dooling and Robenaker placed Weyhing under arrest. At the jail, he gave his name as William Joyce. He denies any knowledge as to how the pigeons came to be in his basket, and says his arrest was a very unjust one.*

—Louisville Courier-Journal, *Tuesday, January 26, 1892*

NOTE: How Weyhing resolved the case is not known. However, he did pitch the entire season for the Phillies that year, going 32-21 for the National League's fourth-place finisher. Weyhing, 264-232 lifetime, worked in four different leagues between 1887 and 1901 and holds the major-league record for hit batsman (277).

[Outfielder William "Farmer"] *Weaver created quite a sensation in right field yesterday in an appropriate manner. He is the possessor of a horse pistol that rivals the famous weapon of "Fighting Bob." He loaded the cylinder to the brim before the game yesterday, and placed the weapon in his sliding pad. Someone knocked a high fly into his territory. Weaver ran under it, steadied himself and pulled the pocket cannon from his trousers. He fired five shots at the ball as it descended, knocked it back up with the free hand and fired the remaining two shots at the ball as it descended for the second time. He then quickly dropped the weapon to the ground, catching the ball as it passed. He was heartily cheered for the successful performance of his original Independence Day feat.*

—Louisville Courier-Journal, *Wednesday, July 5, 1893*

*Leech Maskrey, of the Louisvilles, is managing a rink at his home in Mercer, Pa. He is quite an artist and writer, and expects to soon publish a book entitled "Trips of the Louisvilles." He has been with the club since the American Association was formed.*

—Sporting Life, *Wednesday, January 13, 1886*

NOTE: The subject of the story was outfielder Samuel Leech Maskrey (1854–1922), who split his fifth and last major-league season between Louisville and Cincinnati of the fabled American Association. Founded in 1882, the American Association was the first competitor to the National League.

# Yesteryear

*Constant brooding over his failure to make good with the Louisville American Association club last season is given as the reason for the suicide of Clay Dailey, 25 years old, found dead in a cave near here. Dailey, a promising ballplayer, left his home in a suburb of Frankfort yesterday, after telling his parents he would never return. His threat was not regarded seriously at the time, but when he failed to appear last night, a search was begun. The body was found in Pepper's Cave, a mile and a half from Frankfort. Dailey had shot himself with a revolver. He was the son of Ossie Dailey, a carpenter.*

—Louisville Courier-Journal, *Monday, May 23, 1921*

# Acknowledgements and Dedication

To Daniel Wayne Jackson—always a star in my book. To David Nemec and Ray Nemec, the two best historical baseball men I know. To Gary Ulmer, the best of Louisville baseball. To Dick Bresciani and Debbie Matson of the Boston Red Sox, who provided the final missing link in this book with numerous invaluable photographs and, in doing so, completed the final chapter in the saga that is Louisville baseball history. To Pat Kelly of the National Baseball Library, who once again came to the aid of a struggling baseball writer and made this book everything that it is. To Casey Hutchinson: every writer needs a computer genius; he's mine. To Dixie Davis, a true Louisville ace. To Billy Chapel, my kind of pitcher. To Jon Miller, my kind of baseball announcer. To my "brothers" in Chicago—George and William. To Jeanne, Jenny, Timothy, Carol and Steve Frederick—five of Chicago's best. To my physician, Dr. Tim Winchester, who takes great care of me, and to his son, Graham, a fine right-hander. To the very best of my generation—Anne (Rooney) McIntosh Stith, Dave Stith, Addison Andrew "Andy" Stith, John Alexander "Johnny Mac" McIntosh and Ron and Janie Kissling. To Ryan, Conor and Colin. To Ken Sowers, a fellow admirer of Willie Mays. And to my father, Frank, a Louisville-born ballplayer and writer who believed in defense above all else.

# Introduction

Louisville baseball, both minor league and major league, is a microcosm of American baseball. This may be shocking news to some who have always considered Louisville to be a minor-league city, but it's a fact.

It is the home—the birthplace—of the National League (regardless of what New York revisionists say). It is the city where the first open black major leaguer, Fleet Walker, made his career debut (not New York, Chicago, Boston, Philadelphia, St. Louis, Cincinnati, Detroit or anywhere else, regardless of what baseball revisionists claim). It hosted major-league ball for twenty years in the nineteenth century. It was the site of the first players' strike. Its major-league team of 1889 still holds the major-league record for consecutive losses: twenty-six. And, along the way, Louisville turned out a host of major-league stars—Honus Wagner, Jimmy Devlin, Pete Browning, Fred Clarke, Rube Waddell, Jimmy Collins, Tommy Leach and Deacon Phillippe. That roster also includes Guy Hecker, the only major-league pitcher ever to win a batting title and the only major-league hurler ever to win both a batting title and the pitching crown—something that could only happen in Louisville.

Louisville played in the 1890 World Series and tied that fall classic with Brooklyn—again, something that could only happen in Louisville. It was a charter member of this country's first two major-league outfits—the National League and the American Association. Now in its fourth era of diamond play, Louisville has a singularly extraordinary baseball history.

That immense and wondrous 150-plus-year history includes 116 seasons of professional play (through 2010)—20 at the major-league level and the rest at the minor-league level—the genesis of which was the city's first boxscore in 1858. The antique-era time frame (pre-1876) also numbered a handful of contests between Louisville and the immortal Cincinnati Reds of 1869 and 1870, baseball's first professionally contracted (play-for-pay) team.

The next baseball era, the premodern era (1876–99), included the co-founding of the National League (this nation's oldest continuously active major-league circuit); Louisville's charter memberships in both the National League and the American Association; the debut, in Louisville, of the sport's first recognized black major leaguer; and the birth of the world's most famous bat (Louisville Slugger) and bat maker (Hillerich & Bradsby). It also featured three major-league batting titlists—one of them a notorious drunk, one a pitcher by trade and one nicknamed "Chicken"—who accounted for a total of five batting crowns in a nine-year period; two decades of topsy-turvy big-top action; one major-league pennant; one World Series appearance; and six Hall of Famers.

The River City's third baseball era, the modern era (1901–99), commenced shortly after the turn of the twentieth century, when Louisville began minor-league play.

Already indelibly stamped as a grand American baseball city of major importance and rank, Louisville has, for the past century, further added to that reputation by becoming a sanctuary of minor-league baseball. Its four most hallowed stars were Joe McCarthy, Earle Combs, Pee Wee Reese and Billy Herman, all of whom went on to enjoy Hall of Fame careers in the Major Leagues.

The Louisville minor-league baseball annals also incorporate every major fiber of American being and democratic experience. Those venerable roots notably include the likes of American Indian stars Ben Tincup (Cherokee) and Joe Guyon (Chippewa)—foundation players of the 1920s juggernauts—and Merito Acosta, one of the game's earliest Hispanic stars and also a major part of the championship teams of the 1920s.

Besides Tincup, Guyon and Acosta, other minor-league "lifers" who have worn a Louisville uniform over the years include such standouts as Jay Kirke, Jake Northrop, Dud Branom, Bunny Brief, Nick Cullop, Butch Simons and Nick Polly. Indeed, if there were a Cooperstown for minor leaguers, all ten of these Louisville players would be in there. The elegant Louisville minor-league panorama also embodies a prodigious and lengthy list of players who made it on the major-league level in one form or another: as "knock-around" journeymen, genuine stars or Hall of Famers, eventual or potential.

Stars like Babe Ruth, Lou Gehrig and Satchel Paige barnstormed in Louisville during their legendary careers (which coincided with Louisville's minor-league time frame). And Red Sox stars like Carlton Fisk and Dwight Evans, who came through here in the late '60s and early '70s, and the Cardinal stars after them in the '80s and '90—like Vince Coleman and Louisville's most recent gift to the Major Leagues, Adam Dunn—are merely more big names in a line that traces back decades.

This is nothing new in Louisville. The city's been doing big-time baseball for years, as evidenced by its record million-fan season of 1983, its numerous pennant-winning and Junior World Series championship teams and the 1921 squad, author of the greatest upset in minor-league World Series history.

In 2000, Louisville opened its fourth baseball era, the millennium era, with an all-new, high-tech, state-of-the-art baseball stadium downtown near the riverfront: Louisville Slugger Field. The latest jewel in Louisville's glittering diamond history, the new park is a star-struck wonder that is *mirabile dictu* on all levels. And taken together with the new century, it symbolizes all that is Louisville baseball—past, present and future.

So we celebrate this most unique of baseball cities and its big-time baseball tradition and history with this book, because quite frankly, there just is no other baseball city like it in the country. In his definitive work, *The American Association: A Baseball History, 1902–1991*, author Bill O'Neal wrote: "Few cities can claim as rich a baseball heritage as Louisville." The following pages show why.

# PART I

# Louisville Baseball History

## Scarlet Diamonds: The Louisville Baseball Timeline, 1858–2001

### *1858*

The city's first organized club, the Louisville Base Ball Club (LBBC), was formed in 1858. Teams played at an open lot on the northwest corner of Fourth and Breckinridge Streets. The first known boxscore in the city's history appeared in the *Louisville Democrat* on July 15. The game quickly became so popular that, in August, the city's second organized club, the Phoenix, was formed to provide competition for the LBBC. One of the twelve largest cities in America, Louisville had four daily newspapers, one-quarter of its population was slave and five foreign consuls lived there.

### *1865*

After the Civil War, two more teams were formed—the Louisville Eagles and the Louisville Eclipse. Louisville witnessed its first post–Civil War organized baseball game when the Louisville Eagles met the Nashville Cumberlands in an open field at what are today Nineteenth and Duncan Streets. Louisville triumphed 22–5. (The date of this game has never been documented. At the time of this book's publication, at least three different dates have been given for this game: April 19, 1865; July 19, 1865; and "the latter '60s." It remains under historical review.)

By the next year, the young team was playing at a diamond bounded by Third, Fifth, Oak and Park Streets, although the ballpark was soon moved to a site now occupied by St. James Court.

## *1869 and 1870*

In a series of games against the fabled Cincinnati Red Stockings of 1869–70, Louisville got the worst of it. The most egregious example was an April 21, 1870 contest between the Louisville Eagles and the Red Stockings, in which Louisville was demolished 94–7. About one month later, on May 23, 1870, the Cincinnati powerhouse destroyed the Lexington Onions 74–0. Other available Louisville–Cincinnati boxscores include a 58–9 lancing on November 3, 1869 (Cincinnati played with just eight men), and a return contest the following day, with the Kentucky Picked Nine being whipped 40–10.

## *1871*

The Olympics, Louisville's fifth formal ball club, was formed in 1871. They played at Twenty-eighth and Elliott Streets. That park was taken over by the Eclipse in the late 1870s. Major-league ball was later played there from 1882 through 1892.

## *September 16, 1874*

The Globes, Louisville's first black baseball team, played a charity game for yellow fever sufferers, shaming a pair of local white clubs into following suit to avoid, in the words of the *Louisville Courier-Journal*, "being outdone by the darkly-complected portion of the human race." Contemporaries of the Globes, incidentally, included the Acorns and the prosaically named Black Diamonds.

## *1875*

In early December 1875, Chicago baseball magnate William Hulbert initiated the establishment of the National League, this country's oldest continuously active major-league circuit, in Louisville.

The site was Al Kolb's bar at 323 West Liberty Street, where Hulbert secretly met with representatives of the other three western clubs: St. Louis, Cincinnati and Louisville. (The bar was turned over to Kolb by Larry Gatto, a family member and another seminal name in early Louisville baseball history.) Armed with the western clubs' proxies, Hulbert completed the establishment of the National League the following February in New York City, where he met with the representatives of the four eastern teams: New York, Boston, Philadelphia and Hartford.

In time, Louisville's role in the establishment of the National League would be forgotten (as was the fact that Louisville was a charter member of the senior circuit).

Remarkably, or perhaps not so remarkably, the culprit was none other than New York City, the same body responsible for the Abner Doubleday/ Cooperstown myth. New York partisans shrewdly used Louisville's subsequent demise as a major-league city and the passage of the years to claim sole paternity of the National League.

In time, these myths reached the point of gospel truth, though they were, in fact, nothing more than cartoon history. With the emergence of Renaissance baseball writers/scholars like Harold Seymour in modern times, however, both stories would go the way of the wind.

## *1876*

Louisville began major-league play by losing its opener—at home on Tuesday, April 25, 1876, before some six thousand fans—to Chicago, the National League's inaugural flag winner. The Chicago club was a powerhouse that included the league's champion pitcher, Albert Spalding; the loop's champion batter, Ross Barnes; and future Hall of Fame first-sacker, Cap Anson.

After a brief hiatus, a revamped Chicago club came back in the 1880s and became the game's first dynasty, churning out five flags in the space of seven years behind the likes of Anson, George Gore, Billy Sunday, eventual Hall of Famer King Kelly and an infield called the "Stone Wall," which included Louisville native Fred Pfeffer.

The 1876 Louisville National League Grays, the city's first major-league team. *Reclining*: George Bechtel (OF) and John J. "Johnny" Ryan (LF). *Seated*: John Carbine (1B/OF), Bill Hague (3B), Chick Fulmer (SS), John Chapman (Manager/OF), Joe Gerhardt (1B) and Art Allison (RF). *Standing*: Scott Hastings (CF), Jimmy Devlin (RHP) and Charles "Pop" Snyder (C). *Eclipse BBHR.*

The opening-day score was 4–0; it was the first shutout in the National League (and in the annals of major-league baseball). The pitcher of record for the Louisville Grays was the brilliant Jimmy Devlin, a rising gold-and-silver-laden star who would destroy himself the following season.

The season ended the way it began—with a loss. Louisville's Jim Clinton dropped an 11–2 decision on Thursday, October 5, 1876, at home to Hartford.

## *1877*

Favored to win the National League pennant, the Louisville Grays fell victim to a late-season tailspin that was initially attributed to poor hitting and star pitcher Jimmy Devlin's bout with a case of the boils. As a consequence, it ran a disappointing second to Boston.

## Early History and Growth

Louisville's position as a great American city—and by extension, a major-league baseball town—was the product of sound geography. Founded in 1778, the settlement was named Louisville the following year in honor of Louis XVI, the French king who aided the cause of the American colonies during the Revolutionary War. Granted city status by the Kentucky legislature in 1828, it became Kentucky's largest city two years later and remains so today.

Located on the Ohio River, just above the point where that river pours into the Mississippi, Louisville was originally a frontier settlement. Its growth was directly related to westward expansion (due to the Ohio River, a major conveyor of people and goods).

The first big break for Louisville was the Louisiana Purchase of 1803. That freed navigation to the sea (the lower Mississippi and New Orleans), opening a major shipping lane that had been previously held by the Spanish. This, in turn, made Louisville a vital link in the shipping of goods between the Deep South and the big cities of the North. Louisville's importance was firmly realized in 1830 with the construction of the Portland Canal, opening the way for free and unrestricted traffic from Pittsburgh to New Orleans (prior to that, boats had disembarked in Louisville and then reentered the Ohio below the falls). As a result, Louisville was transformed from a frontier outpost into a booming river town that was an essential port city along the heavily trafficked Ohio River.

The city grew substantially more with the advent of railroads in the mid-1800s. That form of transportation changed the face of the country, sparking a slow shift of the nation's major transportation from water to land. Goods could be transported much more quickly and directly via railroads, and Louisville was a part of it all via the Louisville and Nashville (L&N) Railroad, founded in 1850 so that Louisville could maintain its mercantile economy.

A logical consequence of this commerce was growth, and at one time, Louisville ranked as one of America's biggest cities. This, of course, helped its cultural and sporting growth. By the end of the nineteenth century, however, Louisville had stagnated; it was bypassed by such cities as Cincinnati (a major competitor for southern trade and at one time the pork capital of the world); Chicago (still the railroad crossroads of America and at one time a major venue for stockyards and steel mills); Pittsburgh (an industrial giant nicknamed "Iron City"); and St. Louis, (yet another mid-America mecca via its location at the doorsteps of the Missouri and Mississippi Rivers).

## LOUISVILLE'S BALLPARKS

The 1877 flag-pitching fiasco was a startling contrast to the elegant home of the 1876 and 1877 Louisville National League club, a ballpark that had been modeled after the handsome Hartford Ball Club Grounds. During its two decades in the Major Leagues, Louisville used three ballparks. In a side note that is reflective of Louisville's bizarre major-league history, all three parks were either catastrophically damaged or destroyed.

Louisville's first two major-league teams (the 1876 and 1877 squads) played at a ballpark located at St. James Court. Later, that area served as the site of the 1883 Southern Exposition. Opened by President Chester A. Arthur on August 1, 1883, the fabulously successful exposition ran through 1887. A palatial mansion district since the 1890s, St. James Court today is one of the finest extant examples of Victorian architecture.

Known as Louisville Baseball Park as well as St. James Court, the ballpark was located just a few blocks south of downtown Louisville. Its boundaries were Magnolia, Fourth, Hill and Sixth Streets (home plate was at the intersection of Fourth and Hill). In mid-April 1876, the ballpark's grandstand was heavily damaged by a tornado. The violent storm, however, did not delay the season opener and the city's major-league debut.

The opening game took place, as scheduled, on April 25, 1876, with Louisville losing 4–0 to Chicago, the inaugural National League champion. The loss was the first shutout in National League history. Just over a week later, on May 3, Louisville posted its first major-league victory, hammering St. Louis 11–0 at home.

Eclipse Park, Louisville's second big-league ballpark, was used by the city during its entire American Association membership (1882–1891) and briefly during its second National League stint. Located at Twenty-eighth and Elliott on the city's west side, it was destroyed by fire in late September 1892.

The city's third and last ballpark, also called Eclipse Park, was located at Twenty-eighth and Broadway, across the street from the original Eclipse Park. Used by Louisville during the bulk of its second National League tenure (1892–1899), it, too, fell victim to fire, the blaze occurring, ironically enough, during Louisville's last major-league season.

Like the two before it, Louisville's last major-league ballpark disaster was a direct product of the wooden style that characterized the game's early sporting edifices. The cost of the conflagration was enormous. Because of the fire, the Louisville club was forced to play the last six weeks of its final major-league campaign on the road.

Though long gone, the second Eclipse Park (also known as League Park) was historically significant. It was there that the last major-league game in Louisville, indeed in Kentucky, was played. The date was September 2, 1899, and Louisville crushed Washington 25–4.

For the record, Louisville was officially known as the Louisvilles during all but two years of its big-top membership. The exceptions were the 1882 and 1883 seasons, when the franchise was known as the Louisville Eclipse, retaining the name of the city's crack semipro club that reigned supreme before Louisville became a member of the American Association.

After the season, the real reason became clear: a mammoth game-fixing scandal that ultimately led to Louisville's ignominious departure from the National League and the lifetime expulsion of five Louisville players: utility infielder Al Nichols, outfielder George Bechtel, shortstop Bill Craver, outfielder George Hall and pitcher Jimmy Devlin.

## *1881*

On August 21, 1881, in Louisville, the Louisville Eclipse and the White Sewing Machine Company of Cleveland played a game in which the latter's best player was not allowed to participate because of his color. The action was decried in many quarters: by the *Louisville Courier-Journal*, the fans and even a Louisville baseball executive.

Stripped of its best player, the Ohio club lost 6–3. It was a hollow victory, to be sure. However, the black player in question—the poetically named and equally talented Moses Fleetwood Walker—would make a historic return three years later.

## *1882*

After a four-year hiatus, major-league baseball returned to Louisville in 1882 in the form of the fabled American Association. The National League's first and fiercest competitor, the American Association (nicknamed the "Beer and Whiskey League" by its National League detractors) would, in its ten-year existence (1882–91), bring to the game a host of innovations that would open it up as never before to the general masses: Sunday baseball, beer and liquor at the ballpark and admission prices half those of the National League (which Associationers derisively called the "Rich Man's League").

Although Louisville—a charter member of this league as well—placed third in the six-team circuit, the campaign was not without distinction. Louisville native Pete Browning set the nails in place for his legendary career by leading the junior circuit with a towering .373 mark. The first true rookie to win a major-league batting title, Browning was backed up by thirty-game winner Tony Mullane and first baseman/pitcher Guy Hecker (.276; 6-6/1.30 ERA), both of whom threw on-the-road no-hitters.

Tony Mullane was 30-24 as a rookie with the Louisville Eclipse, and along with fellow Louisville major leaguers Pete Browning and Gus Weyhing, he

Anthony "Tony" Mullane. *National Baseball Hall of Fame Library, Cooperstown, New York.*

unquestionably belongs in Cooperstown. Like them and all the other players in the "AA Ten," his play in the old American Association major-league circuit was the stumbling block. (The only one to escape that fate to date is Bid McPhee, the premier second baseman of the premodern era.)

The first pitcher to switch-pitch a game (July 18, 1882, versus Baltimore) in major-league history, the ambidextrous Mullane threw right-handed principally. Over a thirteen-year career (1881–94), he amassed a 285-220 slate, the most triumphs by a pitcher not in the Hall of Fame. His stellar work included five 30-win seasons and three 20-win campaigns.

His lifetime total, remarkably enough, would have been even larger had Mullane not been suspended the entire 1885 season for contractual violation. That lost season is significant, since it denied him three hundred lifetime victories, a figure considered automatic for Cooperstown.

The pitcher of record in the 1884 game that marked battery mate Moses Fleetwood Walker's debut as the game's first open black major leaguer, Mullane also left another mark on baseball. Handsome as well as talented, the Irish-born Mullane was known as "the County" and "the Apollo of the Box" because of his smoldering good looks. That countenance, so the story goes, led to the popularization of Ladies' Day as a standard major-league promotion in the 1880s, when Mullane was pitching for Cincinnati in the fabled American Association. Noticing that women flocked to the park whenever he pitched, Cincinnati owner Aaron Stern began to shrewdly schedule Mullane against poor-drawing ball clubs, billing those games as Ladies' Day events. The result was a major marketing tool that endures to this day on all levels of baseball.

## Eclipse

The Eclipse name is believed to be a reference to a famous eighteenth-century racehorse and sire. This necessitates a short but informal history of thoroughbred horse racing, in which Kentucky has long played an iconic role both as the home of the world's greatest horse race—the Kentucky Derby—and as America's most renowned thoroughbred breeding state.

Foaled in 1764 during an eclipse of the sun (thus his name), Eclipse began racing at age five and was undefeated in eighteen starts. That record included eight walkovers—contests in which he had no competition and was merely required to tour or "walk over" the race's prescribed distance to be declared the winner. Walkovers generally occur when one horse so far outclasses all of the other competition that no one will run against it in that race.

As a stud, Eclipse was a grand success also, siring the winners of three Epsom (English) Derbies and one English Oaks, Great Britain's top two classic races for three-year-olds. Eclipse was also one of the game's three foundation sires, which history detailed in a pamphlet entitled *The King of Sports*, published by the Thoroughbred Racing Associations (TRA):

> *In order to be eligible for registry in the stud book of the country where he is born, a Thoroughbred must be traceable, through horses already in the stud book, to one of three foundation sires.*
>
> *While all Thoroughbreds can be traced through the tail-male descent (the top line of their pedigree) to the Byerly Turk, the Godolphin Arabian and the Darley Arabian, it is no longer necessary to go back that far.*
>
> *Some 80 percent of all Thoroughbreds today are traceable to Eclipse, a great-great-grandson of the Darley Arabian. Matchem, foaled in 1748, a grandson of the Godolphin Arabian, accounts for about 15 per cent (of the Thoroughbred breed) while the remainder (roughly five percent) are traceable to Herod, a great-great-grandson of the Byerly Turk, foaled in 1758.*

Eclipse's progeny includes 1948 Triple Crown–winner Citation. The legendary Man o' War came from the Matchem line, along with the fabled Seabiscuit, while Herod's offspring includes Whiskery, the 1927 Kentucky Derby winner.

Thoroughbreds are a mixture of English coldblooded stock (giving them their size) and hotblooded Arabian Desert horses (giving them their speed),

Finally, because of his prolific impact on the sport, thoroughbred racing's highest award was named in honor of Eclipse.

## *1883*

Shortstop Ryerson "Angel Sleeves" Jones (also known as "Ri")—the possessor of, arguably, the greatest nickname in major-league baseball history—was briefly a member of the Louisville club. It also features Jack Leary, a left-handed shortstop.

## *1884*

A monumental year in Louisville—and American—baseball, 1884 included the debut of a seminal black player—Moses Fleetwood "Fleet" Walker—in Louisville on May 1, 1884; the "birth" of the Louisville Slugger bat; and pitcher Guy Hecker's Triple Crown season for Louisville.

Regarding Moses "Fleet" Walker, a detailed technical explanation is due here. Born of mulatto parents, he was once thought to be the first black major leaguer; he is now regarded as the second black major leaguer. According to Peter Morris's lucid entry in David Nemec's landmark baseball book, *Baseball Bios: The Early Years, 1871–1900*, the first black major leaguer was William Edward White (1860–?). The product of a Caucasian father and slave mother of mixed ancestry, White played one game for Providence of the National League in 1879. He is not to be confused with Hall of Fame pitching candidate William Henry White (1854–1911). However, it should be noted that Walker was the first black man to play openly in major-league competition (before being driven out). Furthermore, he was the first black player in the history of the fabled American Association, a major-league circuit obviously far more progressive than the reactionary National League.

Though Louisville finished third in the thirteen-team loop, its 68-40/.630 mark was Louisville's second-best American Association finish, topped only by its 1890 flag-winning campaign.

## *1885*

Pete Browning took his second American Association batting crown with a mighty .362 average in 1885. The 1885–87 Louisville teams produced no fewer than four players who eventually went insane and had to be institutionalized (institutionalization/death years in parentheses): Reddy Mack (1900/1916), Jimmy Wolf (1901/1903), Philip Reccius (1902/1903) and Pete Browning (1905/1905).

## *1886*

Guy Hecker became the only pitcher in major-league history to win a batting title when he led the American Association with a .341 mark in 1886. Also a twenty-six-game winner that year, Hecker had his best day as batter in an August game. In a 22–5 rout, Hecker went six-for-seven (three singles and three home runs) and scored a major-league record seven times.

## *1887*

The National Colored Professional Baseball League (NCPBL) began play in 1887; one of its charter members was the Louisville Falls City team. The NCPBL was this country's second black major-league loop. The first was the Southern League of Colored Base Ballists (SLCBB). Founded the year before, in 1886, that league also failed to survive its inaugural season. Nevertheless, both are worth noting because they were forerunners of the twentieth-century Negro Leagues.

### Nicknames

Frequently referred to as the "Falls City" team, Louisville had a host of other nicknames during its major-league years, the most popular of which was the "Colonels."

Other nicknames included the "Grays" (1876 and 1877), believed to be a reference to the gray uniforms the South wore during the Civil War; the "Cyclones," after a violent windstorm that cut up the city in 1890, the year Louisville captured its only major-league pennant; the "Night Riders," a reference to Kentucky's tobacco wars of the 1890s (during that time, tobacco companies gave unusually low prices for tobacco; some farmers struck back at the big tobacco interests, their battles including night raids against fellow tobacco farmers who went along with the pricing system of the tobacco companies); and the "Wanderers," in 1899, when the team spent the last month and a half of the city's final major-league season on the road after fire destroyed the city's ballpark.

## *1888*

Louisville pitcher Elton "Icebox" Chamberlain (157-120 lifetime), so named because of his refrigerator-like build, became the only recorded winner of a switch-pitched game in major-league history with an 18–6 triumph over Kansas City on May 9. In 1894, playing for Cincinnati, he would make history again, becoming the first pitcher to give up four home runs in a game (to Boston's Bobby Lowe).

## *1889*

Louisville staged the first players' strike in major-league history in 1889. Also that season, the Louisville franchise set the all-time major-league record for consecutive losses (26) en route to an atrocious 27-111/.196 mark and the American Association cellar.

On Wednesday, July 17, the *Louisville Courier-Journal* ran the following priceless baseball note, datelined "July 16, Wheeling, West Virginia":

> *Squire Arkle, who made the second arrest of the Wheeling and Dayton baseball clubs Sunday, this evening refused to discharge them and demanded a bond from each. The players refused to give bond, and were ordered committed to jail, but were afterward paroled until 9 a.m. to-morrow, when a writ of habeas corpus will be applied for to the Circuit Court.* [They were later released.]

## *1890*

The first team in big-top history to go from last-place to the pennant in the course of one season, Louisville copped its only major-league flag (88-44/.667) behind the championship stickwork of outfielder William "Chicken" Wolf (.363 and a circuit-topping 197 hits) and aces Scott Stratton (34-14) and Red Ehret (25-14). A foundation part of Stratton's regular season ledger was a sixteen-game winning streak that equaled the American League total and was just four short of the all-time major-league mark.

In the World Series that year against National League champion Brooklyn, Wolf continued his fine plate work for the American Association champion Louisvilles, leading the team with a .360 average that included three doubles, one triple and eight RBIs.

Ehret, however, was the kingpin of the Louisville staff, posting two wins, one save and a 1.35 ERA (Stratton was just 1-1 in three appearances). The World Series that year ended in a tie (each team having three victories, three losses and one tie to its credit) when inclement weather forced cancellation of the postseason classic.

Over in the Players League, where he had jumped after the horrendous 1889 campaign, Pete Browning earned the third and last batting title of his fabulous career, batting .373 for Cleveland.

A detailed sketch of Louisville's only pennant winner and World Series participant, the 1890 American Association flag winner and co–world champion Louisville Cyclones, graced the August 16, 1890 cover of the *Sporting Life*, one of the era's top sporting journals. *Top row*: Michael "Mickey" Jones (LHP), Charlie Hamburg (LF), John Chapman (Manager), Herb Goodall (RHP) and Ned Bligh (C). *Middle row*: John B. Ryan (C), Phil Tomney (SS), Dan O'Connor (1B), Tim Shinnick (2B), Philip "Red" Ehret (RHP) and William A. "Farmer" Weaver (CF). *Bottom row*: Scott Stratton (RHP), William "Chicken" Wolf (RF), George Meakim (RHP), Harry Raymond (3B) and Harry Taylor (1B). Certainly its greatest casualty was shortstop Phil Tomney, who injured his shoulder in the 1890 World Series against the National League champion Brooklyn Bridegrooms and never played major-league ball again. *Eclipse BBHR.*

## *1892*

Louisville began its second stint in the National League, the three-league war of 1890 having disassembled first the Players' League (the 1890 season was its lone campaign) and then the American Association (which ended its ten-year operation after the 1891 season).

While Louisville would never realize .500 baseball in its last eight years of major-league play—though it would come within two games of that percentage in its final major-league season of 1899—it would nonetheless be home to many fine players during that time.

One stellar example was Louisville native Nathaniel Frederick "Dandelion" Pfeffer, a member of the 1892, '93, '94 and '95 Louisvilles. One of the two greatest second-basemen of the nineteenth century (along with Bid McPhee), Fred Pfeffer made his name with Cap Anson's National League dynasty teams of the early and mid-1880s, when he was a member of a seemingly impenetrable infield known as the "Stone Wall."

## *1893*

The National League Louisvilles included the likes of three notables closing out their careers: former St. Louis Browns star outfielder Curt Welch; Matty Kilroy, who, as a twenty-year-old rookie with Baltimore in 1886, had set the all-time strikeout mark with 513 Ks (beating out Louisville's hard-drinking Toad Ramsey, the latter logging 499 strikeouts off a 38-27 mark); and ambidextrous third-baseman Jerry Denny, the last position player to play the game barehanded for his entire career

## *1894*

Fred Clarke began his Hall of Fame career (as outfielder/manager) at Louisville with a brilliant five-for-five debut on June 30 versus Philadelphia in a 13–6 loss at home. The work, which included four singles and a triple, remains to this day the greatest debut by a future Cooperstown inductee.

A playing manager for most of his career (1894–1915) who is credited by historians with inventing flip-up sunglasses, Clarke entered baseball's pantheon in 1945 with a career .312 batting average, 2,672 hits, a thirty-five-game hitting streak (in 1895), sixteen-hundred-plus lifetime managing victories, four National League flags and one World Series championship (1909).

Also in 1894, J. Frederich Hillerich registered the Louisville Slugger bat trademark. By the turn of the century, this would prove to be an extremely wise business move. Initially, the elder Hillerich had wanted no part of the new bat-making "fad" (only begrudgingly allowing his son to continue the "sideline" activity) because his business was booming with orders for wooden swinging butter churns, as well as for bedposts and a trio of items used for staircases (handrails, balusters and newel posts). In addition, his company also made roller skids, tenpins, duckpins and wooden bowling balls.

The bat making, however, proved to be the Hillerichs' salvation at the turn of the century, when progress dried up the market for his top seller: the wooden swinging butter churn. Instead of going under, the firm smoothly switched to bat manufacturing and, in the process, became an American icon.

On August 17, 1894, Louisville pitcher Jack Wadsworth yielded a major-league-record thirty-six hits to the Phillies in a 29–4 loss.

## *1895*

The 1895 Louisville assemblage included five-time batting titlist and future Hall of Fame first baseman Dan Brouthers; Jimmy Collins, who eventually would earn Cooperstown laurels for defining the way third base should be played; and a pair who should be in the Hall of Fame—high-class shortstop Jack Glasscock and strong-armed pitcher Gus Weyhing (a 264-game winner for also-rans).

## *1896*

On April 6, 1896, Louisville National League infielder Pete Cassidy became the first major leaguer to be X-rayed (a splinter of bone was subsequently removed from his wrist).

## *1897*

Hall of Famers Honus Wagner and Rube Waddell began their major-league careers in Louisville in 1897. The latter was signed—and then sold to Louisville—by Ed Barrow (of Babe Ruth renown).

A charter member of the Hall of Fame and considered by many to be the game's greatest shortstop, Wagner spent the bulk of his career with Pittsburgh, where he was an integral part of its early twentieth-century championship teams. His lifetime work included a .327 average, over thirty-four hundred hits and eight batting titles. Able to hit both for average and with power, he also enjoyed a reputation as one of the game's finest glove men.

A fun-loving man-child who drove every manager he had to despair, southpaw Rube Waddell (193-143 lifetime) became a mainstay on Connie Mack's early Philadelphia Athletics pennant-winning team. His tragic death of tuberculosis in 1914 at age thirty-seven underscored the lost talents of this man who loved chasing fire engines, tending bar, playing sandlot baseball and fishing as much as he did pitching.

On June 29, 1897, Louisville lost a National League game 36–7 to Chicago. Chicago's total remains the record for most runs ever scored by a winning team in a major-league contest. Also this year, John A. "Bud" Hillerich became a partner in his father's business.

## *1898*

This Louisville National League team included three major standouts: William Ellsworth "Dummy" Hoy, Tommy Leach and Tully Frederick "Topsy" Hartsel.

A gifted glove man and hitter, Hoy was also a deaf-mute whose handicaps—according to some historians—helped popularize the practice of umpires "calling" strikes by emphatically raising their arms in the air.

Very nearly the first man to play one thousand games at two positions (third base and outfield), Leach was part of a foursome that instantly established the Pittsburgh Pirates as a major National League power in the ensuing decade.

A consummate leadoff man, Hartsel enjoyed his greatest career success with Connie Mack's turn-of-the-century Philadelphia Athletics championship clubs.

## *1899*

The curtain came down forever on Louisville major-league baseball in 1899. After this season, Louisville was one of four cities dropped by the National League. The bulk of the Louisville franchise was transferred to Pittsburgh by eventual Hall of Fame owner Barney Dreyfuss (1865–1932), who bought half of the Pittsburgh franchise and then wound up as the sole owner of the Pirates shortly thereafter.

Yet another long-lost Louisville baseball figure, Dreyfuss is worthy of a note because of his election by the Veterans Committee to Cooperstown. Creator of the modern World Series (Pittsburgh versus Boston, 1903) and builder of the first modern steel-frame, triple-tier stadium (Forbes Field, 1909), Dreyfuss also led the successful battle to obtain Major League Baseball's first commissioner. Fellow baseball executive and Hall of Famer Branch Rickey once called Dreyfuss "the best judge of players" he had ever seen.

The case now rests for Dreyfuss, whose Hall of Fame election in December 2007 was as deserved and long overdue as it was shocking, coming from a committee renowned for its historical ignorance and apathy.

Dreyfuss did not have to wait long for success thanks to the likes of Fred Clarke, Honus Wagner, Tommy Leach and Deacon Phillippe. Spearheaded by that group, the Pirates ran second in the National League in 1900 and then went on to garner three straight National League flags (1901, 1902 and 1903) and one World Championship (1909).

A rookie with the 1899 Louisvilles (his 21-17 log including a no-hitter), Phillippe ran off a 189-109 lifetime mark and six 20-win seasons in thirteen years of play (1899–1911).

Just four years later, in the inaugural 1903 World Series, he became the first hurler in World Series history to win three games. Incredibly, Phillippe and his Pittsburgh teammates ended up losing the series to American League champion Boston, whose star pitcher, Bill Dinneen, became the second slinger in World Series history to win three games.

## *1901*

Louisville's first minor-league foray in 1901 was temporary and strange. A member of the Western Association, it opened with a 7–2 loss (losing pitcher: Gus Weyhing) to Indianapolis on April 25. It played at the "old stand" at Twenty-eighth and Broadway, home of the city's last major-league team.

In early June, the Grand Rapids, Michigan franchise was moved to Wheeling, West Virginia. One month later, Grand Rapids regained its team when the Louisville franchise was moved there. Grand Rapids went on to win the pennant.

The 1901 National League champion Pittsburgh Pirates were a team whose lot in life—that year and for a number of years afterward—was substantially enhanced by the aforementioned four ex-Louisville stars: Tommy Leach, Deacon Phillippe and future Hall of Famers Honus Wagner and Fred Clarke. Other notables included Hall of Famer Jack Chesbro, Jesse Tannehill and "Ginger" Beaumont.

Chesbro (198-132) won twenty games four times and forty games once. In 1904, with the Yankees, he set the modern-day record for most wins in a season (41-12). Tannehill was a six-time twenty-game winner.

Clarence Howeth "Ginger" Beaumont, so nicknamed because of a shock of red hair, was a brilliant leadoff man whose chunky five-foot-eight, 190-pound build belied his speed (in an 1899 game, the up-and-coming rookie beat out six infield hits and scored six times).

Also known as "Beauty," he spent twelve years in the big leagues. His work included a career .311 batting average, the 1902 National League batting title (.357), 1,759 hits, four National League crowns in hits (1902, '03, '04 and 07), 955 runs scored, four straight seasons with 100 or more runs scored (including a league-leading 137 in 1903) and 254 stolen bases.

The 1901 Pittsburgh Pirates. *Back row:* Jack Chesbro (RHP), Charles Louis "Chief" Zimmer (C), George Merritt (RHP), Deacon Phillippe (RHP), Ed Poole (RHP), Honus Wagner (SS) and George Yeager (C). *Middle row:* Jimmy Burke (IF), Ed Doheny (LHP), Fred Clarke (Manager/LF), Jack O'Connor (C) and William "Kitty" Bransfield (1B). *Front row:* Alphonzo "Lefty" Davis (RF), Tommy Leach (3B), Jess Tannehill (LHP), Clarence "Ginger" Beaumont (CF) and Claude Cassius "Little All-Right" Ritchey (2B). *National Baseball Hall of Fame Library, Cooperstown, New York.*

The first batter in the inaugural World Series (1903), Beaumont could do it all, and like many others in this book, he deserves to be remembered.

Two other worthies included Charles Louis "Chief" Zimmer and Claude Cassius Ritchey. The former caught 1,230 games and batted .268 during his nineteen-year big-league career. Ritchey, who was nicknamed "Little All-Right," was indeed that. His diminutive size (five feet, six inches, and 167 pounds) was in vivid contrast to his fine major-league totals: a .273 batting average and 1,618 hits.

One final note: In 1903, on the eve of the first modern World Series between Pittsburgh and Boston, Pirates pitcher Ed Doheny was forcibly removed to a mental hospital. He never pitched again.

## *1902*

Minor-league baseball returned permanently to Louisville in 1902 when the city became a charter member of the eight-team American Association (Louisville, Minneapolis, St. Paul, Indianapolis, Kansas City, Milwaukee, Toledo and Columbus). Louisville replaced Omaha, which was scrapped when officials decided it posed major travel problems for the other clubs in the circuit.

For its inaugural year, the American Association (AA) was classified as an "independent" league. Thereafter, until its final season in 1997, the AA operated under the highest minor-league classification available at the time: Lone-A (1903–11), Double-A (1912–45) and Triple-A (1946–97).

As was to be expected, the inaugural "junior-diamond" season was a doozy that defied comprehension and description. Battling neck and neck with longtime geographical rival Indianapolis the entire season, Louisville lost the pennant race on the last day of the season as Indianapolis snatched a tripleheader from St. Paul.

Indianapolis needed those wins because Louisville took a triple-header from Minneapolis, one by forfeit and the other two going to southpaw Patsy Flaherty, the city's opening-day starter. In its first complete minor-league season, "The City of the Bat" fashioned a fine 92-45/.671 worksheet that was just two games behind Indy's.

The powerhouse Louisville club, managed by "Derby Day" Bill Clymer, included batting champion John Henry "Babe"/"Jack" Ganzel (.366 off a league-leading 194 hits) and Ed Dunkle, the loop's winningest pitcher with a 30-10 mark (the most wins ever in a season by a Louisville minor-league hurler). Other standouts included shortstop Lee Tannehill (.324), catcher Pop Schriver (.315), outfielder/pitcher Dan Kerwin (.318, 114 runs scored, 9-7) and pitchers Pat Flaherty (26-16) and John Coons (24-10).

On April 29, thirty-five-year-old catcher Harry Spies became the first Louisville (and American Association player) to hit for the cycle. Louisville's first home game was on April 23 (a 16–6 loss to the Kansas City Blues); its first home win followed the next day (a 13–0 shutout of the Blues).

## *1903*

Louisville's Tom Walker was the loop's winningest pitcher in 1903 with a 26-7 ledger. He was backed up by Aloysius Jerome "Wish" Egan (24-16).

Playing manager Bill Clymer led the team in batting (.350) and also had thirty-one steals. For all that, Louisville finished second again.

Also in 1903, one of Louisville's old-time, major-league batting champions—William Van Winkle "Jimmy" Wolf—died four days after his forty-first birthday on May 16.

Following a short stay with the Phillies, Ohio native Roy Brashear (1874–1951) became a regular for the Colonels, manning second base through 1907. The Ohio native racked up 2,082 career hits and a .274 average during his minor-league career.

A staple of the early Louisville teams (1903, 1905–10) was first/third baseman Suter Sullivan, the club's playing manager for part of the 1906 season.

## *1905*

On September 1, 1905, Hillerich made modern endorsement-advertising history by signing a contract for its first autographed bat model with future Hall of Famer Honus Wagner, who had inaugurated his career at Louisville in 1897. Wagner was the first major leaguer to have his name on a bat. A few years later, Wagner would become the centerpiece of the most famous and valuable baseball card in existence—the legendary T206 series put out by the American Tobacco Company between 1909 and 1911. Only fifty to sixty such Wagner cards, termed the "Mona Lisa" of baseball cards by collectors, are known to exist; one in almost mint condition sold for a record $2.8 million in early September 2007.

On September 10, the original Louisville slugger—Pete Browning—died at age forty-four at old City (then General, now University) Hospital. Namesake of the Louisville Slugger bat, he left behind an enduring folk legend and a .341 lifetime batting average.

Browning's death, interestingly enough, came weeks after another major native Louisville sporting figure, Marvin Hart (1876–1931), won the heavyweight championship when he knocked out Jack Root in Reno, Nevada, on July 3, 1905. Hart lost the title on February 23, 1906, to Tommy Burns in Los Angeles. Hart's career work included a win over Jack Johnson.

Though the team narrowly escaped a serious train accident in mid-May near Lafayette, Indiana, that killed the engineer and fireman, it was not so lucky later in the summer. On August 31, a Kansas City, Missouri trolley accident injured seven players and the team secretary. Most seriously hurt was right-hander Ed Kenna, whose season ended at 16-13.

This was the last good season for the talented Kenna, whose career ended two years later without him ever having a sustained shot at the Major Leagues.

## *1906*

In 1906, Louisville Colonels outfielder Billy Hallman (1876–1950) topped the loop in batting (.342) and stolen bases (fifty-four).

## *1907 and 1908*

Lefty Ambrose Puttman, one of Louisville's earliest star pitchers, turned out a pair of twenty-win campaigns, going 21-20 in 1907, with a circuit-best 174 strikeouts, and 26-12 in 1908.

He was backed up in 1908 by two other twenty-game winners—southpaw John Halla (22-16) and right-hander Babe Adams (22-12)—as well as right-hander Jesse Stovall, the author of the club's first no-hitter, a 2–0 decision over Minneapolis at home on April 28 that year, and outfielder Orville Woodruff, who at one point reeled off a streak of sixty-two consecutive errorless games.

Interestingly on that same talent-rich 1908 club was a player with one of baseball's most iconic names: "Bull" Durham. Born Louis Raphael Staub on June 27, 1877, in New Oxford, Pennsylvania, he played professional baseball under the name of Louis Raphael "Bull" Durham.

He was 2-0 in four years of major-league play (1904, '07, '08 and '09) with the Brooklyn National League Superbas, the Washington Senators and New York Giants. His 19-7 slate in 1908 with Louisville and Indianapolis included five double-header wins. The prosaically named moundsman, 16-18 with the 1907 Colonels, died the day after his eighty-third birthday on June 28, 1960, in Bentley, Kansas.

Also in 1908, Ty Cobb contracted for a Louisville Slugger bat.

Harry Joseph "Swats" Swacina (1881–1941), whose twenty-three-year professional career included twenty-six games with the Colonels toward the end of the season, was also a member of the 1908 club. A native of Missouri, he registered 2,336 hits and a .291 average in the minors. Originally a catcher, first baseman and outfielder, he was switched permanently to first base the year before he joined Louisville. Swacina's career numbers also included historically interesting stints with Baltimore in the renegade Federal League both years that it operated (1914 and 1915).

## *1909*

After some up-and-down times and near-misses, Louisville picked up its first minor-league flag in 1909, finishing two and a half games in front of Milwaukee off a 93-75 (.554) mark. A notable member of that squad was outfielder Frank Delahanty (1883–1966), the youngest brother of the famed Delahanty baseball family, a unit that included Hall of Famer Ed Delahanty (1867–1903), Tom Delahanty (1872–1951), Joseph Delahanty (1875–1936) and Jim Delahanty (1879–1953).

The 1909 Louisville Colonels squad also included pitcher and baseball trivia curiosity Gene Packard, the only hurler to win twenty games in both seasons the eclectic Federal League was in operation.

The last organized competition to modern-day organized baseball (the National League and the American League), the Federal League numbered future Hall of Famers Mordecai "Three Finger" Brown, Joe Tinker, Eddie Roush and Eddie Plank in its ranks.

This team also included right-hander Bill Hogg, who went 17-14 in his only season as a Colonel. Tragically, on December 8, he died of Bright's disease in New Orleans. He was twenty-eight.

## *1911*

With his career rapidly coming to a close in 1911, former major-league star pitcher Jack "The Giant Killer" Pfiester logged a 7-12 mark for the Louisville Colonels. The numbers notwithstanding, he was a figure of major baseball importance. A member of the 1906–10 dynasty Chicago Cubs teams, Pfiester earned his nickname for his mastery of the New York Giants (15-5 lifetime).

Another pitcher in the 1911 Louisville club was left-handed Bunn Hearn (1891–1959). Though he went 2-11 with the Colonels after opening the season with the St. Louis Cardinals (0-0), the Chapel Hill, North Carolina native finished his twenty-two-year organized baseball career (1910–31) with a 247-166 minor-league mark that included three twenty-win campaigns.

Early Louisville minor-league star Myron Frederick "Moose" Grimshaw closed out his fourteen-year (1898–1911) professional career as a first baseman/outfielder with Louisville in 1911.

The six-foot-one, 173-pound Grimshaw began his play with London in the Canadian and International Leagues in 1898. Along the way, he had stops at Guelph (Canadian, 1899) and Chatham (1900, International); three years at Buffalo in the Eastern League (1902, '03 and '04); three years in the Major Leagues with the Boston Americans (1905, '06 and '07), his best being a .290 mark in 1906; and three years at Toronto in the Eastern League (1908–10). His career work included batting titles with Buffalo in 1904 (.325) and a .309 mark with Toronto in 1909.

For some curious reason, Grimshaw's 1901 baseball record is unavailable. Nonetheless, to the end, the switch-hitting Grimshaw—who threw right-handed—swung a big stick. For the 1911 Colonels, this long-forgotten star batted .363 in ninety-seven games, his 135 hits including fourteen doubles and fourteen triples. Born on November 30, 1875, in St. Johnsville, New York, Grimshaw died in Canajoharie, New York, at age sixty-one on December 11, 1936.

## *1913*

Right-hander Grover Cleveland Lowdermilk, another great pitcher from Louisville's early minor-league years, recorded a league-leading 197 Ks en route to a 20-14 mark in 1913. (Lowdermilk's lifetime work included the single-season minor-league record for strikeouts, 465 in 1907 split between two teams). Will Osborne (.333) banged out a league-leading 214 hits.

Another major chapter in Louisville's baseball history was written that year in the form of epic major-league pitcher John Joseph (Jack/"Red") Powell, a seventeen-game winner for the Colonels.

A four-time twenty-game winner in the Major Leagues, where he compiled a brilliant 2.97 ERA over a sixteen-year period (1897–1912), Powell remarkably still holds the big-top record for most wins by a pitcher with a losing lifetime win-loss percentage (245-254/.491). None of that was Powell's doing, however.

A member of two of the worst clubs in major-league history (first the Cleveland Spiders of the late 1890s and then the early twentieth-century

St. Louis Browns), the workhorse right-hander—one shy of figuring in five hundred career decisions—was plagued by low run support and poor defense the majority his career.

With any kind of a break, John Joseph Powell would today be a member of the Baseball Hall of Fame, instead of a mercurial statistical sidebar who, interestingly enough, was a .500 pitcher in eight of his sixteen major-league seasons.

The five-foot-eleven, 195-pound Powell closed out his long, distinguished professional career in 1914 with Venice (California) of the Pacific Coast League.

For the record, John Joseph Powell (b. July 9, 1874, in Bloomington, Illinois/d. October 17, 1944, in Chicago) is frequently confused with another pitcher named Jack Powell (given name: Reginald Bertrand Powell). The latter was briefly with the St. Louis Browns in 1913, the year after John Joseph Powell had concluded his major-league career with the same team.

Unlike John Joseph "Jack" Powell, Reginald Bertrand "Jack" Powell (b. August 17, 1891, in Holcomb, Missouri/d. March 12, 1930, in Memphis, Tennessee) went early and hard. His last words reportedly were "Watch this!" as he choked to death at age thirty-eight in 1930 while trying to eat an entire steak in one bite.

Before being called up to the Reds late in the season, third baseman John Albert "Bert" Niehoff swiped an American Association–best forty-eight bases and batted .298 in 170 games. A native of Louisville, Colorado, Niehoff finished off his twenty-one-year career as a player in organized baseball with 2,140 minor-league hits and a .272 average. His lifetime minor-league numbers included twenty-five years as a manager (two of them at Louisville), a 1,824-1,713 record and three minor-league pennants.

A lifelong baseball man, Niehoff also worked as a coach, scout and general manager. The last assignment in his extraordinary career was eight years as a scout (1961–68) for the Los Angeles Angels.

## *1914*

Louisville's first superstar minor-leaguer, George Howard "Jake" Northrop (frequently misspelled "Northrup") enjoyed his best season ever in a Louisville uniform. He went 26-10 and tied Melvin Gallia of Kansas City for the league leadership in wins.

As the American Association's all-time victory leader, Northrop, in his fourteen-year American Association tenure (1912–25), posted a 222-189 career total. The worksheet also included American Association marks for most innings (3,516), strikeouts (1,176) and losses.

A four-time twenty-game winner in the American Association, Northrop followed up his 1914 work with a 25-15 mark for Louisville in 1915 and a 16-13 worksheet for the 1916 pennant winners. His Louisville career numbers also entailed a 12-15 tab sheet in 1912 and a 17-10 account in 1913.

Overall, Northrop's minor-league totals came to 266 triumphs versus 212 defeats. The fine work included a gargantuan 27-4 record at Reading in the Tri-State League in 1911, a 20-10 ledger at Indianapolis in 1917 and a 20-17 worksheet for Milwaukee in 1920. As a major leaguer, the 1910 graduate of Bucknell University (also the alma mater of Christy Mathewson), went 6-6 in his lifetime with the 1918–19 Boston Braves.

Born in Monroeton, Pennsylvania, on March 5, 1888, the five-foot-eleven, 170-pound right-hander died there at age fifty-seven on November 16, 1945. Northrop was scarcely a one-man pitching show, however.

For the second year in a row, the aforementioned Grover Cleveland Lowdermilk led the league in strikeouts (254 Ks). This was the third of five times that he would lead his league in strikeouts; Lowdermilk's magnum opus was his rookie 1907 campaign when he struck out a minor-league seasonal record 465 batters.

Hippo Vaughn. *National Baseball Hall of Fame Library, Cooperstown, New York.*

The opening day winning pitcher was Fred Toney (1888–1953), who beat Columbus 7–2 at home. His solid twelve-year National League career (1911–1923) produced a 139-102 record, two twenty-win seasons and a pair of World Series titles with the Giants. It was capped by Major League Baseball's first—and to date, only—extra-inning double no-hitter. The historic and unusual record work occurred on May 2, 1917, when the Nashville, Tennessee native pitched a ten-frame 1–0 no-hit victory for the Reds against the Cubs.

The losing pitcher, no less, was another Louisville product, James Leslie "Hippo" Vaughn (1888–1966). In thirteen years of play (1908, 1910–21), Vaughn rolled out a 178-137 mark with the Yankees, Senators and Cubs. The ledger included five twenty-win seasons and one World Series. As a Louisville Colonel, Vaughn's work included taking the top half of Louisville's 1909 closing day double-header, a 6–5 win versus Kansas City.

An outfielder on the 1914 team and a first sacker on the 1915 outfit—seeing action with Nashville in both years—was Illinois native Dave Callahan (1888–1969). His seventeen-year-career minor-league totals included 2,127 hits; one batting title, .365 with Eau Claire in 1910 in the Minnesota-Wisconsin League; and a .271 average.

Another top name on the team was second baseman Howard Zell "Polly" McLarry (1891–1971), a Texas native who batted .316 in his only season with the Colonels. An eighteen-year veteran of professional baseball (1911–28), McLarry accumulated 2,723 hits, a .317 average, 1,457 runs, 1,292 RBIs and one batting title during his minor-league career. That championship came in 1918, the year McLarry was switched to first base for good. Sent over from Shreveport of the Texas League to Binghamton, he topped the International League with a .385 average.

## *1915*

Though he went 12-14 for the Colonels, right-hander James Blaine Middleton (1889–1974) came through in 1916 with a fine 21-9 mark and 2.01 ERA. The Indiana native appeared briefly with the Louisville Colonels in 1917 and then was called up to the Giants.

A twenty-one-game winner as a rookie in 1910, Middleton retired following the 1929 season with a 259-182 minor-league mark and six twenty-win campaigns.

Also a member of the 1915 squad was first and second baseman Ed Miller (1880–1980), who finished off his nineteen-year career (1909–27) with a lifetime minor-league average of .276, 2,227 hits and one base-stealing title (eighty-seven thefts in 1919 with Newark of the International League).

Yet another 1915 Colonels notable was outfielder Alfred Joseph "Al" Platte (1890–1976), who hit .321 in seventy-nine games. He spent all of the 1916 season with the Colonels (batting .277) and then, in 1917, split the year between Louisville and Chattanooga. His fifteen-year minor-league career statistics (1910–26) showed 1,983 hits, a .313 average and two batting titles: .367 with Cadillac of the Michigan State League in 1912 and .360 with Peoria of the Three-I League in 1922.

## Death on the Diamond

In addition to the somewhat unusual Kentucky connection of the Toney-Vaughn extra-inning double no-hitter, there are the somewhat eerie logistics of the diamond's only on-the-field fatality, whose principals were both born in Kentucky in the same year.

On August 16, 1920, at the Polo Grounds, Yankees pitcher Carl Mays (1891–1971) beaned Cleveland Indians shortstop Ray Chapman (1891–1920). The much-beloved Chapman was carried off the field and died the following day of a fractured skull, never having regained consciousness.

A native of Beaver Dam, Kentucky, Chapman was just twenty-nine and left behind a young widow plus a set of handsome career statistics in just nine seasons of play: a .278 batting average, a trio of .300 seasons and 1,053 hits.

The incident short-circuited two potential Hall of Fame careers, but for vastly different reasons.

Surly and unpopular, Mays—a native of Liberty, Kentucky—spent fifteen years in the big leagues (1915–1929) with the Red Sox, Yankees, Reds and Giants, amassing a 208-126 slate, five twenty-win campaigns and membership on four World Series champions. (His career work, notably enough, also included a stint with the 1931 Colonels.)

However, this single pitch, in the eyes of many experts, continues to deny Mays a clear shot at Cooperstown.

Many of those same experts also point out that Chapman and his batting style—he was a right-handed batter who habitually crowded the plate—put him in harm's way.

As a consequence, Mays—a submarine-style right-hander who had no problem backing a batter off the plate—"froze" Chapman with a pitch that came under, up and then into him. (Robert W. Creamer noted in his classic, *Babe*, that Mays's pitching "style was so extreme that he often scraped the knuckles of his pitching hand on the ground as he threw.")

Despite the loss of Chapman, the Indians nonetheless made it to the 1920 World Series, which they took by a 5-3 margin over National League champion Brooklyn. Highlighting that fall classic was the first, last and only unassisted triple play in World Series history, pulled off by Indians second baseman Bill Wambsganns in the fifth game.

Following the 1920 World Series, the Cleveland players voted a full World Series share—$3,986.34—to Chapman's widow.

Carl Mays. *National Baseball Hall of Fame Library, Cooperstown, New York.*

Dave Danforth struck out fifty-nine batters in four consecutive games. Danforth later became a dentist and for years ran a successful dental supply house in Baltimore. In April 1915, Babe Ruth made his first appearance in Louisville as a member of the Bosox.

## *1916*

The aptly nicknamed "Derby Day" Bill Clymer, who had piloted the club in its first two AA years (1902 and 1903), returned to the helm in 1916 and restored the Colonels to respectability in a grand way. Under his tutelage, Louisville—home of the world-famous Kentucky Derby—recorded its first "century-win" season, logging a splendid 101-66 (.605) mark that was five and a half games better than that of runner-up Milwaukee.

Louisville finished up the season by whipping Omaha, the single-A Western League champion, four games to one in the minor-league championship series.

This season was also another epic year in Louisville's minor-league baseball history, marking the local debut of Jay Kirke, who was sent over from Milwaukee. In action split between the two clubs, he sent up a .303 average that included a league-leading forty doubles. The following year, he again led the league in doubles (thirty-seven) while batting .318 in his first full season in a Louisville uniform.

However, this was just a prelude of things to come from one Judson Fabian Kirke, a six-foot, 195-pound first baseman/part-time outfielder who batted left but threw right.

Kirke's masterpiece season came in 1921. Off league-leading totals of 730 at-bats and 168 games, he established the all-time American Association record for hits in a season (282) en route to a .386 league batting championship (the highest seasonal mark ever by a Louisville minor-league hitter). The mark easily broke the former AA record of 254 hits, set by George Stone in 1904 with the Milwaukee Brewers (and was the most by a non–Pacific Coast League player).

The road to the minor-league mark was narrow, however. Because of the size of the old minor-league record—280 hits, set just the year before by Hack Miller of the Oakland Oaks in the Pacific Coast League—Kirke did not overtake Miller until closing day, when he notched three hits in a double-header against the Milwaukee Brewers. His numbers that season for Joe McCarthy's first flag winner included a circuit-topping 422 total bases, plus 125 runs scored, 43 doubles, 17 triples, 21 home runs and 157 RBIs. In

The 1916 American Association champion Louisville Colonels. *Top row*: Lefty James (LHP), Jay Kirke (1B), John Michael "Red" Corriden (3B) and Al Platte (OF). *Second row from top*: Bill Killefer (C), Bert Daniels (RF), Ralph "Sailor" Strand (RHP), Rube Schauer (RHP), Jimmy Middleton (RHP), Jake Northrop (RHP) and Joseph Waddell (C). *Seated*: George Whiteman (RF), Claude Williams (OF), Pete Compton (OF), Otto Wathen (Owner), Bill "Derby Day" Clymer (Manager), Adolfo "Dolf" Luque (RHP) and Hub Perdue (RHP). *Bottom row*: Emilio Palmero (LHP), Rex Barney (RHP), Josh Billings (C), Roxy Roach (SS) and Joe McCarthy (2B). *National Baseball Hall of Fame Library, Cooperstown, New York.*

1922, his final campaign with Louisville, Kirke again led the team in batting, with a .355 mark that also included 135 RBIs.

A lifetime .316 minor-league hitter with 3,165 hits to his credit, Kirke began his career as a shortstop in 1906 at Kingston of the Hudson River League. He played through the 1927 season and then, after a seven-year absence (1928–34), returned in 1935 as a playing manager for Opelousas in Louisiana's Evangeline League. Despite his age (forty-seven) and the long layoff, the magic was still there: in sixty games, Kirke batted .281.

One of the few players to have played in four different decades, Kirke also left behind a fine .301 major-league batting average; only a weak glove denied him a protracted major-league career. The best of that big-top work, taken in seven years of action with the Tigers (1910), Boston Braves (1911–13), Cleveland (1914–15) and Giants (1918), was a .320 mark in 103 games with the 1912 Braves and a .310 average in 87 games with the 1915 Indians. A giant of the game, the redoubtable Kirke (born June 16, 1888, in Fleischmanns, New York) died at age eighty in New Orleans on August 31, 1968.

Another leading figure on the local baseball scene was Louisville's first major Hispanic star, Adolfo Domingo de Guzman "Dolf" Luque (1890–1957). The Cuban-born right-hander went 13-8 for the 1916 Louisville squad, the city's second AA flag winner.

Getting off to an 11-2 start in 1918, Luque was sold to Cincinnati, where he resumed his major-league career. He flourished, retiring with a fine 194-179 lifetime slate in twenty years of big-top play (1914–35). That work notably included two World Series (1919/Reds and 1933/Giants) and stints with the Red Sox and Dodgers.

The 1916 Louisville roster also included outfielder George Whiteman (1882–1947), a Peoria, Illinois native who was also briefly a member of the 1917 club. The longtime star (an even quarter century, from 1905–29) exited with 3,388 hits and a .283 average in the minors, the minor-league record for most games played (3,282 games), star work in the 1918 World Series (his only full season in the majors) and a sound .272 career average in the big leagues.

Also in 1916, the world's most famous bat maker—incorporated as the J.F. Hillerich & Son Company in 1911—again changed its name. The revamped firm was now known as Hillerich & Bradsby. The new name came a few years after Frank Bradsby, previously a buyer for Simmons Hardware in St. Louis (the firm's first national outlet), became the head of sales for the company.

The elder J. Frederich Hillerich retired in 1916. Born in 1834 in Baden-Baden, Germany, he had immigrated to the United States in 1842 and established the first wood-turning shop in Louisville in 1864. He passed away in 1924 in Louisville; Bradsby died on May 11, 1937.

A shimmering page from Louisville's golden past, the priceless photograph of the star-studded 1916 Louisville Colonels features a rare look at the elusive Jake Northrop. As the first century-winning (101-66) team in the club's history, standouts also included Joe McCarthy and the aforementioned Kirke and Luque.

According to sources, the infield of Kirke, McCarthy, Roxy Roach and Red Corriden played the entire season without missing a time at bat. The top pitcher was John Middleton (21-9); the top batter was Kirke (.303).

Also of interest on this team was William Lavier "Reindeer Bill" Killefer, who had a substantial career in the Major Leagues as a player and manager

(1909–33). The batterymate of Cooperstown pitcher Grover Cleveland Alexander on first the Phillies and later the Cubs, Killefer played on two National League championship teams—the 1915 Philadelphia Phillies and the 1918 Chicago Cubs. A workhorse, he caught over one thousand games in the big leagues.

## *1917*

Louisville Colonels hurler Frank "Dixie" Davis notched a 25-11 slate in 1917. In doing so, he denied former Louisville standout Grover Cleveland Lowdermilk the AA pitching Triple Crown outright. Working for Columbus, Lowdermilk went 25-14, with 250 strikeouts and a 1.70 ERA.

A member of the Louisville team for part of the season (.288 in forty-eight games) was legendary minor-league star Anthony Vincent "Bunny" Brief.

Of Polish extraction, Brief was a right-handed first baseman/outfielder who hit .331 lifetime in the minor leagues. His work included 2,963 hits, 1,776 runs, 1,584 RBIs, 594 doubles, 154 triples, 342 home runs, eight home run titles, seven 200-hit seasons; five runs-scored crowns and five RBI championships.

Bunny Brief. *National Baseball Hall of Fame Library, Cooperstown, New York.*

His finest overall season came in 1921, when he knocked out 222 hits and posted career highs in batting (.361), runs (166), homers (42) and RBIs (191) for Kansas City of the American Association, the latter three all circuit-topping figures. His fifty-one doubles also led the league.

In 1923, he racked up a personal-best 230 hits as he batted .359 for Kansas City. The six-foot, 185-pound Brief went on to set American Association marks in career hits (2,196), home runs (276), doubles (458), runs scored (1,342) and RBIs (1,451).

His nineteen-year career (1910–28) also included major-league work with the St. Louis Browns (1912 and 1913), the White Sox (1915) and the Pirates (1917). Born Antonio Bordetzki in Remus, Michigan, on July 3, 1892, he died at age seventy on February 10, 1963, in Milwaukee, Wisconsin.

## *1918*

The league suspended play on July 21, 1918, because of World War I. Louisville notables this year included Missouri native Joseph Berger (1886–1956) and Anna Sebastian "Pete" Compton (1889–1978).

The former played ten games at shortstop for the Colonels. His career minor-league baseball stats (1907–28) included 2,659 hits and a .282 average. Compton, a Texas native, played fifteen games in the outfield. His twenty-year (1909–28) organized baseball career included 2,565 hits and a .307 average in the minors.

Another standout on the 1918 team was John Frank "Jack" Lelivelt (1885–1941), a Chicago native who batted .325 for the Colonels in double duty at first and in the outfield. During a twenty-one-year professional baseball career (1906–31), he batted .301 in the Major Leagues and averaged .331 in the minors with 2,671 hits. His minor-league work also included two batting titles, one of them a towering .416 mark with Omaha in the Western League in 1921. A manager for twenty years in the minors (1920–40), he posted an 1,861-1,439 career mark, recorded six 100-win campaigns and took Pacific Coast League flags with Los Angeles and Seattle.

## *1919*

Illinois native Tim Hendryx (1891–1957) led the AA with a .368 batting average in 1919. Dixie Davis (22-20) topped the AA with 165 strikeouts.

In the Major Leagues, Hendryx put up a solid .276 average over eight seasons, his best a .328 mark in ninety-nine games with the 1920 Bosox. The latter was 75-71 overall in the big leagues, principally with the St. Louis Browns, where he was a teammate of Hall of Famer George Sisler.

Other luminaries included infielder Bruno Betzel, catcher Billy Meyer and outfielder Bob Bescher.

Possessing one of the longest names in baseball history, Christian Frederick Albert John Henry David Betzel had more names than he did years in the Major Leagues: five with St. Louis in the National League (1914–18). He later piloted

Louisville in the 1930s. Another future Louisville manager was Meyer, who ran the club in the mid-1920s, his hallmark being the 1926 championship team.

Bescher was fresh off a solid eleven-year major-league career (1908–18: Reds, Giants, Cardinals and Indians) highlighted by 1,171 hits and four straight National League stolen-base titles (Cincinnati: 1909–12), a feat later exceeded by Louisville Redbirds star Vince Coleman. Well educated, Bescher attended both Notre Dame and Wittenberg (Springfield, Ohio).

## *1920*

Southpaws Ernie Koob and Tom Long threw no-hitters in 1920. The former beat Kansas City 4–0 on May 11. Long prevailed 12–0 against Toledo on July 24. Both came on the road.

## *1921*

Unquestionably one of the most powerful Louisville teams ever assembled, the 1921 club won the AA flag with a 98-70 mark and then shocked International League champion Baltimore 5-3 in the Junior World Series. The series began in Louisville, where the Colonels split the first four games.

One of the losses was a forfeit of the fourth game when rowdy Louisville fans swarmed the field and prevented further play—though the issue was well settled by then. Baltimore was leading 12–4 in the ninth inning when the game was stopped. The series then switched to Baltimore, which temporarily gained momentum with a win in the fifth game to gain a 3-2 edge in the best-of-nine series.

From then on, however, it was all Louisville. Roaring back into the fray with a vengeance—on the road, no less—the Colonels took the next three games and the Junior World Series. Rated as the greatest minor-league Junior/Little World Series upset ever, it came at the expense of Jack Dunn's mega-dynasty, which was in the midst of winning seven consecutive International League flags (1919–25).

Prominent figures on the quasi-major-league assemblage included future Hall of Fame pitcher Lefty Grove (300-141), who topped the IL in strikeouts (254).

Other talents numbered Jack Ogden, the league leader with thirty-one wins; IL batting champion Jack Bentley (.412), also the league leader in hits (246) and homers (24); and ERA titlist Joe Reddy (1.98).

Joe McCarthy. *National Baseball Hall of Fame Library, Cooperstown, New York.*

All of this explained Baltimore's staggering regular season ledger of 119-47 (.717), twenty games ahead of the Rochester Colts. (The runner-up, incidentally, won one hundred games, work that in any normal season would have yielded them a pennant.)

As for Jack Dunn, the owner and manager of the minor-league powerhouse, this was nothing new. A former major-league and minor-league player himself, Dunn sent many top players to the big show, his career prize being Babe Ruth. Besides Ruth and Grove, that group also included Frank Baker, Max Bishop, Bob Shawkey, Bentley, Ogden and George Earnshaw.

A man who truly had a gift for baseball, Dunn died suddenly at age fifty-four in October 1928 while riding a horse in Maryland.

The driving force behind the 1921 Louisville club was an equally great baseball man: playing manager Joe McCarthy (1887–1978). The second baseman on Louisville's 1916 AA flag winning team, he was named manager in 1919. During his tenure (1919–25), Louisville finished worse than third only once (sixth in 1922).

McCarthy won one Junior World Series (1921) and two AA flags (1921 and 1925). He was runner-up in 1920 and was third three times (1919, 1923 and 1924). Though he never played a day in the Major Leagues, he went on to a Hall of Fame career as a big-league manager.

Over a twenty-four-year span (1926–50), the Philadelphia native notched nine pennants—one with the Cubs, the rest with the Yankees—and seven World Series titles (all with the Yankees, those teams including the likes of Ruth, Gehrig, DiMaggio, Combs, Dickey and Lazzeri).

The winningest manager in major-league history, McCarthy retired with a 2,125-1,333/.614 account, none of his teams ever finishing out of the first division.

As was to be expected, the 1921 Louisville club was loaded with talent, notably beginning with record-setting league batting champion and first baseman Jay Kirke.

*Above*: With afternoon shadows dripping off of them like rich ink, the 1921 American Association and Junior World Series champion Louisville Colonels are seen in this rare picture from yesteryear. *Back row*: Roy Hardee "Red" Massey (OF), Herbert Miller (P), Alfred Ellis (OF), Ernie Koob (LHP) and T. Gaffney (SS). *Middle row*: Nick Cullop (LHP), Wayne Bromley "Rasty" Wright (RHP), Ben Tincup (RHP/OF), Jay Kirke (1B), Roy Sanders (RHP), Brad Kocher (C), Pelham Ashby Ballenger (SS), Tommy Estell (RHP) and Merito "Cubie" Acosta (OF). *Front row*: Tom Long (LHP), Buck Herzog (2B), Joe McCarthy (Manager), Billy Meyer (C) and Joe Schepner (3B). *Eclipse BBHR.*

*Right*: Ben Tincup, the all-time winningest pitcher in Louisville minor-league history with 180 triumphs. *National Baseball Hall of Fame Library, Cooperstown, New York.*

Other headliners were pitcher Ben Tincup and right fielder Merito Acosta, a pair of lost giants from Louisville's grand minor-league history.

The all-time winningest pitcher in the history of the Louisville minor-league franchise, Tincup—a full-blooded Cherokee Indian—spent thirteen seasons with the Colonels (1919–31). During that time span, the fabulous right-hander won 180 games for them. Also a tough left-handed batsman who often saw action as a pinch hitter and in the field, Tincup enjoyed his best seasons in 1921 (9-0/.284 batting average), 1922 (20-14), 1924 (24-17), 1926 (18-7) and 1930 (14-3 at age thirty-nine).

Dealt to Minneapolis during the 1931 season, the six-foot, 180-pound Tincup pitched his last contest in 1942 at age fifty-one in the Northern League. A lifelong baseball man, Tincup pretty much did it all.

At the end, his glittering diamond resume included major-league action with the 1915 National League champion Phillies, a perfect game for Little

Rock in the Southern Association in 1917, a lifetime .271 minor-league batting average, work as a scout and coach on the big-league level and stints as a minor-league umpire and manager.

Born on December 14, 1890, in Adair, Oklahoma, Austin Ben Tincup was truly one for the baseball ages. He died in Claremore, Oklahoma, at age eighty-nine on July 5, 1980.

Merito "Cubie" Acosta. *National Baseball Hall of Fame Library, Cooperstown, New York.*

No less a significant minor-league baseball figure was the regally named Merito "Cubie" Acosta (given name: Baldomero Pedro Acosta y Fernandez). One of Louisville's and the game's earliest Hispanic stars, Acosta (1896–1963) came to the Colonels in 1919 and spent a decade with them. While this may surprise many, it is nonetheless absolutely true. Louisville began producing major Hispanic talent during the World War I era. The baby-faced Acosta, a gifted outfielder, was one of three from that era. He was preceded by pitchers Dolf Luque and Emilio Palmero.

The Cuban-born right fielder was a key element for the 1921 AA/Junior World Series champions (.350, 135 runs, 116 walks) and the 1925 AA flag winners (.310). Acosta also logged time in the big leagues (1913–18) with Washington and Philadelphia in the American League.

Other principal position players on the dynamic 1921 Louisville Colonels club included second sacker Bruno Betzel (.313), shortstop P.A. (Pelham Ashby) Ballenger (.283), third baseman Joe Schepner (.317, 109 RBI), left fielder Roy Massey (.316, 134 runs scored), center fielder Rube Ellis (.336, 100 RBI) and backstoppers Bill Meyer (.312) and Brad Kocher (.271).

On the mound were pitchers Ernie Koob (22-9), Roy Sanders (18-11) and Nick Cullop (14-10). Running the whole show was playing manager McCarthy (.278 as a pinch hitter).

## *1922 and 1923*

Though Louisville slipped to sixth place in 1922, it still had some bright spots; one of them was newcomer Earle Combs (1899–1976). Signed off the campus of Eastern Kentucky State Teachers College (now Eastern Kentucky University), Combs was an immediate impact player for Louisville.

In 1922, the swift, hard-hitting outfielder batted .344 and led the circuit with eighteen triples. He followed that up in 1923 with a whopping .380 average that boasted forty-six doubles, 145 RBIs and a circuit-topping 241 hits. The work earned Combs a trip to the New York Yankees, where he spent his entire twelve-year Hall of Fame career (1924–35) and was the teammate of such fellow Hall of Fame luminaries as Babe Ruth, Lou Gehrig and Waite Hoyt.

The leadoff hitter and center fielder for the legendary 1927 Yankees, for whom he racked up a personal-best 231 hits, Combs three times led the league in triples—yet another indication of his fabulous deer-like speed: 1927 (23), 1928 (21) and 1930 (22).

In 1970, Combs was elected to Cooperstown off a brilliant portfolio that included a lifetime .325 batting average, four World Series appearances (.350 overall) and his storied defense (a career .974 fielding average).

Briefly, a member of the 1922 club was outfielder Lyman Lamb (1895–1955), who pinch-hit in one game. Two years later, though, the Nebraska native made his mark, pounding out an all-time organized baseball record of one hundred doubles in a season for Tulsa in the Western League.

A member of the 1923 Colonels for seventy-four games as an outfielder and first baseman—following a transfer from Portland in the Pacific Coast League—was Philadelphia native Emmett McCann (1902–1937). His seventeen-year professional career (1919–35) saw him play

Earle Combs. *National Baseball Hall of Fame Library, Cooperstown, New York.*

every position but pitcher and catcher. As a minor leaguer, he stroked out 2,244 career hits and batted .284.

Other major events of those two years included the burning down, in late November 1922, of Eclipse Park, the city's first minor-league ballpark at Seventh and Kentucky with a capacity of 8,500; Hillerich & Bradsby becoming the nation's number one bat maker in 1923; and the opening of the city's new minor-league ballpark, Parkway Field, on May 1, 1923. Inspired by Chicago's Wrigley Field, Parkway Field seats almost 16,500 people and cost $250,000 to build.

## *1924*

In January 1924, Louisville sold star right-handed pitcher Wayland Dean (21-8 the previous year) to the New York Giants for $50,000. He lasted just four years in the Major Leagues (Giants, Phillies and Cubs) before arm trouble did him in. His best work was a 10-7 mark with the 1925 Giants.

His mound work also included some relief work in the 1924 World Series, which the Giants lost in seven games to the Senators. A solid batsman as well, Dean went six for twenty-six as a pinch hitter in 1926. In April 1930, Dean died of tuberculosis. He was just twenty-seven.

Outfielder Elmer Smith (1892–1984) led the American Association with twenty-eight homers. His work for the Colonels also included 216 hits and a .334 average. He returned in 1929, and he batted .285 in 156 games for Louisville. During a twenty-one-year professional career (1911–32), the Ohio native hit .317 in the minors with 1,909 hits. Three times Smith led his league in home runs. On the major-league level, he logged a solid .275 average with the Indians, Senators, Red Sox and Yankees. His best full-time big-league mark was a .316 average in 129 games with the 1920 World Champion Cleveland Indians. Smith died in Columbia, Kentucky, on August 3, 1984, at age ninety-one.

## *1925*

Manager Joe McCarthy set Louisville back on top in 1925, when the Colonels won the AA flag via the most victories in the club's history (106-61/.635). One of the prime reasons for that gargantuan success was the work of near mythical outfielder Joe Guyon.

Joe Guyon, a double Hall of Famer. *Courtesy Georgia Tech Sports Information Office.*

Unquestionably the greatest all-around athlete ever to play Louisville baseball (minor league or major league), Guyon remains one of the most fascinating stories in the city's long baseball history. A full-blooded Chippewa Indian, Guyon was born *O-Gee-Chidea* ("brave man") on a reservation in White Earth, Minnesota, on November 26, 1892.

Guyon began his epic athletic career playing football at Carlisle (Pennsylvania) Academy, where he was a teammate of the legendary Jim Thorpe. Their coach was the celebrated Glenn "Pop" Warner. One of their games came against West Point, a team that included a young halfback named Dwight Eisenhower. He was subsequently a part of Georgia Tech's undefeated 1917 national champion team and an all-American tackle in 1918. The fabled John Heisman, the namesake of college football's most prized trophy, coached both teams. From there, Guyon moved on to professional football.

A triple-threat halfback and a teammate of Thorpe on four teams, in 1920 Guyon began his National Football League (NFL) career with the undefeated Canton Bulldogs. He concluded it in 1927 with a touchdown pass that gave the New York Giants a victory over the Chicago Bears for that year's NFL title.

A precursor of two-sport star Bo Jackson (NFL football and Major League Baseball), Guyon also began his minor-league baseball career in 1920. His best career work came in 1925, when he led the league in batting (.363), hits (228) and runs scored (152). He followed that up with a .343 average and 209 hits the next year as Louisville repeated as AA champion. In 1927, he hit .353 for the Colonels, though they fell to seventh place.

Then, the roof fell in.

In the eighth inning of the second game of a May 30, 1928 doubleheader in Indianapolis, the five-foot-eleven-and-a-half, 172-pound Guyon severely reinjured his left knee after running into a fence chasing a triple by Indy's shortstop, Matthews. Suddenly, both his athletic careers were over—along with his dream of playing Major League Baseball, though he played minor-league baseball on and off through 1936, retiring with a career .329 mark. (Ironically, Guyon's replacement in right field the next day was the aforementioned Merito Acosta, who was making his first appearance in a Louisville uniform since a near-fatal beaning the previous August by Minneapolis's Pat Malone.)

Following the injury, Guyon was the coach of Louisville's St. Xavier High School football team for three years. Also, during the 1930s, he was employed by the Colonels. In later years, he worked as a bank security officer in Flint, Michigan, but returned to Louisville when he retired.

In 1966, he was elected to the Pro Football Hall of Fame and, in 1970, to the College Football Hall of Fame. On November 27, 1971, one day after his seventy-ninth birthday, Joseph Napoleon Guyon died in a Louisville hospital. He was buried at that city's Resthaven Memorial Park, where another Louisville great—Pee Wee Reese—was also interred.

The 1925 club also featured a trio of twenty-game winners in Nick Cullop (22-8), Joe DeBerry (20-8) and Ed Holley (20-7).

## *1926*

Louisville again reached the century mark in wins (105-62) en route to its second straight AA flag, this one under new helmsman Billy Meyer. The postseason action quickly ended when Toronto swept the Colonels 5-0 in the Junior World Series.

A big force on the club was outfielder Earl Webb (1898–1965). The Tennessee native batted .333 with 158 hits, 32 of them two-baggers. Five years later, with the 1931 Boston Red Sox, he got serious and set an all-time seasonal major-league record of sixty-seven doubles, a mark that still stands.

And former Louisville star Albert "Ty" Tyson broke into the Major Leagues at age thirty-four as an outfielder for John McGraw's New York Giants. He played for the Giants for two years (.293 and .264) before closing out his big-top career with the Brooklyn Robins in 1928.

## *1927*

The extraordinary opening day winning streak of Norman Andrew "Nick" Cullop (1887–1961) came to a halt in 1927. It took some doing, though, as

Southpaw Norman Andrew "Nick" Cullop, one of Louisville's greatest and most forgotten pitchers. *National Baseball Hall of Fame Library, Cooperstown, New York.*

Minneapolis went twelve innings to win 1–0. The skein had begun with a 4–0 shutout of Indianapolis in 1923 and then continued with a 6–4 defeat of St. Paul in 1924, a 3–2 victory over Milwaukee in 1925 and a 10–5 whipping of Milwaukee in 1926.

An integral part of Louisville's fabled Roaring Twenties teams, the durable southpaw racked up over 100 wins for the Colonels during an eight-year period (1921–28). Highlighting the star's Louisville numbers were a 22-8 mark in 1925, a 20-8 record in 1926 and a 14-win campaign in 1921. A career 57-53 in the Major Leagues, Nick Cullop logged a 20-win season for Kansas City of the renegade Federal League in 1915.

The Virginia native followed that up in 1916 with a 13-6 worksheet for the Yankees, at one point reeling off ten straight victories.

For the record, pitcher Norman Andrew "Nick" Cullop is not to be confused with the famed minor-league slugger Henry Nicholas "Tomato Face" Cullop (1900–1978), also known as "Nick." (They are not related.)

Though the latter batted just .249 in five years of major-league play, when it came to minor-league pitching, he absolutely feasted. A lifetime .312 hitter in the minors (1920–44), Henry "Tomato Face" Cullop rang up 2,670 hits, 420 homers and a ranking as minor-league's all-time RBI king (1,857).

A manager from 1940 to 1959, Henry "Tomato Face" Cullop (born in Missouri as Heinrich Nicholas Kolop) was twice named the *Sporting News* Minor League Manager of the Year for his work with a pair of upset Junior World Series champions: the 1943 Columbus Red Birds and the 1947 Milwaukee Brewers.

Outfielder Simon Rosenthal (1903–1969), a native of Massachusetts, hit .276 in 76 games for the 1927 Colonels. The work came in the season after he played his only big-league full-time campaign, batting .267 in 104 games for the Bosox. Totals for his fourteen-year career (1922–35) show a .333 average and 1,654 hits in the minors.

## *1928*

Though Louisville fell into the cellar, a fall somewhat softened by a next-to-last-place finish in 1927, the 1928 season was not a total loss. The reason was Texas-born Edgar Dudley "Dud" Branom (1897–1980), who topped the league in RBIs (128). The following year, Branom—a pure southpaw who batted and threw left—hit .332 with 129 RBIs.

Still another fabulous minor great to wear the Louisville uniform, Branom spent five years with the Colonels (1928–32), his RBI output ranging from a "low" of 110 to a high of 134. A lifetime .317 minor-league hitter with over 2,500 hits and 1,459 RBIs to his credit, the six-foot-one, 190-pound Branom tallied fifteen years in the game (1920–34), that play including a brief stint with the 1927 Philadelphia A's.

Second baseman Eddie Sicking (1897–1978) led the league in hits (242) en route to a .368 average. He followed that up in 1929 with a .310 average in 148 games for the Colonels. Also with Louisville on a part-time basis in 1927, the Ohio native wound up with 2,534 hits and a .306 average in the minors. His eighteen-year organized baseball career (1916–33) also included time with the Giants, Phillies, Reds and Pirates.

One of the few players to wear a Colonels uniform in parts of three decades, left-handed hitting and throwing Earl James Browne (1911–1993) started his twenty-two-year career (1928–49) with his native Louisville,

Dud Branom. *National Baseball Hall of Fame Library, Cooperstown, New York.*

following up with cups of coffee in 1929 and 1930. Brought back toward the end of the 1942 season, he played first base through the 1945 season. Then, in the twilight of his career, Browne took back-to-back KITTY League batting titles with Owensboro in 1946 (.429) and 1947 (.424).

Browne's career stats included 2,309 hits, a .304 average, 1,222 runs and 1,301 RBIs in the minors. One of minor-league baseball's more versatile players, he played three positions during his long career: pitcher, first base and outfield. As a major leaguer (Phillies and Pirates), Browne hit a career .284; his best was a .292 mark in 105 games for the 1937 Phillies.

Foster Pirie "Babe" Ganzel (1901–1978) came over from the Senators for the final part of the season, batting .322 in 79 games. It was a sign of things to come. In 1929, he hit .322 in 157 games for the Colonels, playing both outfield and the hot corner.

Permanently converted to third base in 1930, he responded with a .338 average, following that up with a .306 mark in 1931. A seventeen-year veteran (1922–41), the Massachusetts native exited with 2,032 hits and a .317 mark in the minors and a lifetime .311 average in the Major Leagues.

## *1929*

Yet another all-time minor-league great, Melbern Ellis "Butch" Simons made a notable debut with Louisville in 1929, hitting .340 and punching out 214 hits in 150 games. The next season, the five-foot-ten, 175-pound outfielder—who batted left but threw right—was even better.

A major force in Louisville's last championship until 1939, Simons hit .371 with a league-leading 248 hits, 49 of them doubles (also top in the AA).

Following major-league service with the White Sox and action with AA rival Toledo, Simons rejoined the Colonels in 1932 (batting .314). A fixture through 1938 with the Colonels, where he was a marquee name in a series of also-rans, Simons stroked out 201 hits in 1933 (.324) and 1934 (.328). In 1935, he batted .352 with 185 hits and the next year led the AA again in hits (220) off a .353 average.

Though he "dropped" to .316 in 1937, he just missed another 200-hit season, ending with 199 hits. He concluded his long Louisville run with a .272 mark in 1938. A career .329 minor-league hitter with 3,031 hits to his credit, Simons went out with a bang, taking the 1941 KITTY League batting title with a .386 average. It was his next-to-last year in organized baseball; he was forty-one.

The following year, he polished off a stellar nineteen-year career (1924–42) with a .313 average for Quebec of the Canadian-American League. A playing manager toward the end of his career, Simons made a brief return to baseball in 1955, managing Fulton (Kentucky) in the KITTY League. Born on July 1, 1900, in Carlyle, Illinois, Simons died in Paducah, Kentucky, at age seventy-four on November 10, 1974.

An interesting figure on Louisville's "Depression Year" club was right-hander Walter William "Boom-Boom" Beck.

## *1930*

A diamond on the 1930 Louisville squad was future Hall of Famer William Jennings Bryan "Billy" Herman. Signed out of semipro ball for $250 a month in 1928, Herman batted .305 in 1930. His .350 average the following year for the Colonels earned him a big-league promotion; his contract was sold to the Cubs for $60,000. In retrospect, the Depression-era sale turned out to be a bargain.

*Above, left*: Mel Simons. *National Baseball Hall of Fame Library, Cooperstown, New York.*

*Above, right*: Billy Herman. *National Baseball Hall of Fame Library, Cooperstown, New York.*

Gifted with both the glove and the bat, the slick-fielding, sure-hitting second baseman spent fifteen years in the Major Leagues (1931–47) with the Cubs, Dodgers, Boston Braves and Pirates. In 1975, Herman was inducted into the Hall of Fame off the following career numbers: a .304 batting average, 2,345 hits and play in four World Series.

Born on July 7, 1909, in New Albany, Indiana, Herman died on September 5, 1992, in West Palm Beach, Florida, at age eighty-three.

In 1930 postseason action, the Colonels won the AA flag under Al Sothoron but lost the Junior World Series to International League champion Rochester five games to three.

Another major headliner on the 1930 Colonels team was Indiana native Ken Penner (1896–1959), who began a six-year stay with the Colonels that season (1930–35). He posted his best numbers in a Louisville uniform the following year when he went 17-8. When Penner concluded his twenty-eight-year pitching career (1913–43), he was a member of minor-league baseball's elite 300-win circle, ranking seventh on the all-time minor-league wins list with 330 victories against 284 defeats. The right-hander's work included four 20-win campaigns.

Standouts on the 1930 Colonels team included outfielder Herman Layne (1901–1973), a West Virginia native who hit .333 and notched 209 hits. Following a pair of .300 seasons, he started the 1933 season with Louisville and ended it with Toledo, batting .274 overall. During his thirteen-year organized baseball career, Herman Layne amassed 2,097 hits and a .327 average in the minors. But this is only half the story.

In an identical thirteen-year career (1922–34), twin brother Harry Layne knocked out 1,607 hits and averaged .316 in the minors. Highlighting the work was a .360 batting title with Peoria of the Three-I League in 1926.

Curiously, though the pair—both outfielders—opened their careers together at Bristol in the Appalachian League, the brothers never again played on the same team. And unlike brother Harry, Herman Layne did get a brief ticket to the Major Leagues, appearing in eleven games with the Pirates in 1927.

While right-hander Louis Americo Polli went 8-13 for the 1930 Colonels, he finished his twenty-one-year professional career (1922–45) with a 263-226 slate that numbered a pair of 20-win seasons and two ERA crowns—all in all, not bad for a man who was brought to this country when he was only months old. Born in Baveno, Italy, on July 9, 1901, Polli died in Denmark on December 19, 2000, months short of his 100th birthday.

Also in 1930, Louisville fielded its first Negro League team: the Louisville White Caps of the Negro National League. They were followed over the next quarter century by the Louisville White Sox (1931/Negro National League), the Louisville Black Caps (1932/Negro Southern League), the Louisville Buckeyes (1949/Negro American League) and the Louisville Black Colonels (1954/Negro American League).

A notable member of the 1930 Louisville Colonels squad was Bill Wambsganns, the only player in World Series history ever to pull off an unassisted triple play. Despite that remarkable work (game five—October 10, 1920), Wambsganns (1914–26 in the Major Leagues) and his Cleveland Indians lost the 1920 World Series to the National League champion Brooklyn Robins.

## *1931–39*

In step with the times, Louisville saw its first professional night game on Wednesday, May 25, 1932.

Playing before 5,063 fans at Parkway Field, the Colonels defeated the Columbus Redbirds 5–4 in dramatic fashion. With the bases loaded and one out in the bottom of the ninth, pinch-hitter Clarence Nachand lifted a sacrifice fly to center field that sent winning pitcher Phil Weinert home with the deciding run. The losing pitcher was none other than eighteen-year-old Paul "Daffy" Dean, brother of future Hall of Fame pitcher Dizzy Dean. The game lasted for two hours and seven minutes.

The new lights cost $12,000 to construct, according to the *Louisville Courier-Journal*. Thirlwell Electric Company installed the lights, placing four towers in the outfield and four groups of lights in the roof of the grandstand. They also installed four floodlights to illuminate the parking space west of the field.

Though the game was the first organized (minor- or major-league) night baseball game in the history of Louisville, it was not the city's first night game. Not by a long shot.

In September 1931, a Louisville All-Stars outfit met the House of David club at Parkway Field, which was illuminated via lighting equipment carried by the House of David team. However, this contest was not the first night in Louisville baseball annals either. That honor, incredibly, belongs to a recently discovered Friday, September 11, 1903 contest at old League Park at Twenty-eighth and Broadway, where the Reccius Baseball Club met the Sioux Indian Baseball Club of Spokane, Washington.

That this was Louisville's first night game ever is unequivocal because of the *Louisville Courier-Journal*'s game-day story, which stated that "the game at night by electric light has never been seen in this city before." A barnstorming team from the reservation in Washington and Oregon, the Sioux Indian Baseball Club, was en route to California, where it would close its season on December 1. The team had its own car and provided fifty arc lamps for the game.

The contest was confined almost entirely to the infield due to a special ball that had been made for the occasion. Called at 8:00 p.m., the game resulted in an easy 8–3 victory for the traveling team, which was used to playing night baseball.

Another memorable aspect of the game was the visitors' lineup, which read as follows: Afraid of the Moon (catcher), On the Trail (pitcher), Likes the Snow (first base), Kakimah (second base), Red Blanket (third base), Walk in Smoke (shortstop), Rolling Clouds (left field), Little Wolf (center field) and Swift Water (right field).

A curious epilogue to all of this is that the teams made history without knowing it, a phenomenon that is both indicative of history in general and Louisville baseball history in particular.

Hall of Famers Pee Wee Reese (left) and Ducky Medwick. *National Baseball Hall of Fame Library, Cooperstown, New York.*

The innovative night-game concept, which later revolutionized Major League Baseball, saved minor league baseball during the depths of the Depression, providing cost-effective and enjoyable entertainment to people who spent the day working or looking for employment.

In every way, it was one of the few bright spots in Louisville as the Colonels went through their longest postseason-action dry spell, eight straight years (1931–38) without an appearance. During that time frame, the franchise ran through five managers, one of them future Hall of Fame pitcher Burleigh Grimes (270-212), who put in a one-year stand in 1936. However, in 1938, a dazzling light of hope appeared on the horizon in the form of one Harold Herman "Pee Wee" Reese, who in time, along with folklore hero Pete Browning, became one of the two signature names in Louisville's rich baseball history.

A product of Manual High School in Louisville, where he was coached by the peerless Ralph Kimmel, the young phenom batted .277 as rookie in 1938 for a cellar-dwelling Louisville team. The following year, Reese was the fulcrum of a Cinderella baseball story as fourth-place Louisville, three games under the .500 mark at 75-78 in regular season action, rocked the 1939 baseball world with its off-season play.

First, the team emphatically whipped Minneapolis and Indianapolis by twin 4–1 margins in the playoffs; then, it topped it all off by stunning International League champion Rochester in the Junior World Series, scoring four runs in the eleventh frame of the seventh and deciding game.

Reese's contributions in the field and at the plate were enormous, as the precocious wunderkind shortstop—also a natural-born leader—batted .279, led the league in triples (eighteen) and stolen bases (thirty-five) and topped the circuit's shortstops in putouts. This was merely a sign of things to come. His major-league statistics during a sixteen-year career (1940–58), all with the Dodgers, first in Brooklyn and then Los Angeles, included a .269 batting average; 2,170 hits; NL titles in walks, runs scored and stolen bases; and a .272 average in seven World Series.

An incomparable gloveman who could make all the plays at short, a heady leadoff hitter and base runner and the consummate captain, Reese was a major force behind Jackie Robinson's successful transition into Major League Baseball in 1947. And together, they were a part of the great "Boys of Summer" Dodger teams of the 1940s and 1950s, a cast that also included the likes of Carl Erskine, Roy Campanella, Preacher (Elwin) Roe, Duke Snider, Clem Labine, Billy Cox, Joe Black, George Shuba, Carl Furillo and Gil Hodges.

Inducted into Cooperstown in 1984 and a member of the Veterans Committee in his retirement years, Reese enjoyed success in every facet of his career: as a player, private businessman, broadcaster and business executive with Hillerich & Bradsby.

Though slight in stature, the five-foot-ten, 170-pound Reese was a giant of the game—and life—in every way. Born on July 23, 1918, in Ekron, Kentucky, Reese died at age eighty-one in Louisville on August 14, 1999. With his passing, Louisville lost its most beloved baseball figure, who—in thought, word and deed—was the absolute essence of what every human being should be. His lifelong example will live forever.

Also in 1938, Louisville's last surviving old-time major-league batting champion, Guy Hecker, died in Wooster, Ohio, at age eighty-two on December 3. The only pitcher ever to win a major-league batting title (1886), he also was the only player ever to win a big-top batting title and a pitching Triple Crown (1884).

Waxahachie, Texas native James Aubrey "Jimmy" Adair (1907–1982) played shortstop and second base for the 1932 squad and then became a fixture at second for the next four years (1933–36). He retired in 1944 with 2,034 hits and a .285 lifetime average off a nineteen-year career (1927–44) in the minors.

Adair's teammates included right-hander Claude Alford Jonnard (1897–1959), a Nashville native who went 18-15 in 1932 for the Colonels and 1-7 for them the next year. In a twenty-four-year career in organized baseball (1917–46), Claude Jonnard ran off a 219-219 win-loss record in the minor leagues, four times winning twenty games or more.

Part of yet another set of twins with Louisville connections in whole or in part, Jonnard's twin brother was catcher Clarence James "Bubber" Jonnard (1897–1977), whose organized baseball career ran from 1917 through 1936.

One of the few sets of twins to have played big-top baseball, both men logged six years in the Major Leagues during their expansive careers.

The 1935 squad included third baseman Frank Sigafoos (1904–1968). The Pennsylvania native began the season with Memphis but ended it with the Colonels, batting .314 in ninety-eight games. During his fourteen-year stay in professional baseball (1925–38), this handy gloveman played second base and shortstop. His lifetime minor-league numbers showed 2,003 hits, a .313 average and one batting title (.370 with Indianapolis in 1933) that included a then American Association record thirty-nine-game hitting streak.

The 1935 Louisville aggregation also boasted pitcher Truett Banks "Rip" Sewell (143-97), inventor of the famed "Eephus" pitch.

In 1937, Ellis Foree "Mike" Powers (1906–1983) saw action with Toledo and Louisville, batting .306 overall. Playing through 1942, Powers accumulated fifteen-year minor-league totals of 2,228 hits, a .334 average, 1,265 runs scored and 1,056 RBIs. His work included league crowns in hits, doubles, triples, RBIs and a .383 Cotton States League batting title in his 1928 rookie season. Born in Crestwood, Kentucky, on March 2, 1906, the aptly named Powers died in Louisville at age seventy-seven on December 2, 1983.

Yet another notable during this time frame was versatile Tennessee native Bill Lewis (1904–1977), who batted .327 in the Major Leagues and .308 (with 1,734 hits) in the minors. The first eight years of his twenty-one-year career in organized baseball (1924–45) saw him play every position with the exception of pitcher.

In 1933, he was converted to catcher and spent the rest of his diamond career backstopping. After splitting the 1939 season between Indianapolis and the Colonels, he logged a full season with Louisville in 1940.

In 1939, outfielder Chet Morgan (1910–1991) began a five-year run with the Colonels. The Massachusetts native enjoyed a seventeen-year career (1933–50) in organized baseball, collecting 2,159 minor-league hits along the way and batting a lifetime .301 in the little show. His work also included a .342 batting title in the Texas League in 1934.

## *1940*

Louisville very nearly duplicated its 1939 "miracle" season in 1940. Though it was a dead-even .500 club in regular season play (74-74), it far exceeded its fourth-place finish in postseason action. After besting Columbus 4–2 in the playoff openers, the Colonels then took out regular season AA champion

Kansas City 4–2 in the playoff finals. It all ended in the Junior World Series, however, when International League champion Newark upended Louisville in six games.

For the second year in a row, right-hander Woodrow "Woody" Rich (1917–1983) spent part of the season with the Colonels. Though the North Carolina native only bagged one 20-win season during his career, he nonetheless came up with a 250-174 career minor-league slate that included 2,405 strikeouts.

His twenty-two-year tenure (1937–58) in professional baseball also included a 6-4 mark in the majors, all with Boston in both the National and American Leagues.

Outfielder Fred Sington (1910–1998), an Alabama native, closed out his ten-year career (1931–40) at Louisville with a .271 average and 115 hits. His lifetime minor-league numbers read: 1,171 hits; a .317 average; league crowns in runs, doubles, triples, home runs and RBIs; and a pair of batting titles (.368 with Beckley in the Middle Atlantic League in 1932 and .384 with Chattanooga in the Southern Association in 1936). His major-league average with the Senators and Dodgers was .271. His other work with Louisville included eighty-three games with the 1939 Colonels. A two-time all-American football player at Alabama (1929 and 1930), Sington was elected to the College Football Hall of Fame in 1955.

A.H. (Albert Henry) Tarvin published the first history of Louisville baseball in 1940: *75 Years on Louisville Diamonds*. His work also includes another collectible: *A Century of Baseball, 1839–1939*.

A Louisville-born baseball king and trailblazing pioneer died on November 17, 1940, at age seventy-eight. Nicknamed the "Father of the Texas League," John McCloskey either founded or helped establish numerous other minor-league operations during his life. Besides the Texas League (1888), that group also included the Pacific Northwest League (the forerunner of the modern-day Pacific Coast League) and the Southern League. All three operate today in powerful fashion, a sterling tribute to the baseball genius of McCloskey and his indefatigable work at the grass roots of the game.

A generous man who often used his own money to sustain struggling ballplayers, clubs and circuits, McCloskey is reputed to have established more professional baseball leagues than any other man in the history of the sport. Though he never played in the majors, McCloskey managed several big-top clubs, including his hometown's National League aggregation in 1895 and, briefly, 1896. It was one of some three dozen major- and minor-league teams (at all levels) that he piloted during his venerable thirty-six-year managing career (1888–1932), a figure believed to be a record. The vast majority of that work came in the minors, where he spent thirty-one years, turning out a 1,713-1,632/.512 mark and a number of flag winners.

Possessing a strong eye for baseball talent, McCloskey discovered a number of fine players over the years, including Fred Clarke, Jimmy Collins, Joe Tinker, Joe "Iron Man" McGinnity, Herman Long, Red Ehret and Jack Pfiester.

Nicknamed "Honest John," McCloskey started his extraordinary diamond career as the batboy for the 1876 Louisville National League team. By the time he retired in 1930, McCloskey had held every major position in the game: player, coach, manager, scout and executive.

McCloskey was buried at Louisville's Calvary Cemetery, within sight of the final resting place of another Louisville baseball great and should-be Hall of Famer, pitcher Gus Weyhing. McCloskey's grave is watched over by a two-sided marker. On the front is his name and life dates; the reverse contains his name, nickname ("Honest John") and a mighty inscription that reads: "This tribute of grateful memory is dedicated by the youth and manhood of America, benefited by his life spent as a player, manager and league organizer of his beloved game, baseball."

It is a great epitaph for a giant of the game, a man who was truly the "Johnny Appleseed of baseball."

## *1941*

Shortstop Johnny Pesky, born John Michael Paveskovich on September 27, 1919, in Portland, Oregon, batted .325 in 1941. The next year, Pesky commenced a fine ten-year major-league career (1942–54) that would see him bat .300 or better six times. A career .307 batter with the Red Sox, Tigers and Senators, his work also included three seasons with 200 or more hits: 1942 (205), 1946 (208) and 1947 (207).

Both a shortstop and third baseman in the majors, Pesky for years unfairly bore the brunt of Boston's loss in the 1946 World Series to the Cardinals, which saw future Hall of Famer Enos Slaughter, on first, score the winning run in the seventh and decisive game via Harry Walker's double. In truth, according to numerous sources, Pesky had no chance for two reasons: first, because Slaughter was running on the pitch, and second, because the relay throw to Pesky was late. As one person said, Pesky couldn't have gotten Slaughter out with a shotgun (throw).

Johnny Pesky. *Courtesy Boston Red Sox.*

Another bright star was pitcher Tex Hughson (7-1/2.97 in his second year with Louisville), who would finish out the 1941 season with Boston. His 96-54 career big-league work, all with the Bosox, included a pair of twenty-win seasons, one of them a 20-11 mark for the pennant-winning 1946 Bosox; two World Series starts; and the 1944 AL win-percentage crown (.783) off an 18-5 record. Born Cecil Carlton Hughson in Buda, Texas, on February 9, 1916, he died in Austin, Texas, at age seventy-seven on August 6, 1993.

Making its third straight postseason appearance, Louisville beat Minneapolis 4–2 in the playoff openers but lost the AA playoff finals to regular season AA titlist Columbus 4–1.

During the season, Hall of Fame and Negro League star Satchel Paige pitched before five thousand fans at Parkway Field. He was yet another big-league luminary to make an appearance at Parkway; this list over the years included the likes of Babe Ruth, Lou Gehrig and Honus Wagner.

## *1942*

The skipper of the 1942 AA All-Star team was also one of the successful managers in Louisville baseball history: Bill Burwell. Taking over for Donie Bush in the 1939 season, Burwell immediately and completely reversed the decade-long slide of the club with three straight postseason appearances (1939, '40 and '41), two AA championships (1939 and '40) and one Junior World Series title (1939). This work was not by chance, however; Burwell came to the job with impeccable credentials and experience.

A fine right-handed pitcher during his playing days, the five-foot-eleven, 175-pound Burwell, much like Hall of Famer "Three Finger" Brown of the

Chicago Cubs did before him, used a serious hand injury to his advantage. In action during World War I, Burwell's index finger was severely shot up by an enemy machine gun. Back in civilian life, Burwell discovered that the wound actually improved his breaking pitch. The results were unmistakable, as evidenced by his career 239-206 slate in the minors.

The bulk of that was taken in the American Association, where Burwell won 193 games. His work included back-to-back twenty-win campaigns with the AA Indianapolis Indians in 1925 (24-9) and 1926 (21-14), the former season leading the circuit in victories. In the twilight of his career, Burwell continued to ring them up.

At age forty-two in 1937, he rolled out a combined 9-2 record in action divided between Minneapolis in the American Association (4-0) and Rock Island in the Western League (5-2). His active career (1915–38) also included a 9-8 major-league total with the Browns and Pirates.

But that is merely the tip of the iceberg. A playing manager and then a manager and coach in the minors, Burwell went on to coach in the majors with the Boston Braves and Pittsburgh Pirates. Burwell's final baseball assignment came at age sixty-eight in 1963 as a scout for the Pirates. Born on March 27, 1895, in Jarbolo, Kansas, Burwell died on June 11, 1973, in Ormond, Florida, at age seventy-eight.

Also in 1942, Hillerich & Bradsby converted to wartime production, making carbine stocks, tank pins and billy clubs for the U.S. Armed Forces.

## *1943*

For the second year in a row, southpaw Chester Rogers "Chet" Covington (1910–1976) made a brief stop in Louisville (0-1). From there, he went on to a 21-7 mark with Scranton in the Eastern League, topping the circuit in wins. One of them was a 6–0 perfect game on May 23 against Springfield. At season's end, he received the Minor League Player of the Year award.

During a fifteen-year haul (1939–53), Covington four times won twenty games or more. He also led his league in ERA four times, strikeouts and victories three times and twice in innings pitched. The end results were a towering 220-126 lifetime minor-league record, a sterling .636 win-percentage rate and a 2.57 ERA.

His glistening career work included a 3-2 tab with Louisville in 1942, a season that found him opening with the Colonels, transferring to Birmingham and then finishing up with Springfield.

Outfielder Arthur Anthony "Art" Rebel (1914–2004) split his time between Louisville and American Association foe St. Paul, batting .262 overall. The Cincinnati native's seventeen-year (1936–52) organized baseball totals are impressive: 2,099 hits, a .301 average, 1,127 runs scored and 1,230 RBIs in the minor leagues, plus a .333 average (twenty-seven for eighty-one) in the majors with the Phillies and Cards.

## *1944*

Under new manager Harry "Nemo" Leibold, Louisville ran a good third. It followed up with triumphs over regular season AA champion Milwaukee (4–2) and St. Paul (4–0) in the AA playoffs. However, it lost the Junior World Series to International League titlist Baltimore, 4–2.

A key element on the improved team was another minor-league star from yesteryear: third baseman Nick Polly (1917–1993), born Nicholas Polachanin in Chicago on April 18, 1917. The American Association leader that year in RBIs (120), Polly also set the American Association's all-time record for walks (147). It was all part of a campaign that saw Polly hit .290 and homer twenty times. His baseball resume included short stints with the Dodgers and Red Sox.

Right-hander James Wilson (19-8) led the league in strikeouts (147) and tied Earl Caldwell of Milwaukee for wins. Fellow right-hander Mel Deutsch captured the ERA crown (2.47), giving Louisville a pitching Triple Crown of sorts.

Nick Polly. *Courtesy of Brace Photo, Chicago, Illinois.*

And outfielder Frank ("Chico," "One Hop") Genovese, an outfielder on the 1944–46 Colonels, began a phenomenal defensive streak during the 1944 season. When the skein finally ended in 1946, the Staten Island, New York native had played 268 games without an error, an AA record for an outfielder. Aiding the record substantially was Genovese's avoidance of making shoestring catches. Instead, he preferred to catch them on one bounce, thus making for fewer errors and also accounting for his nickname.

## *1945*

For the second year in a row, in 1945 outfielder Cosmo Como "Tony" Cotelle (1904–1975) split his time between two teams, one of them Louisville. In 1944, he saw action with Indianapolis and the Colonels. In 1945, he started off the season at Louisville and then transferred to Scranton in the Eastern League. The five-foot-five, 155-pound Louisiana native ended his twenty-one-year baseball career (all of it in the minors) in 1946. Though built small, Cotelle still left some big numbers: a .323 average, 2,730 hits, 1,319 runs scored, 1,199 RBIs and three batting titles.

On May 14, Byron Laforest went six for six, duplicating Eddie Morgan's work in 1937.

And in a near mirror image of its previous season's work, third-place Louisville won the playoff opener and playoffs against Milwaukee and St. Paul respectively by identical 4–2 margins. This time, however, the team nailed the big prize, capturing the Junior World Series 4-2 from International League titlist Newark.

## *1946*

Manager Nemo Leibold's magic continued in full force as Louisville reached the much-vaunted Junior World Series for the third straight season. Capturing the American Association flag outright for the first time since 1930, it defeated St. Paul 4-1 in the playoff opener (the team's lone loss being a no-hitter thrown by Tom Sunkel) and then swept Indianapolis 4-0 in the playoff finals. In the ensuing Junior World Series, it built up an early 2-1 lead, but IL batting champion Jackie Robinson (.349) got staggering game-winning hits in contests four and five to give the Montreal Royals a 3-2 advantage. Montreal went on to win it all in six games.

A part-season member of the 1946 and 1947 Louisville Colonels was catcher/first baseman Otto George Denning (1912–1992), a career .309 hitter in the minors.

## *1947 and 1948*

Making its fourth straight postseason appearance, Louisville beat Minneapolis 4–3 in the 1947 AA playoff openers. However, a narrow 4–3

Billy Goodman. *Courtesy Boston Red Sox.*

loss to Milwaukee in the AA playoff finals denied it its fourth straight trip to the Junior World Series. However, it had been an impressive run by Louisville helmsman Harry "Nemo" Leibold, the pilot of that year's All-Star team. One of the franchise's most successful managers, Leibold departed the following year after the club tumbled to the cellar of the eight-team circuit.

A noteworthy member of the 1947 Louisville team was North Carolina native William Dale "Billy" Goodman (1926–1984), who hit a robust .340.

The consummate utility man, Goodman went on to a sixteen-year major-league career with the Bosox, Orioles, Chisox and Astronauts, playing every position but catcher and pitcher. A lifetime .300 hitter, he registered 1,691 hits. His big-show highlights included the 1950 American League batting championship (.354) and the 1959 World Series with the "Go-Go" White Sox.

Also in 1947, Clem Dreisewerd (18-7) topped the AA in wins and ERA (2.15).

## *1949*

Ward Hillerich died in 1949; he was succeeded as CEO of Hillerich & Bradsby by his son, John F. Hillerich II.

In local baseball action, Louisville's Thomas Everette "Tom" Wright led the league with a .368 batting average via 202 hits in 151 games. The work included thirty-eight doubles, eighty-nine RBIs and ninety-one runs scored and in part obscured his fine 1948 numbers with the Colonels: .307, 173 hits, thirty-one doubles, eighty-five RBIs and eighty-nine runs scored. He spent nine years in the majors with the Red Sox, Browns, Chisox and Senators.

The '49 squad was hardly a one-man show, though. Besides Wright, it also included pitcher Mickey McDermott and outfielder Jimmy Piersall, each exciting, dynamic ballplayers in his own right.

Born on August 29, 1928, in Poughkeepsie, New York, tall and reed-thin southpaw Maurice Joseph "Mickey" McDermott struck out seventeen batters in a Wednesday, April 19, 1949 opening day 4–3 victory versus Minneapolis. It was just one short of the AA loop record of eighteen, co-held, interestingly enough, by two other Louisville lefties: Dave Danforth in a September 12, 1915 contest against Kansas City, and Archie McKain in a June 19, 1934 night contest with St. Paul.

McDermott got the record outright on May 24, 1949, when he struck out twenty hitters in the second half of a double-header versus St. Paul. This was part of a mesmerizing 116 strikeouts in seventy-seven innings that year for the six-foot-two, 170-pound McDermott, who went 6-4.

During a twelve-year career (1948–61), McDermott was 61-61 with the Red Sox, Senators, Yankees, Kansas City Athletics, Tigers and Cardinals; his best season was an 18-10 mark with Boston in 1953. A member of the 1956 World Champion New York Yankees, McDermott was also a fine hitter (.252 lifetime), his two best marks both coming with the Red Sox: .364 in 1950 and .301 in 1953.

One of baseball's most colorful, entertaining and intelligent players, Connecticut native Jimmy Piersall (b. 1929) overcame a nervous breakdown to have a fine major-league career. With Louisville in 1949, he batted .271. The next year, he initiated a seventeen-year big-show career (1950–67) with the Red Sox, Indians, Senators, Giants and Angels that produced a lifetime .272 batting average. His major-league stats also included a .990 fielding average (many forget that Piersall was a brilliant-fielding outfielder).

Many also forget that Piersall had the last—and ultimate—laugh at his youthful problems with a courageous bestselling book entitled *Fear Strikes Out*, later made into a hit movie of the same name starring Anthony Perkins in the title role.

A success in everything he did, after his retirement from the game, Piersall became a noted and insightful sportscaster.

One of the more unusual players with the 1949 and 1950 Colonels was outfielder George Washington "Teddy" Wilson (1925–1974). In 1949, he batted .267 in 141 games and then followed that up in 1950 with a .274 mark in 126 games.

During a twenty-year career (1942–64), the North Carolina native logged time in the majors, the minors and Japan. Wilson's best work came in the American minor-league system, where he rolled out a .311 average highlighted by 1,901 hits. Remarkably, these substantial numbers (and his

*Above, left*: Mickey McDermott. *Courtesy Boston Red Sox.*

*Above, right*: Jimmy Piersall. *Courtesy Boston Red Sox.*

lengthy career) came despite the loss of three prime years to military service (1943, '44 and '45).

On September 3, 1949, Cotton Deal went the route in a twenty-inning, 4–3 win over the Colonels at Toledo. The contest tied the American Association record for the longest game in league history, set twice before, both of those times also road contests involving Louisville. The first occurred on June 9, 1914, when the Colonels lost 3–2 at Minneapolis; the second was on July 11, 1942, when the Colonels and Toledo played to a 6–6 tie.

Also a member of the 1949 and 1950 squads was big Walt Dropo (six feet, five inches/220 pounds). The AL Rookie of the Year in 1950, when he batted .270 and hit fifteen homers for the Red Sox, Dropo—of Yugoslavian descent—spent thirteen years in the big leagues (1949–63).

## *1950*

A major member of the 1950 Louisville Colonels was outfielder Taft Shedron "Taffy" Wright (1911–1981). A former major leaguer embarking on a second baseball career at the minor-league level, he was the Colonels'

The lion at rest: Taft Shedron "Taffy" Wright. *National Baseball Hall of Fame Library, Cooperstown, New York.*

top batter for three straight years: .318 (1950), .335 (1951) and .297 (1952). With good reason.

A lifetime .311 hitter in the majors, Taffy Wright batted .300 or better six times. His best full-time season came with the White Sox in 1940, when he batted .337 in 147 games. Besides the Chisox, he also saw action with the Senators and Athletics during a fine big-top career (1938–49) substantially compromised by three prime seasons lost to military service (1943–45).

Because of an extraordinary number of similarities, Taft Shedron "Taffy" Wright and the previously profiled Thomas Everette Wright have been frequently confused over the years. Besides their surnames, both men played for the Colonels in the 1950s as outfielders, each was born in North Carolina, both batted left but threw right and each had a nine-year career in the majors. However, Thomas Everette Wright and Taft Shedron "Taffy" Wright were distinct and separate entities in Louisville and American baseball.

## *1951*

During the Golden Jubilee (fiftieth) anniversary season of the AA (and Minor League Baseball in Louisville), the club won its last fourteen games, matching the streak of Joe McCarthy's 1925 pennant winners. Incomplete records prevent the confirmation of this skein as record-tying club work, no data having been being compiled on this statistic before the 1925 streak. Nevertheless, the 1951 Colonels victory run was both impressive and well timed.

And that season, Michael Franklin "Pinky" Higgins (1909–1969) began a rather unusual but lucrative stint. Though his teams never won the AA flag outright, they still landed in the playoffs three times in four years. Higgins's zenith came in 1954, when Louisville took the Junior World Series. Higgins came well heeled for his work. His career stats, all in the American League, included a .292 batting average, nearly two thousand career hits and play in two World Series.

Also, James Atkins led the league in wins (18-9), and Louisville saw brief postseason action as St. Paul beat it 4–1 in the AA playoff openers.

## *1952 and 1953*

The shortstop on the '52 Colonels team was Carl Francis "Buddy" Peterson (b. 1925). A native of Portland, Oregon, he enjoyed a fourteen-year stay in professional baseball, the highlight of which were 2,146 career hits and a .280 batting average in the minors.

Major Louisville names in 1953 included Frank Baumann and the ill-fated Harry Agganis.

Baumann went 10-1 and batted .368 in thirteen games. During an eleven-year major-league career (1955–65), the St. Louis native compiled a 45-38 mark with the Red Sox, White Sox and Cubs. His personal best came in 1960, when he went 13-6 and racked up a league-leading 2.67 ERA for the Chisox.

Of Greek descent, the regally named Aristotle George "Harry" Agganis was one of the most heralded athletes in New England history. At Boston University, he earned all-American quarterback honors and was a standout on the diamond. Choosing Major League Baseball over the NFL, he was signed by the Bosox, and in 1953, his only season of minor-league play, he turned out a .281 average, twenty-three homers and 108 ribbies for the Louisville Colonels.

Called up by the parent club the following year, the six-foot-two, two-hundred-pound rookie first baseman got 109 hits (eleven of them home runs) in 132 games for the 1954 Red Sox. The next season, the "Golden Greek" was batting .313 after twenty-five games and the future was infinite—until the budding twenty-six-year-old superstar died suddenly of a pulmonary embolism in late June 1955.

A major name on both the 1952 and 1953 clubs was Ken Aspromonte, older brother of Bob Aspromonte.

## *1954*

Though it was second in the regular season, Louisville ended 1954 in spectacular fashion. Taking out Columbus 4-3 in the playoff openers, it upended AA regular season champion Indianapolis 4-1 in the playoff finals. That was a substantial piece of work, since the Indy squad included the original "Gold Dust Twins": Herb Score and Rocky Colavito. Louisville finished off its season and its postseason play by copping the Junior World Series in six games from International League foe Syracuse.

One of the more interesting players on the club was Albie Pearson, who, despite his diminutive five-foot-five, 141-pound stature, went on to a make a big name for himself in the big leagues.

## *1955*

One of the top names on the club in 1955 was third baseman Frank Malzone (b. 1930), who batted .310. The Bronx, New York native spent twelve years in the majors (1955–67), eleven of them with the Boston Red Sox. A career .274 hitter, the sure-handed Malzone reeled off 142 hits or more in eight straight big-top seasons.

Also, Louisville lost the playoff openers 4-3 to Omaha.

Frank Malzone. *Courtesy Boston Red Sox.*

## *1956*

In Parkway Field's final year, Ted Abernathy posted a league-best 212 strikeouts (despite a 12-16 mark). At the helm for the Colonels during the latter part of the season was future Hall of Famer Max Carey. Significant players included Pompeyo "Yo-Yo" Davalillo (brother of longtime major-league star first baseman/outfielder Vic Davalillo: sixteen years, 1963–80; .279; four World Series) and Jiro Nakamura.

## *1957*

In 1957, the Colonels commenced play at Fairgrounds Stadium, part of the newly completed Kentucky State Fairgrounds & Exposition Center. Fairgrounds Stadium was later renamed Cardinal Stadium.

## *1958*

For the third straight year, in 1958, the Colonels occupied the cellar. But there was at least one bright light. His name was outfielder Willie Tasby, and at season's end, he earned AA Rookie of the Year honors for his exemplary work: a league-leading 174 hits, a .322 batting average, twenty-two homers and ninety-five RBIs. A fine fielder as well, he was the complete package. Louisville's first major black minor-league star, the Shreveport, Louisiana native (born January 8, 1933) spent six years in the majors with the Orioles, Red Sox, Senators and Indians.

Also a member of the 1958 Louisville club was future Hall of Fame Orioles manager Earl Weaver.

Willie Tasby. *National Baseball Hall of Fame Library, Cooperstown, New York.*

## *1959*

Though Louisville had on its staff the league's two winningest pitchers in right-handers Georges Maranda (18-6) and Don Nottebart (18-11 and a sparkling 13-5 the next year), the Eastern Division titlist was still swept 4-0 in the AA playoff openers against Fort Worth.

Other standouts on the team included switch-hitter Ken Wise (.302) and Puerto Rican–born pitcher Juan Pizarro, who went 4-1 with a 1.07 ERA. One of those wins was a no-hitter, allowing the southpaw to join the select company of Jesse Stovall (1908), Ernie Koob and Tommy Long (both 1920), Don Thompson (1945) and Bob Alexander (1950).

Yet another fine Hispanic talent in Louisville's long baseball history, Pizarro went on to an extensive eighteen-year major-league career (1957–74) that included a 131-105 record, a personal-best 19-9 mark with the White Sox in 1964 and action in two World Series.

In 1959, Louisville's club was the ninth one in eight years for the well-traveled outfielder/first baseman Dave Roberts (b. 1933). A native of Panama, he finished off his twenty-two-year career (1952–73) having played in the majors, the minors (.282 average; 1,858 hits) and Japan (.275).

Another notable was Pennsylvania native Ray Shearer (1929–1982), who played for Louisville, Atlanta and Nashville that year. A thirteen-year veteran of professional baseball (1950–62), the outfielder/first baseman left the game with 1,581 minor-league hits and a .288 average. His career work also included a brief stop with the 1957 world champion Milwaukee Braves.

## *1960*

In postseason action in 1960, Louisville took the Junior World Series from International League champion Toronto after cutting down St. Paul and Denver in the AA playoff openers and finals, respectively. Interestingly enough, all three postseason showdowns were decided by identical 4-2 margins.

Much of the credit for the Colonels success went to gifted manager Ben Geraghty (1914–1963). In 1959, he inherited a club coming off three straight last-place finishes, and he responded with three consecutive postseason appearances (1959, '60 and '61) and one Junior World Series title (1960).

A member of the team that year was future Hall of Famer Phil Niekro (born April 1, 1939). Coming over from Jacksonville in the South Atlantic

League, with a 6-4 mark, the Ohio native was 1-0 in six games for Louisville. Niekro returned to the Colonels in 1962, sending up a 9-6 mark for that team.

A twenty-four-year veteran of the majors (1964–87) with the Braves, Yankees, Indians and Blue Jays, Philip Henry Niekro turned out a brilliant 318-274 lifetime record that featured three twenty-win seasons. His younger brother, Joseph Franklin "Joe" Niekro (born 1944), also did well in the big leagues, going 221-204 lifetime and twice winning twenty games or more.

Michigan native George Brunet (1935–1991) went 4-1 for the 1960 Colonels, part of a career 244-242 lifetime minor-league ledger. An active hurler in organized baseball for thirty-three straight years (1953–85), Brunet held the minor-league record with 3,175 strikeouts. A top name for years in the Mexican League, the lefty wound up winning, and losing, over three hundred games in baseball. Overall, with his 69-93 major-league numbers factored in, he was 314-335; his best mark was 13-13 with the 1966 California Angels.

Also, Howie Koplitz no-hit Indy 2–0 on May 30, and a notable member of the 1960 squad was Tommie Aaron, brother of home run king Hank Aaron.

## *1961*

For most of the 1961 season, outfielder Howie Bedell led the American Association in batting, but in late August, he was sidelined for the rest of the campaign with a chipped bone in his shoulder. This cost Bedell.

In a closing day, September 7 double-header with Houston, Denver's Don Wert went five-for-eight. The work enabled Wert to narrowly win the batting crown, .328 to .327. For the statistically inclined, the actual margin was .00041, Wert posting a .32756 mark to Bedell's .32715 average.

Bedell's numbers that year for the Louisville club included a league-leading 194 hits and a sensational forty-three-game hitting streak that tied shortstop Eddie Marshall's 1935 AA standard with Milwaukee. Though he only got a cup of coffee as a major leaguer, he did have one memorable moment. On June 8, 1968, his sacrifice fly for the Phillies stopped Don Drysdale's consecutive scoreless streak at fifty-eight and two-thirds innings, though the Dodgers won 5–3. Ironically, it was Bedell's only RBI of the season—and his last as a major leaguer.

In the AA playoff openers, Louisville decked Denver 4-3 and then dispatched Houston 4-2 in the AA playoff finals. It all came to a halt in

Howie Bedell. *National Baseball Hall of Fame Library, Cooperstown, New York.*

the Junior World Series, though, where International League foe Buffalo summarily brushed Louisville aside 4-0.

Other standouts on the 1961 team were Frederico Olivo, who rolled out a circuit-topping 2.66 ERA, principal catcher and future funnyman/Hall of Fame broadcaster Bob Uecker (.309) and receiver Joe Torre.

Starting the 1961 season with the Louisville Colonels, Joseph Paul "Joe" Torre hit .342 in 27 games and then moved up to the Milwaukee Braves, where he hit .278 in 113 games. Though few knew it at the time, this was the beginning of a two-part player/manager career deserving of Cooperstown admission.

Born on July 18, 1940, in Brooklyn, New York, Torre went on to a durable and productive eighteen-year career (1960–77) with the Braves, Cardinals and Mets. His apex was the 1971 National League batting crown off a hefty .363 mark that included a league-leading 230 hits and a circuit-best 137 RBIs for the Cardinals.

When Torre retired as an active player, he left behind a set of imposing career numbers: a .297 batting average, 2,342 hits, 344 doubles, 252 homers, 1,185 RBIs and 996 runs scored.

A versatile player and fine gloveman as well, during his extended career, Torre logged 903 games at catcher, 787 at first, 515 at third and 2 in the outfield. Possessed of a keen baseball mind, Torre then managed for fourteen years (1977–84, 1990–95) with moderate success in the National League. His lone prize was the 1982 NL West title with the Braves.

A change of scenery often produces positive results, and in 1996, Torre jumped to the American League to take over the rusty New York Yankees. Finally given some horses to run with, he immediately initiated another dynasty reign for the sport's signature name, taking four world championships in five years (1996–2000).

The 1996 triumph, which saw the Yankees surprise the 1990s NL dynasty Braves in six games, ended a long dry spell. For the Yankees, it was their first

World Series title since 1978. For Torre, it was his first World Series after thirty-one years in the Major Leagues as a player and manager. (That the title also came in Torre's first season in the Steinbrenner/Yankee pressure cooker is perhaps most impressive of all.)

Further enriching the 1996 World Series victory was the human triumph of Torre's older brother, Frank, a former National League and Louisville standout (.282 in 1960), who received a heart transplant during the postseason classic.

Torre's Yankees then followed that up with facile, back-to-back World Series sweeps of the Padres (1998) and the Braves (1999) and a near sweep (4-1) of the Mets in 2000.

Torre's long-running World Series show came to an end when the Yankees fell to the Arizona Diamondbacks in the 2001 World Series, a seven-game postseason classic that ranks as one of the greatest ever. (In 2008, he was hired by the Dodgers, for whom he continues to be a force as a manager.)

## *1962*

Under new manager Jack Tighe, Louisville made its third straight Junior World Series appearance and fourth consecutive postseason appearance in 1962—despite a sub-.500 regular season record (71-75/.486).

The wild and mercurial postseason action had something for everybody.

In the playoff openers, Louisville swept Indianapolis 3-0 and then followed that up with a 4-2 drubbing of Denver in the AA playoff finals. In the ensuing Junior World Series, Louisville held a 3-2 edge over its International League foe, the Atlanta Crackers, after five games.

However, Louisville wound up losing the series 4-3 after the Crackers took a twi-night double-header from it; the unusual two-for-one finale was necessitated by a desire to end the series before it was terminated by cold weather.

At season's end, the venerable American Association, in operation since 1902, was disbanded. There would be no more baseball in Louisville until 1968 and no American Association baseball in the River City until 1982.

Top names on the 1962 club included pitchers Connie Grob, who posted a league-best 2.86 ERA en route to a 14-10 mark; Frederico Olivo, the circuit's strikeout champion (151 Ks; 13-11); and Denny Lemaster (10-4; 125 Ks), who registered seven consecutive strikeouts—and 14 Ks overall—in an April 23 win over Omaha. The amazing performance tied the AA successive-strikeout record set by Toledo's Monte Pearson in 1933.

## *1964*

Louisville baseball executive and sportswriter Bruce Dudley, a landmark figure in Louisville baseball history, died on June 24, 1964, at age seventy-two.

President of the Louisville Colonels minor-league baseball club from 1940 to 1949, Dudley also was president of the American Association from 1948 until 1953.

Born in Flemingsburg, Kentucky, Dudley had come to Louisville in 1916 as a reporter for the old *Louisville Herald*. From 1918 to 1923, he was sports editor of that paper and then served in the same position with the *Louisville Courier-Journal* from 1923 through 1938. While at the latter newspaper, he became well known via his "The What-Not" column.

A skilled football and thoroughbred horse racing writer as well (his specialties were the Centre football team, Louisville's annual Male-Manual High School football showdown and the Kentucky Derby), Dudley wrote sports in a humorous tone, devoid of any mean-spirited jabs. His baseball writing also included an award for best minor-league baseball story of the year in 1924, the only year that Major League Baseball writers cited their minor-league counterparts.

Leaving the *Louisville Courier-Journal* and joining the Louisville Colonels minor-league baseball franchise in 1938, Dudley became president two years later. The first man to be voted the nation's outstanding minor-league baseball executive twice, during his long career, Dudley was also vice-president of the National Association of Professional Baseball Leagues and chairman of its executive committee.

During Dudley's tenure with the Louisville team, attendance records were repeatedly broken, substantial improvements were made to Parkway Field and the team was well marketed, that work including a number of revamped or new promotions for both fans and civic organizations.

Executive director of the Kentucky Independent College Foundation from 1953 until his retirement in July 1962, Dudley remains today a major page in Louisville's—and this country's—spectacularly rich baseball history.

## *1968*

Baseball returned to Louisville in 1968 after a six-year hiatus, although in a much different package. The Colonels were now a Red Sox affiliate in the International League. This was Louisville's second stint with Boston, and it lasted five years.

For the record, Louisville has served as a farm club for the following major-league teams to date: the Pittsburgh Pirates, 1936–38; the Boston Red Sox, 1939–55 and 1968–72; the Washington Senators, 1956; the Baltimore Orioles, 1958; the Milwaukee Braves, 1959–62; the St. Louis Cardinals, 1982–97; the Milwaukee Brewers, 1998–99; and the Cincinnati Reds, 2000 to present.

In IL action, Louisville's Galen Cisco posted a league-best 2.21 ERA as the Colonels tied Syracuse for fifth place in the eight-team loop under new manager Eddie Kasko.

A notable member of the 1968 and 1969 Colonels was pitcher Ken Brett, brother of Hall of Famer George Brett and the youngest pitcher ever to appear in a World Series game (age nineteen in 1967).

## *1969*

Billy Conigliaro. *Courtesy Boston Red Sox.*

John A. Hillerich II died in 1969. John A. Hillerich III became the new president and CEO of Hillerich & Bradsby.

On the local baseball scene, Luis Alvarado earned International League MVP honors off league leaderships in hits (166) and runs (89). And Jerry Janeski (15-10) shared the league leadership in victories with Fred Beene of Rochester and Ron Klimkowski of Syracuse. The performances pushed Louisville up to second place. In postseason action, the Colonels lost to Syracuse 3-2 in the AA playoff openers.

A notable member of this team was Billy Conigliaro, brother of ill-fated Bosox superstar Tony Conigliaro.

Jim Lonborg. *Courtesy Boston Red Sox.*

## *1970*

Hillerich & Bradsby marketed its first aluminum bat in cooperation with ALCOA in 1970.

A noteworthy member of the 1970 Colonels, briefly, was pitcher Jim Lonborg, who went 1-1. In 1971, he compiled a 4-2 ledger for the Colonels. Both stints were temporary "rehabs."

Born James Reynold Lonborg, the powerfully built California native (six feet, five inches/200 pounds) went 157-137 in a fifteen-year career (1965–79) with the Bosox, Brewers and Phillies. His best season came in 1967, when Lonborg (22-9) led the Boston Red Sox to the American League flag with a circuit-best 246 strikeouts and the co-leadership in wins.

His work included a pennant-clinching victory over Dean Chance and the Minnesota Twins on the final day of the season. The victory gave the AL flag to Boston at the expense of the Twins and Tigers, the other two parts of a three-way knock-down, drag-out pennant fight that year.

That year's American League Cy Young Award winner, Lonborg almost ended the city's longstanding drought for a world championship, going 2-1 in the fall classic. However, the defeat came in the seventh and decisive game of that year's World Series, albeit under extenuating circumstances. After just two days' rest, Lonborg went down by a 7–2 score to future Hall of Famer Bob Gibson and the St. Louis Cardinals.

Also, Billy Farmer no-hit Toledo 8–0 on August 24.

## *1971*

Darrell Johnson took over the Louisville club, and it became a .500 club again. Its fortunes ascended even more dramatically the next year. A major contributor was Carlton Fisk, one of the game's greatest catchers ever.

*Above, left*: Darrell Johnson. *Courtesy Boston Red Sox.*

*Above, right*: Carlton Fisk. *Courtesy Boston Red Sox.*

Fisk's pertinent career numbers, in twenty-four years as a championship backstop with first the Red Sox and then the White Sox (1969–93), included a .269 batting average, 2,356 hits, 1,330 RBIs, 1,276 runs and 376 home runs.

The most famous home run of Fisk's career, far and away, occurred in the twelfth inning of the sixth game of the 1975 World Series against the Cincinnati Reds. Even today, the footage of that moment remains undaunted by time. Classic and epic, Fisk waved his up-reached arms and cajoled the ball to stay fair (it barely did, hitting Fenway Park's left-field pole).

Considered by many to be the greatest World Series game ever, the electrifying sixth game was also part of arguably the greatest fall classic ever played. Five of the seven games were decided by one run, including the 4–3 finale at Fenway Park that gave the world title to the Reds.

In historical retrospect, however, there were no losers.

American League Rookie of the Year in 1972, Vermont native Fisk (born December 26, 1947) batted .263 in ninety-four games for the 1971 Colonels. His stats included forty-three RBIs, forty-five runs, ten doubles and ten homers.

*Above, left*: Ben Ogilvie. *Courtesy Boston Red Sox.*

*Above, right*: Luis Tiant. *Courtesy Boston Red Sox.*

In mid-January 2000, Fisk—along with Tony Perez, another star from the 1975 World Series—became one of the millennium's first two inductees to the Baseball Hall of Fame in Cooperstown.

Also members of the 1971 Louisville Colonels squad were future American League star Ben Ogilvie, who hit .304, and Luis Tiant (229-172), who would go on to win two games in the 1975 World Series.

## *1972*

Behind MVP outfielder Dwight Evans, first baseman Cecil Cooper and pitcher Craig Skok, three of five Louisville players selected for that year's International League All-Star team, Louisville took the IL flag in heart-stopping fashion.

On the last day of the season, Monday, September 4, the team clinched the pennant via a brilliant 1–0 shutout by Mike Nagy over Toledo, putting its final record at 81-63 (.563). It was a close call as the Charleston Charlies finished just one game back in second with an 80-64 (.556) account. Only Louisville's 1998 divisional title would be by a smaller margin, a microscopic half-game advantage.

Evans won MVP and All-Star honors off a .300 batting average, a league-leading ninety-five RBIs, 149 hits, 17 home runs; 23 doubles and 90 runs. The California native (born 1951) then went on to spend twenty years in the majors (1972–91), nineteen of them with the Red Sox. His career numbers included a .272 batting average, 385 homers, 2,446 hits and superlative action in two World Series.

But Evans was more—much more—than just a hitter.

He was a gloveman of consummate grace and brilliance (.987 lifetime fielding average), who relentlessly patrolled right field for the Boston Red Sox for years. His highlights included an electrifying catch of Joe Morgan's homer-to-be and subsequent doubling up the runner at first in the sixth game of the 1975 World Series. More than a quarter of a century later, they remain two of the finest defensive masterpieces ever seen at Fenway Park, in World Series play and in all of baseball history.

Power-hitting first sacker Cecil Cooper (born 1949), who would make it to the majors for good the following year, led the International League in hits (162). His .315 average included thirty-one doubles, ten home runs, eighty-six runs and seventy-eight RBIs in 134 games.

The Texas native was just as big in the big leagues, running up an impressive array of career numbers during his seventeen-year career (1971–

*Above, left*: Dwight Evans. *Courtesy Boston Red Sox.*

*Above, right*: Cecil Cooper. *Courtesy Boston Red Sox.*

87) with first the Red Sox and then the Brewers: a .298 batting average, 2,192 hits, 241 home runs, 415 doubles, 1,125 RBIs, 1,012 runs and two World Series appearances.

And fifteen-game winner Skok led the loop in victories.

Piloted by Darrell Johnson, whose managerial apex would come in 1975 when he guided Boston into the World Series via such former Louisville standouts as Carlton Fisk, Dwight Evans and Cecil Cooper, Louisville won its IL playoff opener versus Rochester but lost the IL playoff finals to Tidewater.

Still, despite the championship season and a bumper crop of stars during the last two seasons, Louisville lost its baseball team for a decade after the club was evicted from its stadium. This curious state of affairs occurred when the University of Louisville Cardinals' football program gained exclusive use of the Fairgrounds Stadium, which it later renamed Cardinal Stadium.

## *1975*

Hillerich & Bradsby introduced a full line of baseball and softball gloves in 1975.

## *1982*

Nothing great is ever lost forever, it has been often said, and after a decade-long hiatus, baseball returned to the River City. And in a big way—the renamed Louisville Redbirds set a minor-league attendance record.

On August 8, 1982 (its fifty-fifth home date), Louisville drew 19,251 fans, raising its season total to 681,479. The figure surpassed the old mark of the 1946 San Francisco Seals in the Pacific League, who drew 670,563 fans in 183 games. The Redbirds closed out the season with a total attendance ledger of 868,418. But this was only a warm-up for the next year.

Managed by Joe Frazier, the 1982 club tied for second with Iowa in the Eastern Division as Ralph Citarella (15-6) led the league in victories.

A budding marquee name on the 1982 Louisville club was that of Willie Dean McGee. Born November 2, 1958, in San Francisco, McGee became a mainstay of the Cardinal outfield and, in time, would be joined by fellow Louisville product Vince Coleman.

National League MVP in 1985, the switch-hitting McGee captured the NL batting title with a .353 batting average. His work also included 216 hits and eighteen triples, both league-leading totals, plus 114 runs scored.

McGee's eighteen-year major-league totals (1982–99) with the Cardinals, A's, Giants and Red Sox, included a .295 batting average, 2,254 hits, 1,010 runs scored, four World Series and two NL batting titles.

## *1983*

With two home dates remaining, the Louisville Redbirds became the first minor-league franchise to draw a million fans in a season. The team concluded its banner, record-setting year with an attendance figure of 1,052,438. Much of this was due to the team's owner, a brilliant baseball promotion man named A. Ray Smith, and the Redbirds' new manager, Jim Fregosi, who was firmly in the tradition and mold of Louisville's finest helmsmen: "Derby Day" Bill Clymer, Joe McCarthy, Bill Burwell, Nemo Leibold, Mike "Pinky" Higgins and Ben Geraghty.

The manager of the AA All-Star team that year, and again in 1985, Fregosi presided over the grand resurrection of Louisville, which took the Eastern Division crown. Making its first postseason appearance since 1972, Louisville nipped Oklahoma City 3-2 in the AA playoff openers. The Redbirds' highly successful season and their championship run ended in the AA playoff finals, where they were swept 4-0 by Western Division champion Denver.

Truly a man for the times, Fregosi's overall Redbird work included the aforementioned record-breaking million-fan season, the first in minor-league history; a pair of back-to-back American Association playoff champions (1984 and 1985); two Eastern Division crowns (1983 and 1985); and three straight appearances in the AA playoffs (1983, '84 and '85).

In late June 1986, Fregosi got another call to manage in the majors, this time with the White Sox. Later, he went to the Phillies, which he guided into the 1993 World Series. They lost a six-game set to the powerful Toronto Blue Jays, who were repeating world champions.

The minor-league and major-league managing success of James Louis Fregosi, born April 4, 1942, in San Francisco, was a reflection of his savvy and skills as a major-league player. A classy fielding All-Star shortstop who could also hit, Fregosi put together a stellar eighteen-year career (1961–78) with the Angels, Mets, Rangers and Pirates that featured a .265 batting average, 1,726 hits and 151 homers. Fregosi's 1983 Louisville Redbirds

Jim Fregosi. *National Baseball Hall of Fame Library, Cooperstown, New York.*

squad included the league RBIs leader in Jim Adduci (101), plus future major-league standouts Todd Worrell and Andy Van Slyke.

A flame-throwing right-hander, Worrell (born 1959) had several stints with the Redbirds. One of them was the 1985 season, when the California native—as a starter and reliever—chalked up a league-leading 126 strikeouts off an 8-6 record.

In 1986, the top-built six-foot-five, 222-pound right-hander topped the National League with 36 saves for the Cardinals, a feat Worrell duplicated with the Dodgers in 1996, when he recorded 44 saves. Worrell's pertinent big-league numbers with the Cardinals and Dodgers included 221 saves and two World Series appearances during an eleven-year career (1985–97).

Getting his final major-league polish with the Redbirds, Utica, New York native Andrew James "Slick" Van Slyke (born 1960) batted a resounding .368 in fifty-four games for the 1983 Redbirds, contributing twenty-one doubles and forty-one RBIs along the way.

A brilliant defensive outfielder, Van Slyke went on to spend thirteen seasons (1983–95) in the majors with the Cardinals, Pirates, Orioles and Phillies. His substantial career work included a .274 batting average; 1,562 hits, 293 of them doubles; one World Series ring; a league-leading fifteen triples in 1988; three straight National League Championship Series (1990–92); a .988 fielding average; and a personal-best .324 mark in 1992 that included league leaderships in hits (199) and doubles (45).

## *1984*

Speedy Florida native Vincent "Van Go" Coleman (born 1961) set an all-time American Association record with 101 stolen bases. (The work came the year after he stole an all-time minor-league record 145 bases for Macon in the South Atlantic League.) He also scored a league-leading ninety-seven runs for the Redbirds.

Sent up to the majors in 1985, Coleman wasted no time at all making a name for himself, topping the big show in stolen bases six straight seasons, three of them century marks: 110 (1985), 107 (1986), 109 (1987), 81 (1988), 65 (1989) and 77 (1990).

A longtime running mate of former Louisville standout Willie McGee in the Cardinals outfield, Coleman logged thirteen years (1985–99) with the Cardinals, Mets, Royals, Mariners, Reds and Tigers. His big-top career credits included a .264 average, 752 stolen bases and World Series play.

Vincent "Van Go" Coleman. *National Baseball Hall of Fame Library, Cooperstown, New York.*

Also on the 1984 team was Terry Pendleton, who went on to a fifteen-year career (1984–98) with the Cards, Braves, Marlins, Reds and Royals. The 1991 NL MVP and batting champion (.319), he logged a .270 career average, 1,897 lifetime big-top hits and action in five World Series.

Postseason action saw the Redbirds defeat Wichita in a one-game playoff for fourth place and then beat Indianapolis 4-2 in the AA playoff openers and Denver 4-1 in the AA playoff finals. It was a most remarkable season for a team that finished just three games over the .500 mark in regular season play.

Also in 1984, the new Pete Browning grave marker was dedicated.

## *1985*

Future St. Louis Cardinals outfielder Curt Ford pilfered a circuit-topping forty-five bases in 1985. His major-league career numbers included a .308 mark in the 1987 World Series, which the Cards lost in seven games to the Twins.

Louisville won the Eastern Division for the second time in three years and took the AA playoffs 4-1 from Western Division titlist Oklahoma City.

## *1986*

In late June 1986, Jim Fregosi resigned to take over the reins of the Chicago White Sox, and a fabulous era ended.

One of the standouts on the 1986 squad was Jim Lindemann, who led the American Association in RBIs (ninety-six). His work also included thirty-eight doubles, twenty homers and eighty-two runs scored for the Redbirds, who finished last in the East Division.

## *1987*

Cincinnati native Lance Johnson (born 1963) won the MVP award via a fine season that included a .333 batting average, 159 hits, eleven triples, eighty-nine runs scored and forty-two stolen bases.

His highly productive fourteen-year big-league career (1987–2000) included stops with the Cardinals, White Sox, Mets, Cubs and Yankees. Major numbers for the speedy Johnson included a .291 batting average, 1,565 hits (117 of them triples), five triples titles in the NL and AL, two league leaderships in hits (one each in the NL and AL) and one World Series.

On the same team was Tom Pagnozzi (.313), a solid catcher who went on to a durable journeyman career (1987–98) with the Cardinals, one that included World Series play.

Under new manager Mike Jorgenson, Louisville finished second in the American Association race, just one game back of the Denver Zephyrs, the regular season AA champion. In postseason action, the Redbirds lost their AA playoff opener to Indianapolis 3-2.

Lensman R.G. (Richard Gilbert) Potter (circa 1901–1987), the name most synonymous with premodern and early modern Louisville historical baseball photographs, died on December 15.

## *1988*

In the September 1 closer in 1988—a 4-1 loss to Indianapolis—Billy Lyons played all nine positions. His feat duplicated that of Jim Ryburn, a former Auburn football player and member of the 1958 Louisville club.

## *1989*

While last in the Eastern Division for the second year in a row, Louisville had some top-notch names. Chief among them was California native Todd Edward Zeile (born 1965), a high-class receiver whose .289 batting average, 131 hits, twenty-six doubles, nineteen homers and eighty-five RBIs earned him Rookie of the Year honors and a promotion to the majors.

Though a catcher by trade, Zeile spent the bulk of his sixteen-year career (1989–2004) at third base and first base following one full-time season as a backstopper (105 games for the 1990 Cardinals). Besides the Cardinals, the durable and well-traveled star also saw service with the Cubs, Phillies, Orioles, Dodgers, Marlins, Rangers, Mets, Rockies, Yankees and Expos.

A descendant of John Adams, the second president of the United States, Zeile left the game with a .265 average, 2,004 hits, 1,110 RBIs and a .400 average for the Mets in the 2000 New York "Subway Series" against the Yankees.

Other standouts on the 1989 Redbirds included Alex Cole, the league's stolen-base champion (forty-seven), and right-hander Bob Tewksbury. The latter shared the AA pitching-wins crown (thirteen) with Omaha's Steve Fireovid, Nashville's Jack Armstrong and Iowa's Kevin Blankenship.

### Horseshoes and Diamonds

On May 6, 1989, trainer Hank Allen became the first known (and to date, only known) major leaguer to saddle a starter in the famed Kentucky Derby. Allen sent out Northern Wolf to a sixth-place finish in the 1989 Kentucky Derby, won by west coast star Sunday Silence over east coast archrival Easy Goer. Allen's work was also another notable page in the Kentucky Derby's venerable black history.

The oldest of three brothers, all of whom played Major League Baseball, Hank Allen played from 1966 to 1973 for the Senators, Brewers and White Sox.

The best known of the Allen brothers trio, easily, was Richie Allen. A perennial Cooperstown candidate, Richie Allen played fifteen years in the majors (1963–77) with the Phillies, Cardinals, Dodgers, White Sox and A's, compiling a career .292 average with 1,119 RBIs and 351 home runs. A seven-time All-Star, the controversial star was the National League Rookie of the Year in 1964 and the American League's Most Valuable Player in 1972.

Filling out the triad was Ron Allen, who played one year for the St. Louis Cardinals (1972). His lone major-league hit, interestingly enough, was a home run.

Terry Francona. *Courtesy Brian Babineau and the Boston Red Sox.*

## *1990*

Cris Howell Carpenter (b. 1965, not to be confused with the 2010 Cardinals hurler Chris Carpenter), Stan Clarke and Omar Olivares all notched ten wins in 1990, while Mike Perez posted a league-leading thirty-one saves.

In other notable action, St. Louis native Bernard Gilkey (born 1966) got 3 hits in an inning during a May 9 contest against Nashville. Gilkey's pair of singles and three-run homer were part of a sixteen-run, third-inning outburst that produced an 18–4 Louisville victory. At season's end, Gilkey had a team-best 147 hits. Gilkey went on to a solid twelve-year career (1990–2001) with the Cards, Mets, Diamondbacks, Red Sox and Braves, retiring with a .275 average and 1,115 hits.

Another top Louisville product, Ray Lankford, also began his fourteen-year major-league career (1990–2004) with St. Louis in 1990. He accrued 1,500-plus hits, 238 of them homers, and a .272 average for the Cardinals and Padres.

A member of the 1990 Louisville club was Terry Francona, who gained fame in his first season as a major-league manager when he led the 2004 Bosox to their first World Series since 1918. He added a second a few years later, giving Boston two titles in four years after none in nearly a century.

## *1992*

Top performers on the 1992 Louisville team included pitchers Rene Arocha and Jeff Ballard, part of a five-way tie for the league's victory crown (twelve wins); Mark Grater, a league-leading twenty-four saves; and Chuck Carr, a circuit-topping fifty-three stolen bases.

The 1992 team also boasted Ozzie Canseco, twin brother of major-league star Jose Canseco, and longtime major-league star Andres "the Big Cat" Galarraga (1985–2004: .288 batting average, 399 homers, 1,425 RBIs).

## *1994*

Making its first postseason appearance since 1987, Louisville fell to regular season AA champion Indianapolis, which swept it 3-0 in the AA playoff opener.

Allen Battle's statistics included a league-leading 104 runs. He also tied with Scott Bullett of Iowa for most hits (163).

Members of the '94 squad included Rick Sutcliffe (171-139 lifetime), the 1979 NL Rookie of the Year and the 1984 Cy Young NL winner, and Mark Whiten, who the previous September 7, in a contest against the Reds, had become one of the few men in baseball history to homer four times in a single game

## *1995*

In 1995, Hillerich & Bradsby relocated to its present location at Eighth and Main, near the Ohio River, in downtown Louisville.

For the second year in a row, Manager Joe Pettini sent Louisville into postseason play. Returning the favor of the year before, Louisville swept regular season AA titlist Indianapolis 3-0 in the playoff openers and then took out Buffalo 3-2 in the AA finals.

A notable member of the 1995 Louisville club was Chris Sabo, the 1988 National League Rookie of the Year. Nicknamed "Spuds" during his rookie season by manager Pete Rose (because of his resemblance to a bull terrier character in Bud Light beer commercials named Spuds MacKenzie), Sabo was recognizable by his wraparound protective eyeglasses commonly known as "Rec Specs." A three time All-Star and member of the 1990 World Champion Cincinnati Reds, Sabo closed out his injury-plagued nine-year major-league career in 1996 with the team he had started with—the Reds. His work along the way included stints with the Orioles, White Sox and Cardinals.

## *1996*

Hillerich & Bradsby opened the Louisville Slugger Museum (now called the Louisville Slugger Museum & Factory) in 1996.

In local baseball action, future major-league standout Dmitri Young (born 1973) won the AA batting title with a .333 mark (off 153 hits) and also topped the league in runs (ninety).

Through 2008 (his last major-league season; he played minor-league ball exclusively in 2009), the Mississippi native showed a .292 batting average, over thirteen hundred hits and five .300 seasons with the Cards, Reds, Tigers and Nationals.

## *1997*

The American Association disbanded at the end of the season in 1997.

## *1998*

With a new manager, a new league affiliation and a new major-league sponsor, Louisville bounced back from two consecutive cellar-dwelling seasons to narrowly take the International League's Western Division crown in 1998 under Gary Allenson.

The team won the title by a half game over runner-up Indianapolis, the thinnest title-winning margin in club history. In the ensuing playoffs, Louisville—now a part of Milwaukee's farm system—was swept 3-0 by Durham.

Second baseman Ron Belliard provided substantial offensive force with 163 hits, thirty-six doubles and 114 runs scored.

## *August 14, 1999*

Dodger Hall of Fame shortstop Harold Herman "Pee Wee" Reese, one of the four trademark names in Louisville's baseball history—along with Pete Browning, the Louisville Slugger bat and the Hillerich & Bradsby Company—passed away at his home in Louisville. He was eighty-one.

## *September 6, 1999*

Louisville played its last game at Cardinal Stadium, its home since 1957. It lost 8–3 to Indianapolis and finished third of four in the Western Division with a 63-81/.438 account.

Outfielder Lyle Mouton swung some big timber, batting .357 with thirty-four doubles, nineteen homers and seventy-seven RBIs.

## *2000*

A promotional commemorative ticket of the inaugural game at Louisville Slugger Field on April 12, 2000. *Courtesy the Louisville Bats.*

On Wednesday, April 12, 2000, Louisville Slugger Field opened. The high-tech, state-of-the-art baseball stadium is located just east of the downtown area and adjacent to the Ohio River at East Main and Jackson.

The RiverBats lost 8–5 to the Norfolk Tides before an overflow crowd of 13,242. Despite a sub-.500 mark, however, Louisville went on to top the International League in total home attendance: 685,561.

Louisville Slugger Field is the city's fourth minor-league ballpark. The first was Eclipse Park (1902–22), located at Seventh and Kentucky, which, over the years, became famous for nearby "Baseball Alley" (so-named because after fans alighted from Fourth Street trolleys, they avoided the jog in Kentucky Street by continuing down this alley to the ballpark).

Chronologically sandwiched between the city's oldest and newest ballparks were Parkway Field (1923–56) and Cardinal Stadium (1957–99). Located on the University of Louisville campus, adjacent to Eastern Parkway, part of

Parkway Field still stands today. Formerly Fairgrounds Stadium, Cardinal Stadium is located near Louisville International Airport.

Also, on June 29, 2000, a statue of Pee Wee Reese was dedicated at Louisville Slugger Field.

## *2001*

During minor-league baseball's centennial, Louisville hit the mother lode with Houston, Texas native Adam Dunn, who skyrocketed from the midlevel minor-league ranks to Major League Baseball in just a few months.

The Cincinnati Reds' second-round draft choice in 1998, Dunn was a major force in Louisville's runaway divisional championship and eventual International League pennant. His Louisville numbers included a .329 batting average, twenty home runs and fifty-three RBIs in fifty-five games.

The meteoric rise, which saw Dunn play for three different clubs at three different levels, began with the Double-A Chattanooga Lookouts. In just thirty-nine games, the six-foot-six, 235-pound outfielder hit .343, homered twelve times and drove in thirty-one runs.

Called up to Cincinnati in late July, Dunn capped his spectacular season with a .262 average, nineteen homers and forty-three RBIs in sixty-six games. His work for the struggling Reds included a club and NL rookie record twelve home runs during the month of August, breaking a 1956 club and co-NL record (eleven) of another Reds player, Hall of Famer Frank Robinson. Dunn's sixty-four hits also included eighteen doubles and one triple.

Not surprisingly, Dunn was named Minor League Player of the Year by *SportsTicker* and *USA Today Baseball Weekly* at the end of the season off a .334 average, thirty-two homers, eighty-four RBIs and eleven stolen bases in ninety-four games split between Chattanooga and Louisville.

Overall, Dunn's combined 2001 minor-league and major-league stats read: 160 games, 594 at-bats, 181 hits, fifty-one home runs, 127 RBIs, a .305 batting average, 128 runs scored, forty doubles, a .633 slugging average, one hundred walks and fifteen stolen bases.

Though his average dropped to .249 in 2002 and was accompanied by 170 strikeouts, Dunn still produced twenty-six homers, seventy-one RBIs, 133 hits, 128 walks and a .400 on-base percentage. Brought up as an outfielder, he also logged time at first base. In 2008, he was traded to the Diamondbacks, where he continues to star.

*Note*: 2001 was selected as the cutoff point for Louisville's minor-league statistics in this section because that marked the centennial of minor-league baseball in this country. It was also Louisville's 125th mathematical baseball anniversary (1876–2001). Future editions of *The Louisville Baseball Almanac* will carry the post-2001 years.

PART II

# Big Top and Little Top

## *Stories From Louisville's Major-League and Minor-League Days*

## Ole Pete

A genuine premodern national star, one of the game's earliest pioneers and one of the sport's most enduring and intriguing figures, Louis Rogers "Pete" Browning was born in Louisville, Kentucky, on June 17, 1861, at Thirteenth and Jefferson on the city's west side. Because the State of Kentucky did not require the official recording of vital statistics until 1911, no formal birth certificate exists today for Pete Browning or any of his seven siblings.

However, numerous sources from his own life verify his birth date, including federal census records for 1900; the legal documents that authorized his commitment to an insane asylum at nearby Lakeland, Kentucky, in June 1905; the official record of his death as filed three months later in the pages of the *City Mortuary Book* (number 13, page 44); obituaries from Louisville's four leading newspapers of that day (the *Courier-Journal*, the *Times*, the *Herald* and the *Post*); and Browning's first grave marker itself.

A lifelong resident of Louisville, Pete Browning was the youngest of eight children born to Kentucky natives Samuel Browning (1814–1874) and Mary Jane Sheppard Browning (1826–1911). The pair were married in Jefferson County, the county seat of Louisville, the day after Valentine's Day 1849. The couple eventually produced four sons and four daughters (three of them spinsters): Charles L., Henry D., Louis (1861–1905), Samuel L. Jr. (d. 1900), Blanche N., Fannie E. (1859–1907), Mrs. Florence Browning Ramsey (d. 1935) and Ida May.

In October 1874, when Browning was thirteen, his father died at age fifty-nine from injuries sustained during a cyclone. A prosperous merchant, Browning's father had for years run a grocery store at the corner of Fifteenth and Jefferson Streets in Louisville, not too far from the family's residence. Browning's mother, with whom the confirmed bachelor lived all his life, lasted substantially longer. She died of old age on April 6, 1911, at age eighty-four at her home at 1427 West Jefferson Street.

According to her obituary, she had lived there for more than half a century. She was survived by three children: Charles, Henry and Florence. Nothing is left of the Browning residence today. In the 1970s, it was demolished as part of an urban renewal program that cleared out huge blocks of one of Louisville's oldest neighborhoods. A strip mall currently occupies the site.

Unquestionably, the most extraordinary piece of Browning's family history involves his nephew, Tod Browning.

The son of Browning's brother Charles and Lydia J. (Fitzgerald) Browning, Charles Albert "Tod" Browning (1882–1962) ran away from home at age sixteen to join a traveling circus. Later, he became a successful vaudevillian comedian and then joined forces with another Kentucky native and filmdom's first great director, D.W. Griffith, first as an actor and then as an assistant director.

His big break came in 1925 with *The Unholy Three*, starring Lon Chaney, known as "the Man of a Thousand Faces" for his brilliant ability to play numerous characters. In 1931, Tod Browning turned out the horror classic *Dracula*, with Bela Lugosi taking over the title role after the untimely death of Chaney. Browning followed that up the following year with one of the most controversial films ever—*Freaks*. In 1939, Tod Browning went into prosperous retirement in California, where he died in the early 1960s.

This unusual sidebar to Pete Browning's life was picked up by New York–based author David Nemec, whose nonfiction work includes four landmark baseball books: *The Ultimate Baseball Book* (historical text), *The Beer and Whisky League*, *The Great Encyclopedia of 19th-Century Major League Baseball* and *The Rules of Baseball*. His fiction notably includes a magical short story on Pete Browning entitled "Browning's Lamps," which appeared in the June 1982 issue of *Twilight Zone Magazine*.

## *The Early Years: 1877–1881*

As a youth, Browning was a crack athlete and avid sportsman who studiously avoided schoolwork. Frequently, he would hide the schoolbooks his mother had provided him under the doorsteps of the home of John Reccius. A teammate of Browning's on some early Louisville teams and later a pallbearer at Browning's funeral, Reccius was part of a noted Louisville baseball family that also included his brothers William and Philip. Rounding up companions, Browning then would spend the rest of the day shooting marbles, spinning tops or playing ball.

The *Courier-Journal* noted in his obituary: "When a lad, he began playing ball on the commons, and was a good player from the start."

Browning's proficiency as a marble shooter mirrored that of a later Louisville contribution to the Major Leagues, Dodger Hall of Fame shortstop Harold "Pee Wee" Reese. A master of the game in his neighborhood, where he regularly won all the marbles of his friends, Browning began to return the common marbles while keeping only the prized agates for himself. In time, Browning accumulated a trunk full of them. Eventually, his reputation became so great that Browning had to travel to the east end of Louisville, where he was unknown, in order to get up a game.

According to several newspaper accounts, Browning was also a superb skater who "was easily the best in Louisville," possessing an ability to "cut more funny figures and skate faster than any other boy of his acquaintance." A lover of the outdoors, Browning enjoyed all athletics except swimming, which he claimed hurt his ears. This is not exactly insignificant since Browning, a resident of a town nicknamed the "River City," grew up only blocks away from the Ohio River.

Pete Browning. *National Baseball Hall of Fame Library, Cooperstown, New York.*

Browning's habitual absences from the classroom as a young man had the expected repercussions, leaving him uneducated and rendering him a functional illiterate for his entire adult life. And that adulthood came pretty early.

On Friday, April 13, 1877, still some two months shy of his sixteenth birthday, Browning made what is thought to be his debut as an organized ballplayer. And it came against penthouse competition, no less—the city's charter National League club, the Louisville Grays. Picked by many to take that year's National League flag, the powerhouse Grays were just about a month away from their seasonal opener.

Behind Jimmy Devlin's nifty three-hitter, the Grays decimated the Eclipse 22–1. As for Browning, his debut was unremarkable. He went zero for four—perhaps understandably in light of the competition and maybe even the date, Friday the thirteenth. Nevertheless, it was a start all the same, and on July 28, he made his first big imprint as a ballplayer.

Using a fine curveball and deceptive change of pace, Browning hurled the Eclipse to a 4–0 shutout win over the vaunted Grays. The young right-hander's strikeout victims that day included slugging outfielder George Hall and ace pitcher Jimmy Devlin, both participants in that season's National League pennant-fixing scandal, which eventually cost the city its major-league team and resulted in the lifetime ban of four Louisville players.

Browning's reputation progressively increased during the next few years, spent principally with the city's nationally known semipro club, the Louisville Eclipse. And shortly before the end of that apprenticeship (from 1877–81), he also laid the groundwork for his lifelong battle with the press.

On July 2, 1881, Charles Guiteau—a disappointed office-seeker and Republican factionalist—shot newly elected President James A. Garfield in Washington's Baltimore & Potomac Railroad station. Lingering for several months, Garfield finally died on September 19, 1881. When Browning was informed of Garfield's death, so the story goes, he queried an astonished reporter: "Oh, yeah? What league was he in?"

Later, as a major leaguer, Browning gained the moniker "The Gladiator" for his ongoing battles with the fourth estate and his pathological alcoholism, best characterized by another memorable quote: "I can't hit the ball until I hit the bottle!" (Long incidental to that nickname were his epic gaffes with fly balls. However, *American Gladiator: The Life and Times of Pete Browning*, the first biography of Browning, yielded a much different story.)

Deaf and illiterate, the six-foot, 180-pound Browning was eccentric as well, and today he still rates as one of the game's most colorful characters.

In Browning's 1905 *Louisville Times* obituary, teammate and longtime friend John Reccius recounted an oddity of the Gladiator's playing:

> *Pete was afraid of players coming in on the bases. He had a habit, too, of standing on one foot and extending the other knee if he saw a fielder approaching him. He always declared that if the man ran into the bone* [the knee], *he would be put out of business and "Old Pete" would escape injury. After Pete went to the outfield, he would often catch a ball standing on one leg, with the other knee extended. Browning was also timid at the bat when the speedy pitchers were putting them in close.*

That peculiar defense was partially explained in Browning's *Courier-Journal* obituary. "He was one of the best infielders who ever played on Louisville, but he lost his nerve after being run over and spiked by players on several occasions and was shifted to the outfield, where he always played after that time." The fear of being spiked also presumably was behind his refusal to slide.

The *Times* obituary provided yet another rich tidbit on Browning:

> *Old Pete enjoyed notoriety. When traveling over the circuit, the gladiator would frequently alight from the train and exhibit himself to people at the station, and if no one recognized him, he would introduce himself as the champion batter of the American Association. He has been known to impart his identity to a lone station agent.*

The complete package as a legend, Browning also stared into the sun to improve his "lamps" (eyes), treasured his "active" bats because of the hits they still contained, was constantly on the prowl for the next "magical" stick with hits in it, maintained a warehouse of "retired" bats (all of them named, many after biblical figures) in his home and kept his batting statistics on his shirt cuffs.

## *Pete Browning's Major Career Statistics*

Reducing Browning to mere numbers and historical shorts is impossible, but here is a roll call of some of the more pertinent statistics and facts from his career.

During the course of thirteen major-league seasons from 1882 through 1894 (the bulk of that with Louisville in first the American Association and later the National League), Browning compiled a lifetime .341 batting average. His .341 figure is tied for eighth place on the all-time list with Cooperstown inductees Wee Willie Keeler and Bill Terry. It also ranks today as the fourth best among the game's right-handed batsmen. Only Hall of Famers Rogers Hornsby (.358), Eddie Delahanty (.346) and Harry Heilmann (.342) have done better work from that side of the plate.

To date, Pete Browning is one of several dozen players to have legitimately batted .400 in a season: .402 in 1887. He ranks twenty-third on the all-time list of seasonal batting averages.

Browning posted a .467 lifetime slugging average. His personal best was a .547 mark in 1887. Other top marks include .530 in 1885, .517 in 1890 and a league-leading .510 in 1882.

He recorded his personal-best .464 on-base percentage in 1887, one of the one hundred best in the game's history. Other notable on-base percentage marks include .459 in 1890 (second in the Players League) and a league-leading .430 mark in the American Association (1882). His lifetime .403 on-base percentage mark ranks among the top fifty on the all-time list.

Browning twice hit for the cycle (the major-league record is three).

He is the only player to have lost a batting title to a pitcher: to teammate Guy Hecker in 1886 (.341 to .340).

Browning literally swung the big lumber; he reportedly favored bats that were thirty-seven inches in length and forty-eight ounces in weight.

And, he is the namesake of the famed Louisville Slugger, an American icon.

## *1882*

In 1882, Louisville went major league again, this time as a charter member of the American Association, the National League's first great rival. With his skills honed to a fine edge, Browning notched his first two major-league hits (a single and a triple) in his second major-league contest on May 3 at St. Louis. By season's end, he had run away with the American Association's inaugural batting race, posting a .378 average. It was thirty-six points better than that of his nearest rival, Cincinnati's Hick Carpenter (a left-handed third-baseman and source of the phrase, "hot corner"). Moreover, it was the best average in the Major Leagues, topping Dan Brouthers's National League title work by ten points.

Browning's monster rookie season also included the American Association's slugging average (.510) and on-base percentage championships (.430). In addition, he ranked second in hits (109) and fourth in total bases (147) and runs scored (67) and was among the league's leaders in home runs and walks. In total, it was one of the finest rookie seasons ever in the game's history, and more destruction was on the way from the twenty-one-year-old star who was a few years away from his prime.

Though such games are not part of the official records, an exhibition contest against a strong Atlantic City team on May 27, 1882, is noteworthy for several reasons. In the 10–7 Eclipse win, Browning launched a gigantic home run. According to the game account, he drove "the ball over the center field fence, almost on a dead line, for a home run"—no mean feat for the dead ball era, when an inside-the-park *un circuit* (French for "home run") was the norm and not the exception. Yet, the prodigious home run was no optical illusion. It was an accurate reflection of Browning's power, of which he modestly said: "It was the longest hit I ever made, an all-around-the-world hit, and it's still going yet."

The game is also instructive of the times, when regular season exhibition games between big-top teams and semipro clubs were as much a matter of course as were preseason, intraseason and postseason games between National League and American Association clubs.

An instant major-league star, Browning had a virulent drinking problem, which didn't take long to reach major-league proportions either, making its debut in an August 13, 1882 contest against the Athletics. Despite the *Louisville Courier-Journal*'s hard story the following day over Browning's drunken state, the team did not release its star, nor did it tighten the rope on its star—for the most obvious of reasons.

The fabulous homegrown rookie had brought Louisville back to major-league baseball with a flourish, was tearing the league apart with his stick and was clearly a foundation franchise player who was the light of the common man everywhere for the relief he gave him from their daily oppression. Without Browning, the Eclipse club would have quickly found itself playing to an empty ballpark. And everyone knew it: the press thugs, the incompetent management, the jealous teammates and, most of all, Browning's prized and loyal fans.

His state notwithstanding, Browning had gone two for four in the 7–4 Eclipse win over the Athletics.

Though no one will ever know, it seems safe to believe that the alcoholic display was the result of his lifelong mastoiditis condition back on the rampage again. Certainly, the two pathologies were locked at Browning's hip his entire life: wherever the mastoiditis went, the bottle was not far behind.

The close of the season also produced one of Browning's "signature" games. In a September 12 game at Cincinnati that was sandwiched between no-hitters by Tony Mullane and Guy Hecker, Browning unloaded for a pair of home runs and a triple in the 10–4 Eclipse win.

## *Browning and the American Association*

In order to understand Browning in his full and proper historical context, it is necessary to take a look at the league where he spent the bulk of his career: the glorious American Association. What follows is a quick-study look at one of America's greatest and most colorful major-league circuits.

Founded in Cincinnati's Gibson House Hotel in 1881, the storied American Association was given little hope of survival by its National League detractors, who quickly tagged it the "Beer and Whiskey League." The derisive moniker referred to the league owners, many of whom were engaged in the liquor industry. It also was a slap at the American Association's plan to sell beer at all its ballparks.

To date, however, the American Association remains the most formidable opponent that the National League has had in its 125-plus-year existence. In short, it gave the "Rich Men's League," as American Associationers called the senior circuit, all it could handle. And more. As blue in collar as the National League was in blood, the American Association crossed broad sections of class and opened up the game to the working masses with admission prices half that of the National League: twenty-five cents as opposed to fifty cents, a huge sum at that time. The American Association further expanded the game with Sunday baseball. Since the standard workweek at the time was six days, this innovative policy enabled thousands of working people to take in a ballgame on their day off.

The American Association, progressive as it was colorful, also boldly reentered and reopened such fertile western baseball strongholds as Cincinnati, St. Louis and Louisville—all former National League cities.

The so-called "inferior league" also gave the national pastime a number of innovations and historic firsts: the sale of beer at the ballpark, the development of Ladies' Day as a standard baseball promotion, league control of umpires, the percentage system of determining pennant winners, standardized contractual procedures, participation in the first World Series (an abbreviated affair in 1882) and the first African American to openly play major-league baseball in the history of the game: Moses Fleetwood Walker (1884).

Fiercely competitive, the American Association was eventually done in by the aforementioned three-league 1890 war that left the National League the sole survivor. At the end of that season, the Players League folded, and a year later, after a glorious but turbulent ten-year existence (1882–1891), the American Association closed up shop. Interestingly, the bulky one-league concept did not last long as major-league baseball soon learned a basic premise of its existence, thanks to the American Association. Three leagues were too many; one league was too few.

Recognizing this fundamental law of baseball economics, founders of the American League established their circuit at the turn of the twentieth century. Had the American Association survived, it (not the American League) would have been major-league baseball's second companion league.

For the record, there have been two American Associations in the game's history. The first (and the oldest one) was the nineteenth-century major-league circuit that operated from 1882 through 1891. The other was a twentieth-century minor-league loop founded in 1902 that, with several interruptions, ran through the late 1990s. The two are not to be confused. They have nothing in common save their name.

In 1968, the Special Baseball Rules Committee recognized and defined six circuits as having "major-league" status, among them Browning's longstanding home, the colorful American Association (1882–91).

Though many baseball historians and writers have classified the American Association as an "inferior" major-league circuit, this is not so. In point of fact, the exact opposite was the case.

A prime example was the 1890 season. That year, for the only time in history, American Association and National League stars played under the same flag: the Players League. This was a natural consequence of the three-league war that picked off players from both the National League and the American Association. And American Association stars had no trouble holding their own.

The top two batsmen that year were not National League standouts but longtime American Association luminaries Pete Browning and Davey Orr (.3732 and .3728, respectively).

Likewise, the stolen-base king was not a National Leaguer but American Association great Harry Stovey (ninety-seven steals). And though the winningest pitcher—Mark Baldwin (thirty-four victories)—was a member of the senior circuit, tied for second with thirty wins each were American Association kingpins Silver King and Gus Weyhing.

Backing up the Players League statistics were the statistics of postseason play between the American Association and the National League. The American Association operated for a decade. During that 1882–91 time frame, the American Association and the National League met regularly in World Series action. In addition, the two loops regularly engaged in pre- and postseason exhibitions as well. In neither instance—the World Series nor the exhibitions—did either league display overwhelming superiority. (So much for the American Association's long-presumed "second-rate" status, a product of National League elitism.)

American Association statistical data (league, team and individual player) is a part of Major League Baseball's original and greatest reference volume, *The Baseball Encyclopedia: The Complete and Definitive Record of Major League Baseball.* An instant classic when it was first published in 1969 by Macmillan, this watershed and much-beloved statistical work is known to its many admirers as the "Big Mac." (The nickname refers to its size and publisher).

The same American Association data are also an integral part of David Nemec's superb award-winning premodern-era reference volume, *The Great Encyclopedia of 19th-Century Major League Baseball*, as well as *The Sporting News Complete Baseball Record Book.*

Unquestionably, Browning and his American Association colleagues were both pioneers of the game and major stars. And to be gauged most accurately, they must be judged in, by and of the context of the times in which they played. To judge them any other way is like comparing the Wright brothers' plane to a 747.

To date, one American Association star has been elected (in 2000) to the Hall of Fame: John Alexander "Bid" McPhee, the game's best second baseman of the premodern era. Still waiting outside for their rightful entrance are nine others, including three Louisville old-time stars: Pete Browning; ambidextrous right-hander Tony Mullane (284-220; 30-24 as a rookie with Louisville in 1882 and the source of the Ladies' Day promotion); and another right-hander and, like Browning, a Louisville native—Gus Weyhing (264-232, principally for second-division clubs).

Other AA giants excluded because of Cooperstown's longstanding prejudice against the old-time AA major leaguers, aided and abetted by the national baseball media, include Bob Caruthers and Dave Foutz. Co-aces on the first three of the St. Louis Browns four straight AA pennant-winning squads (1885–88), both were right-handers and superb combination players. Caruthers, who also played outfield, posted a 218-99/.688 win percentage and a .282 lifetime batting average. Foutz, the all-time major-league record holder with a .692 win percentage, was 147-66 on the mound. He also saw extensive action at first base, and was a lifetime .276 hitter with over twelve hundred hits to his credit.

Filling out the "AA Ten" are Harry Stovey (born Harold Duffield Stowe), a multidimensional player whose career work included titles in slugging, doubles, triples, home runs, RBIs, runs scored and stolen bases; Davey Orr, a .342 lifetime hitter whose brilliant career was cut short by a stroke; right-

Major League Baseball's second dynasty, the 1888 St. Louis American Association Browns, league champion for the fourth straight year. *Top row*: Arlie Latham (3B), the team mascot and James "Tip" O'Neill (LF). *Second row*: Bill White (SS), James H. Devlin (LHP), William "Yank" Robinson (2B), Tommy McCarthy (RF), Silver King (RHP) and Ed Herr (IF-OF). *Third row*: Jack Boyle (C), Nat Hudson (RHP), Charlie Comiskey (1B/Captain), John "Jocko" Milligan (C) and Tom Dolan (C). *Bottom row*: Elton "Icebox" Chamberlain (RHP) and Harry Lyons (CF). Of special interest in this superb image of a long-forgotten dynasty are owner Chris von der Ahe's beloved and stylish greyhounds, Pooch and Fly (although which one is which remains a mystery). *National Baseball Hall of Fame Library, Cooperstown, New York.*

hander Will White (229-166 in just a decade); and right-hander Silver King (born Charles Frederick Koenig), another St. Louis Browns ace who was 204-153 in a ten-year period.

The cream of the crop, the 1888 St. Louis Browns were champions of the American Association for the fourth straight year. Notable team members included lost AA star Silver King; Tip O'Neill, who hit .435 in 1887, the second-highest mark ever posted in major-league play; Hall of Famers Charlie Comiskey and Tommy McCarthy; and Elton "Icebox" Chamberlain (159-120), who began his career at Louisville.

## *1883*

Unlike many major leaguers, Browning cut a swath through the sophomore jinx in 1883, batting .338 and finishing second to Pittsburgh's Ed Swartwood for league honors. And boxscores from that fine follow-up campaign also correct two longstanding statistical errors about Browning.

Official baseball records credit Browning with two—not a co-major-league-record three—career cycle games. The error surrounds a May 2, 1883 game against Columbus, referred to in Browning's *Louisville Times* obituary. Though he did get four hits in the 13–6 Louisville victory, Browning—horribly sick—actually singled three times and doubled once.

Interestingly enough, the first player to pull off the cycle feat—a unique blend of speed and power—was not a National Leaguer or an American Leaguer. Rather, it was an American Association standout, Cincinnati first baseman Long John Reilly, Browning's bat-pilfering teammate from the 1891 Cincinnati Reds. Reilly posted his first two cycles in 1883, a great season for cycles—real or mistaken. Also the first player to cycle in two different leagues, his third coming in the National League (1890), Reilly presently shares the major-league career-cycle mark with American League record-holder Bob Meusel and National League standard-bearer Babe Herman.

The other error is when Browning was first hit by a pitch.

Prevailing legend has it that Browning played for ten years (yet another error) before being hit by a pitched ball on May 8, 1890, when he was hit in the back. The first documented instance, however, was a July 8, 1883 contest when he was struck on the leg and forced to leave the game. For the record, Browning suffered the most serious HBP of his career in his tenth season of play, when he raised his hand in a September 5, 1891 game to avoid a beanball. The resulting injury cost him the final month of the season.

## *1884, Part I*

The 1884 campaign was a busy season, as Major League Baseball, for the first of several times in its history, had no fewer than three circuits from which the fans could choose. The newcomer was the Union Association, which lasted but a year. The season also witnessed the first World Series, the National League champion Providence Grays besting American Association titlist New York Mets, as well as the debut of Moses Fleetwood Walker, the first black to play openly in the Major Leagues, at Louisville on

May 1, 1884. Two days later, Walker got his first major-league hit, a single in a 5–4 loss to Louisville.

In retrospect, Louisville was a mecca of black American sporting history that year. Across town, Isaac Murphy—America's first great black athlete—notched his first Kentucky Derby win aboard Buchanan. Ironically, the stewards had to force Murphy to ride the fractious colt.

By the time Murphy hung it all up, he had become the first rider to take three Kentucky Derbies and the first to pilot consecutive Derby victors (Riley in 1890 and Kingman in 1891). A charter member of the Racing Hall of Fame, Murphy today is considered by many to be the greatest rider ever in the game.

Hours after Fleet Walker got his first major-league hit on May 3, Browning used his athletic ability in a most extraordinary way off the baseball field. His heroic act was reported thusly in the following morning's *Courier-Journal*:

> *Browning saved a boy from being run over by a street car at Seventeenth and Marinet last night. The little fellow was trying to cross the track, when the mules struck him and knocked him under the car. Browning was standing by, and pulled him out in time to save his life.*

(It is instructive that this majestic story is not a part of the Browning myth and legend, perhaps because it is true and can be documented.)

On May 12, while the team was on the road, Browning underwent ear surgery for the first time for mastoiditis, a bacterial infection of the skull's mastoid bone. Frequently, it is a complication of acute otitis media, or a middle ear infection. The infection spreads from the ear to the mastoid bone, which is located just behind the ears and connected to the temporal bones that run along both sides of the head.

(The mastoid bones—also known as the mastoid process—are two honeycomb-like areas that occasionally aid the human ear by acting as a surplus receiving area for violent sound vibrations that the ear cannot handle by itself, such as a sudden nearby explosion.)

Unchecked or crudely treated, mastoiditis can cause the mastoid bone to deteriorate. Once a leading cause of death in children, mastoiditis is now treated with antibiotics.

For nearly his entire life, Browning was plagued by mastoidal problems, and the results of the surgery were unmistakable. Freed from mastoidal pain for the time being, Browning had a fine season, playing in 103 of 108 games without any major alcohol problems and finishing third in the league with a .336 average.

The significance of this malady cannot be overstated. In the mid-1980s, the tide changed for Browning, when it was discovered in his obituaries that he had suffered from mastoiditis, a condition that had robbed him of his hearing, reduced him to virtual illiteracy, turned him into a raging alcoholic, caused his commitment to an insane asylum and was a major factor in his early death. In short, it was responsible for the majority of his personal and professional problems.

That watershed information instantly, radically and forever changed historical perceptions of Browning. The end result is that Browning stands in complete and sharp historical focus today: an epic ballplayer and longstanding folklore legend, he was also a desperate man relentlessly assailed and pursued his entire adult life by atavistic forces wildly beyond his control.

Those who ignore this information are living in the past.

## *1884, Part II:* *Pete Browning and the True Story of the Louisville Slugger Bat*

In the spring of 1884, so the story goes, John Andrew "Bud" Hillerich custom-made a bat for Browning, who was in a slump. The Gladiator then went out and got three hits the next day, and, as they say, the rest is history. The incident forged modern bat making because it ultimately led to the birth and creation of two American icons: the world-famous Louisville Slugger bat and its equally renowned bat-making firm, Hillerich & Bradsby.

In recent years, this story has come under inspection because no reference to it has ever been found in that season's baseball coverage or in Browning's obituaries. And, as of this writing, there are three other versions.

The second version is that the first Louisville Slugger bat was made for one Walter Arlington "Arlie" Latham, also known as the "Freshest Man on Earth" because of his cocky personality, vile bench-jockeying talents and his vulgar mouth. In a 1937 article, Latham claimed that he was the first recipient of the Louisville Slugger bat, saying that, in 1883 or 1884, he went over to the Hillerich wood-turning shop near his hotel after breaking his bat in a game that day. Hillerich agreed to make him a bat for the next day's game, and that's how it all started.

This story was backed up by a 1942 letter from Bud Hillerich himself. However, that was more likely the product of diplomacy than anything else, since Browning had been long dead and Latham was still very much alive. In addition, it's highly unlikely that the first Louisville Slugger bat would have been made for a player who never spent a day in a Louisville uniform, and was a lifetime .269 hitter to boot, when that city had a demigod hitting legend available from exactly the same time frame in the form of Browning.

The ego-driven Latham story has the least credibility of the four Louisville Slugger versions. (Further confusing the Latham story is an A.H. Tarvin article that says Latham was one of many players who followed Browning's example after seeing the Gladiator's success with the bat.)

The third version is that Bud Hillerich, a fine player as a youngster, either lost or had his "turned" (custom-made) bat stolen while a member of the Morning Star team in 1883. Recovered in time for the 1884 season, it then fell into the hands of Gus Weyhing, a minor-league player who would go on to win 264 games during his big-top career. The problem with this story is that Weyhing was known for his pitching, not his hitting.

Weyhing then passed the bat along to several Louisville major-league players. In due course, its reputation as a quality stick—first called Hillerich bats, then Falls City Sluggers and finally Louisville Sluggers—led to the establishment of the Hillerich & Bradsby Company and the expanded commercial production and distribution of this signature item.

Story number four comes courtesy of Ira Smith's wonderful 1954 book, *Baseball's Famous Outfielders*. In an 1889 home game against Sadie McMahon and the Athletics, Browning broke his favorite bat, "Old Betsy," clean in two late in the game when he swung hard at one of McMahon's pitches.

Smith's story continues:

> *As soon as he could get out of his uniform and into his street clothes, Pete rushed over to a bat factory which had been established in Louisville five years earlier. He got there just as they were closing up shop, carrying the two pieces of the broken bat. The slugger plaintively begged the workmen to remain on the job and turn out a new bat for him—one exactly like the late lamented Betsy.*
>
> *Probably nobody but Pete Browning would have gotten anywhere with such a request. But he was the pride and joy of Louisville's baseball fans. More than that, he was the best, and reportedly the first of the bat factory's customers. So the bat makers put themselves to work.*
>
> *Pete selected the wood himself and hovered over every bit of the production to be sure the new bat was an exact duplicate of Old Betsy. When the job was finished, Pete and the workmen went down the street to have meat and drink at his own expense.*
>
> *Pete's period of mourning for Old Betsy came to an end the next afternoon when the new bat banged out three hits for him.*

This version incorporates many essential and/or documented elements: the 1884 founding of the bat factory, the broken-bat scenario, boxscores of those home games between Louisville and the A's in which both McMahon and Browning played, the presence of both Weyhing (a thirty-game winner that year with the A's) and McMahon (a rookie on his way to a 174-win career) and the rather interesting fact that Browning was the company's first paying customer.

However, the timing is off, not because it's 1889 rather than 1884 but because after the first McMahon-Browning matchup of August 4 in which Browning went one for four, he went into a horrendous slump. He was still in that slump when he met McMahon again on August 12, going hitless in four at-bats. Shortly after that, about August 23, Browning was suspended without pay and did not play for the final two months of the season.

As a result of these contradictory stories, Browning's longstanding historical link with the Louisville Slugger bat appears to be tenuous at the very least, nonexistent at the very worst. This, of course, is predicated on the assumption that the 1884 episode is Browning's only link with the Louisville Slugger bat.

Missed in this rush to judgment, again a product of the errors that have plagued Browning's life and career, is the true nature of the beast: that the Louisville Slugger event is one of those rare historical incidents in which the inaugural event cannot be traced directly to the namesake. Once again, this is something that could only happen to Browning.

To the contrary, the historical link between Browning and the Louisville Slugger bat remains sound, but in a different arena. It stands to reason that it would be so; otherwise, the bond between the pair would not have survived this long. Certainly, the body of materials is there to support the link.

Indeed, Browning's connection with the Louisville Slugger bat—another American baseball icon—is so strong that it has reached metaphysical and literary proportions. To date, he has been the subject of two finely crafted pieces of historical fiction: David Nemec's "Browning's Lamps" and Jo Ann O'Connor's "The Birth of the Bat."

Now, this may not be a record, but it is nonetheless most telling that Browning still has a hold on the game's history as one of the sport's most fabled pieces of folklore via his mythical character, his batting prowess (three batting titles, a .400 season), his colorful personality and his eccentricities regarding his bats.

When the Hillerich & Bradsby Company (then called the J.F. Hillerich Company) registered the trademark name "Louisville Slugger" in 1894, the company had one person and one person only in mind: Pete Browning. Unlike the native birth of the bat, the bat's namesake had a precise genesis.

Newspaper coverage of the times repeatedly identified Browning as the "Louisville Slugger." One example was a Wednesday, June 17, 1891 *Louisville Post* headline that referred to Browning as such. Browning's best-known nicknames were "Pete" and "the Gladiator"; however, he had a third moniker, for some reason lost in the mix: "the Louisville Slugger."

It is not by accident that Browning's last season was the Louisville Slugger bat's first season under that name—kind of a going-away present for the aging star. But it had more than a little edge of sound business and savvy marketing to it.

With Browning's longstanding and enormous local and national popularity, the Louisville Slugger bat would go farther—much farther—in his name than in anyone else's. Browning's shelf life as the Louisville Slugger namesake/trademark player/inspirational spirit is infinite, unlimited and undeniable.

## *1884: Part III*

The 1884 season also included two notable pitching items. One was Guy Hecker's pitching Triple Crown work: 52-20, 385 strikeouts and a 1.80 ERA. The highest single-season American Association total, Hecker's 52 wins stands third on the all-time list behind Hall of Famers Old Hoss Radbourne (60) and John Clarkson (53).

Propelled by that work, Louisville finished third with a 68-40/.630 mark, its second-best American Association finish, bettered only by its 1890 flag-winning campaign.

A few days before the end of the season, on October 6, 1884, Browning came up with his lone career start. Pitching one-third of an inning, he gave up two hits, three walks and three runs—plus throwing one wild pitch—in a 7–6 defeat to Baltimore.

## *1885*

Switched permanently to the outfield in 1885, Browning notched his second American Association batting title, running away with the title by a margin of twenty points: .362 to Davey Orr's .342. This was his second title in four years. This season also marked a curious three-year run in which Browning should have notched three consecutive batting titles, which would have given him five lifetime titles. Instead, he came out with just one and three overall. It was all due to a set of mercurial circumstances that could only have happened to Pete Browning.

The blockbuster season also included league leaderships in on-base percentage (.393), hits (174) and total bases (255). Signature games included a single, triple and home run on May 20; three doubles and a triple in a June 1 contest; a five-for-seven performance on July 10; a trio of four-for-five games on July 16, 21 and 26; and a five-for-five game on August 11.

## *1886*

In 1886, Browning narrowly lost the American Association batting title to Guy Hecker, the only pitcher ever to win a batting crown. Also the only pitcher ever to win a batting title and a pitching Triple Crown, Hecker held off Browning .341 to .340 (.3411078 to .340471) as the race went down to the final day of the season. Hecker's work also included a 26-23 mound slate—clearly, the team got its money's worth.

The major prize of the 1886 season was Browning's first career cycle game. In an August 8 home contest against the New York Metropolitans, the Eclipse won 11–6 as Browning went four for five and scored twice.

Sandwiched around the cycle were three items that were vintage Browning.

**Browning Can Write.**

A statement has been going the rounds to the effect that Pete Browning could not write. This caught the eye of the tall center-fielder, and in refutation he has sent the following autograph, with his compliments to the base-ball editor:

Pete Browning's "autograph." *Eclipse BBHR.*

On June 20, his signature appeared in the *Courier-Journal* as proof that he could write. However, both his first and last names were misspelled. In early July, he was laid off for a month because of "incompetent playing," an absence that undoubtedly cost him the batting title. And in a September 5 home contest against St. Louis, which the Louisvilles won 5–2, something happened to Browning that, a century later, would serve as the lead in a mid-March 1986 *Sports Illustrated* article on the centennial anniversary of the *Sporting News*.

Leading off first base, Browning had his attention diverted. Seeing this, pitcher Dave Foutz ran over and tagged out the astonished Browning for an unassisted pickoff play. To date, it remains the only documented case of a hurler picking off a runner unassisted without the benefit of a rundown.

## *1887*

It isn't often that a man can hit a career-best .402 and finish second, a distant second at that, but that's exactly what happened in 1887 as Tip O'Neill hit a .435. Also lost in the shuffle were career bests by Browning in hits (220), slugging average (.547) and on-base percentage (.464).

In compiling the second-highest average ever in single-season play, bettered only by Hugh Duffy's .440 mark with the 1894 Baltimore Orioles, O'Neill also became the only player in major-league history ever to lead a league in batting, hits, total bases, slugging average, runs, doubles, triples, home runs, RBIs and on-base percentage.

As one would expect, Browning had a number of emblematic games, the best easily being three near-cycle games: a single, double and a triple in a 16–1 demolition of Baltimore at home on August 20; a single, double and two triples on September 3 in a 14–9 loss at Brooklyn; and a double, two triples and a home run on September 6 in a 12–11 road victory over the New York Metropolitans.

## *1888*

In 1888, things returned to normal as baseball dispensed with counting walks as a hit and a time at-bat, a rule that enjoyed a brief one-year run in 1887 before baseball quickly realized its mistake. As a logical consequence, batting averages and ERAs went down.

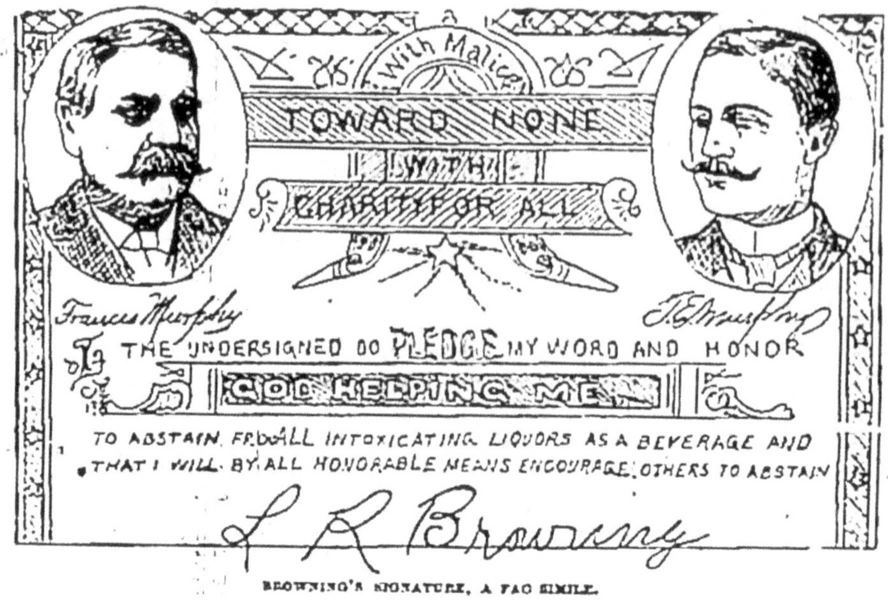


Pete Browning's 1888 temperance pledge. *Eclipse BBHR.*

Browning's .313 average, however, was more the product of an extensive suspension and less the product of the two major rule changes (the other was the restoration of the three-strikes-and-out rule). In retrospect, it undoubtedly cost him a higher finish, maybe even the American Association batting championship. That went to O'Neill in a repeat performance; his .335 was followed by Long John Reilly (.321) and Browning.

The hiatus was in direct contradiction to an April 17 temperance pledge Browning made to nationally known evangelist Francis Murphy at Eclipse Park. Initially, the penance paid dividends. A week later, he went five-for-five (all singles) in a 15–6 win over Kansas City, part of a two-month run that included nine other signature games, the kind of foundation that batting crowns are built on.

The wheels began to fall off on June 19 in Kansas City, when Browning got roaring drunk and landed up fishing in the gutter outside the team's hotel. The drinking escalated, and in late July, he was temporarily grounded with biliousness (a liver dysfunction in which the organ secretes excessive amounts of bile). More good games ensued, but the erratic nature of the situation finally took its toll on Louisville management.

After missing a game on August 10 with a stone bruise on his heel, Browning was shortly thereafter suspended and did not make an appearance again until September 23, when there were only three weeks left in the season. The offense, towering even by Browning standards, more than justified the suspension, as attested by a late August story in the *Louisville Courier-Journal*.

Sporting a black eye of unknown origin and sans a shirt, vest or undershirt (his bare chest was covered only by an overcoat), a drunken Browning had boarded a streetcar one night earlier in the month and insulted a city councilman, whom he later dragged into a saloon.

## *1889*

Spiraling downward, Browning hit rock bottom in 1889, when he batted a career-low .259. His average was a reflection of the doomed season that saw Louisville finish in the cellar with a 27-111/.196 record, sixty-six and a half games back of the league champion Brooklyn Bridegrooms; suffer 26 consecutive losses, still the all-time major-league record; taken over by the league, followed by the sale of the club; charged arbitrary fines and pay dockings by owner Mordecai Davidson; and endure close calls with the lethal Johnstown, Pennsylvania flood and a brief players' strike, the first ever in major-league history, in which Browning participated.

Oddly enough, Browning picked up his second cycle on June 7, his five-for-six work including a pair of singles and two runs scored. Remarkably, it came during the ferocious losing streak. Even more remarkably, the feat had been accomplished from the sixth spot in the lineup. All of this came to naught, as Louisville lost 9–7 to the Philadelphia Athletics, its fourteenth straight defeat.

For Browning, the season ended abruptly on August 11, when he was suspended for the remainder of the campaign (a career-best two months) for drunkenness.

Whether it was chronic alcoholism or mastoiditis-generated pathological drinking will never be fully known. Considering Browning's success during the remainder of his career—in particular, the next season—it was more than likely the former.

One thing was without question, however. Left in the wake of Browning's most self-destructive season were two abstinence pledges he had signed in early April, one with Davidson and another before a local judge.

## *1890*

In 1890, for the second time in its history, major-league baseball presented fans with three leagues, the new addition being the Players League. Despite the 1889 debacle, Browning was still top property and landed with the Cleveland Infants in the newest loop.

Besides Browning, the loop was enriched with other major defections from the National League and the American Association, that group including future Hall of Famers Monte Ward, the founder of the Players League; Connie Mack; King Kelly; Hoss Radbourn; Tim Keefe; Roger Connor; Charlie Comiskey; Jim O'Rourke; Pud Galvin; Ed Delahanty; Jake Beckley; and Hugh Duffy. Other top names included Davey Orr, Harry Stovey and George Van Haltren.

A change of scenery often produces remarkable results, and in retrospect, Browning's 1890 campaign was high baseball art. It was like a managing master putting the final touches and flourishes on a magnificent career with one final grand masterpiece.

Signed for a hefty $4,480 according to one source, Browning responded in price, taking the first, last and only batting title of the Players League with a .3732 average that just barely nipped Davey Orr's .3728 work. Also the league leader in doubles (forty), Browning finished second in on-base percentage (.459), fourth in hits (184) and fifth in slugging percentage (.517).

An ancillary part of this work was a number of signature games starting with a late April game in which he doubled, tripled, scored two runs and overall went three for five in an 18–15 loss. That was followed by the following standouts:

Three for five (two doubles) on May 22
Four for five (all singles) on June 3
Three for five (one triple) on July 14
Three for three (one triple) on July 22
Three for four (one double) on July 23
Four for seven (two doubles, one triple) on July 29
Three for three on August 15
Four for six (one double) on August 30
Three for five (one homer) on September 5
Three for five (one double) on September 27
Three for three (one double) on October 1

But the season wasn't all hitting. There was the matter of Browning's glove, and on Friday, June 6, 1890, the *Cleveland Plain Dealer* carried arguably the best story of Browning's career, one that thoroughly debunks the long-held perception of Browning as a one-dimensional player who was "good hit, no field."

Headlined "In Love with Old Petie," the article contained pickups from two leading Chicago newspapers.

> *Pete Browning has made an unconditional "hit" in Chicago and people there have gone wild over the Gladiator's ball playing. Describing a play in Wednesday's game, the* Chicago Inter Ocean *says: "The one act of the afternoon which stands out like a wart on a man's nose was a catch by Col. Browning in the fifth inning. Mr. (Hugh) Duffy, a distinguished townsman with whom it is a genuine pleasure to deal, tripped to the bat with his teeth set so hard that his jaw bones stuck out like handles on an Etruscan vase. He reached for the first ball which Mr. (Jersey) Bakely was good enough to land over the rubber.*
>
> *"The sound that followed was the same as when the slats fall down in an old-fashioned bed. The ball mounted towards the town of Jefferson until it was lost to sight. It came into view again in a few moments in the extreme left field, and then it was observed that Mr. Browning was only a few rods away.*
>
> *"He rattled his lengthy legs towards his heart's desire as long as possible, and then jumped in a northwesterly direction, turning four times in the air and stretching one arm for the ball in a manner of a boy after his second piece of pie.*
>
> *"He got it.*
>
> *"Then applause went up from the grandstand like an insane man experimenting with a French horn. Pete had to doff his cap a dozen times."*
>
> *Of the same play, the* Chicago Tribune *says: "Browning was the hero of the day. He made one of the most marvelous catches from Duffy's bat ever seen on a ball field."*

This masterpiece was no isolated example. Rather, it was reflective of Browning's defensive work that spanned his entire active career, from a rookie game in 1882 when he posted six putouts, five assists and two double plays (at either shortstop or second base) to the opener of a July 4, 1893 double-header at home, in which Browning made "probably the grandest catch that has ever been made in this city."

It was hardly an overstatement. Seeing that he could not reach a dying quail shot without extreme effort, Browning "gave a grand spurt, and throwing his body forward at almost full length, he grasped the ball with two fingers about three inches from the ground." It brought the house down.

These three catches were hardly freak occurences as the following web gems, all reported in the *Louisville Courier-Journal*, clearly demonstrate:

> *April 25, 1885: Browning's left-handed catch of* [Hugh] *Nicol's hit was decidedly the feature of the game. After a long run in which he covered an almost incredible amount of ground, he reached up his left hand and caught the ball. It was some time before he could check himself, and the crowd all supposed the ball had got past him.*
>
> *July 2, 1885:* [Curt] *Welch came to the bat and hit a terrific liner far out to center field. It appeared good for a home run, but Browning ran back for it, with no apparent chance to make the out. Away went the ball and Browning toward the fence. As the sphere came low enough, Pete reached up one hand and quietly pulled it down. Two men were already out, and this retired the side.*
>
> *May 2, 1887: Browning played a remarkable game in center field. In the seventh inning, he made two brilliant catches, one on a long drive of* [Charley] *Jones to left center, which he captured after a hard run toward the picket fence, and again on a high fly from* [Frank] *Fennelly's bat, which passed over* [right fielder Chicken] *Wolf's head, and was taken in by big Pete close to the right field fence. He was loudly applauded, and was forced to doff his hat several times to the admiring crowd.*
>
> *August 27, 1887: Browning made a nice catch in the same* [fifth] *inning. When big Bill Phillips came to the bat, Pete went back near the fence to the right of center field. The Gladiator knew by experience where the giant knocked his best balls. Phillips got one where he wanted it, and sent the ball high and far into Browning's territory. Pete made a noble effort for the hit, and captured it over his head after a long backward run.*
>
> *April 22, 1888:* [Arlie] *Latham got first on balls and stole second.* [Harry] *Lyons hit a home run to right, which Browning ran for. As the ball was going into home run territory, Pete threw his left hand over the four-foot fence and made a miraculous catch.* [Browning then doubled up Latham.]

*July 10, 1888: Pete Browning led in the work in the field for the Louisvilles. The Gladiator was himself again, and the friends of the club were glad to see him again in the old position in the middle field. No less than three of Browning's four putouts were circus catches, and one was a great, running catch of a ball knocked by* [Ed] *McKean in the third inning, which looked safe for three bases. Recovering himself, Pete completed a neat double play by throwing out* [Cub] *Stricker, who had attempted to leave first base on the hit.*

*May 3, 1892: Then the prettiest play of the game was made.* [Lew] *Whistler drove a fly to short left that many thought would drop short of the benches. The Gladiator turned and ran like a dog. He managed to catch that ball, no one knows how. Such was the impetus of his dash that he almost ran to the top of the benches before he could stop himself. That ended the game.*

*June 26, 1893: In the ninth, the Louisvilles were quickly retired in order.* [Kid] *Nichols was the first man to bat for the Bostons. He hit the ball a terrific whack and it sailed far out into right field. As he swung his bat, Browning started for the scoreboard, and, as it passed over his head, he gave a peculiar jerk with his hands. The crowd did not know he had the ball until he threw it into the diamond.*

Clearly, when Browning was on—that is, not beset by illness, injury, pain or alcoholism—he was capable of the most extraordinary defensive masterpieces, a virtuoso along the lines of Willie Mays. When he was "off," he fielded worse than Mays's godson. Seemingly, there was no in between.

Unquestionably, Browning's alleged defensive liabilities can now be traced to three separate entities: historical embellishment; the ignorance of his times, when the crude equipment made anyone fielding at .950 or better a golden glover; and the contradiction that Browning, for a good portion of his career, played the three most significant positions on the defensive spectrum—shortstop, second base and center field—hardly places where a defensive liability would be put.

In retrospect, the weakest part of Browning's game was not his fielding but his base running. The examples of his base-running gaffes are endless and legendary; the richest of them all was the previously mentioned 1886 game in which Browning was picked off first base unassisted by the opposing pitcher.

The June 6 *Cleveland Plain Dealer* article piece also showed how much cities around the circuit—like Cleveland and Chicago—loved Browning, and certainly he loved them in return. And that leads directly into another salient historical point, overlooked by numerous historians, researchers and baseball writers over the years: the inordinate joy that Browning brought to countless thousands of fans throughout his career.

Nine days later, the *Cleveland Plain Dealer* carried the following short item, which iced the cake of the June 6 article: "President Addison of Chicago is opposed to Peter Browning on principle. 'That fellow,' he says, 'is seven feet high and he jumps six feet into the air to pull down home runs. What does he want to do? To kill the sport off entirely?'"

## *1891*

The 1891 season marked Browning's third different league in as many seasons and his first season in the National League. In hindsight, it's easy to state that had it not been for the 1877 Louisville pennant-fixing scandal, Browning would have probably spent the bulk of his career, instead of his twilight years, in the senior circuit; certainly would have increased his career numbers; and would today be in Cooperstown.

Splitting the season between the Pittsburgh Pirates and the Cincinnati Reds, Browning wasted little time in adding to his legend, bunting into a triple play (4-6-3) against the Chicago Cubs on May 5. Though this was a freak play, it was a sign of things to come.

While hitting decently, he began to run afoul of manager Ned Hanlon over such things as wearing spikeless shoes, which caused him to fall down while chasing a fly ball. On another occasion, he hit into a double play after ignoring Hanlon's orders to sacrifice. As a consequence, Browning and his .291 average in fifty games were sent packing in late June.

Browning was quickly picked up by the Reds, for whom he batted .343 in fifty-five contests. While there, he ran into a mirror image of himself, teammate Long John Reilly, whose obsession with "hit-filled" bats was second only to the Gladiator's. Always on the prowl for any of Browning's bats, it was suspected but never proved that while Browning was conducting an early July interview in one part of the clubhouse, Reilly was in another section picking up a few good sticks. (Undoubtedly, the situation only worsened later that month when Browning went four for four.)

Browning's last fine game of the season came on September 2, when he singled twice and tripled once from four trips to the plate. Three days later, he was done for the season when Kid Gleason came far inside with a pitch that Browning fended off with his hand to avoid being beaned.

It is reasonable to believe that had Browning spent the entire season in a positive atmosphere like Cincinnati and without injury, he could have made the kind of major-league history that would have guaranteed him a spot in Cooperstown by becoming the first and only man to win batting crowns in three different leagues.

The 1891 National League title would also have marked his fourth career batting crown—his second in a row—and his first in the National League. It didn't play out that way, though, and Browning landed with a .313 mark that was third behind Billy Hamilton (.340) and teammate Bug Holliday (.319).

## *1892*

By 1892, major-league baseball found itself with only one league, the Players League having folded after the 1890 campaign and the American Association closing shop in 1891. Back with his old city, Browning hit .247 in twenty-one games for Louisville before being released in mid-May. Once again, he caught on quickly with Cincinnati, batting .303 in eighty-one games and ending the season at .292.

His top game easily was a five-for-six performance (all singles) against Baltimore in early July, but his sloppy defense (trying to stop grounders with his shins) earned him his release shortly thereafter. Signed back by the Reds, he re-debuted for that team on September 2 with a three-for-four performance. A few days later, he left a game following an attack of vertigo, unquestionably the manifestation of growing mastoid problems. Deadly serious, this stood in direct contrast to an October 10 absence due to barnacles (marine crustaceans) on Browning's hands.

## *1893*

In late May 1893, Browning signed a contract with Louisville and delivered on both sides of the diamond, playing sterling defense and batting .355 in just 57 games. One of the team's three stars, along with pitcher George Hemming (18-17 on a team that finished 25 games under .500) and first baseman Willard Brown (.304 in 111 games), Browning was inexplicably released in early August and played no more that year.

## *1894*

True to form, Pete Browning's fabled major-league career came to a close with a storybook ending. On Sunday, September 30, 1894, in the finale of a closing-day double-header, he played right field for Brooklyn and batted sixth in the order. The Gladiator singled twice in two official at-bats, walked once and scored once. The work helped Brooklyn to a 12–4 victory and a split in the twin bill held in Louisville.

## *1895 and 1896*

In early June 1895, Browning played first base for a local team, the Rhodes-Burfords, and led them to a 26–11 smashing of the Rudolphs & Bauers. Obviously, the train was headed home after the usual series of stops: amateur prodigy, major-league rookie sensation, longstanding major-league superstar, major-league journeyman and, finally, aging ballplayer holding back the dawn as a minor-league, semipro and amateur fill-in player.

Officially, the last stop came in 1896, when Browning played his last recorded season of organized baseball at any level, batting .333 in twenty-six games with Columbus of the Western League.

## *1897–1905*

The late 1890s found Browning working as a cigar salesman, his bar—located near his residence at Thirteenth and Market—having failed, perhaps for the most obvious of reasons. Giving that up, Browning turned to caring for his mother, and during baseball season, he was seen frequently at local baseball games. As in previous years, Browning was always well received and well remembered by crowds.

But the peaceful retirement was an illusion.

On June 7, 1905, according to existing court records stored in Frankfort at the Kentucky State Archives, Louis Rogers "Pete" Browning (aka the Gladiator, Line-'em-out Pete, etc.) was brought forth in the criminal division of Jefferson County Circuit Court, where he was declared a lunatic and ordered to the Fourth Kentucky Lunatic Asylum at nearby Lakeland.

As a matter of course, the *Courier-Journal* story the next day recounted Browning's prowess as a hitter, toward the end relating Browning's secret for his batting success: daily washings of his eyes with buttermilk.

Even under the direst of circumstances, Browning was extremely readable copy.

After some improvement, Browning was removed from Lakeland by one of his sisters on June 21, 1905. On July 26, 1905, he was admitted to old City Hospital, later renamed General Hospital and now called University Hospital. There, he underwent surgery for ear trouble and a tumor of the breast on July 29.

Making a rapid recovery, the Gladiator was sent home only to return in early August after experiencing more difficulty. Becoming morbid and losing hope, Browning refused to take his medication or cooperate with doctors. In late August, he slipped away from the hospital and walked to his mother's house, explaining that he didn't like to hear people groan. That same night, he was taken back to the municipal hospital.

On September 1, 1905, Hillerich & Bradsby signed a contract for its first autographed model with future Hall of Famer Honus Wagner, who had begun his career in Louisville in 1897 along with another Cooperstown resident-to-be, pitcher Rube Waddell. The first man to have his name on a bat, Wagner was part of modern endorsement-advertising history.

Wagner was also part of a nucleus of four players transferred to Pittsburgh after Louisville lost its franchise when the National League contracted from a dozen teams to eight clubs following the 1899 campaign. The results were something and immediate. Led by former Louisville standouts Wagner, Deacon Phillippe, Tommy Leach and another Cooperstown resident-to-be—Fred Clarke, the Pirates became an immediate dynasty, winning four pennants (1902, '03, '04 and '09) and one World Championship (1909) in their first decade of play.

But as those new stars began to rise and shine, an ancient star—and the catalyst for all of that history—began to dim.

Around the time of this historic contract, a growth appeared once again on Browning's neck. Deteriorating rapidly, Browning finally yielded to his relentless adversaries on Sunday, September 10, 1905, at 2:15 p.m. Present during the waning hours of the final siege were his mother, Mrs. Mary Jane Sheppard Browning; two sisters, Mrs. Florence Ramsey and Miss Fannie Browning; and one brother, Charles. Another brother, Henry, was unable to come to his bedside because of serious illness.

Pete Browning's old grave marker. *Eclipse BBHR.*

This is in direct contradiction of a commonly reported error that Browning died alone in an insane asylum. Great story, especially if you're a Hollywood screenwriter, but that's all it is. In truth, the end came for Browning, simply and without any earth-shaking fanfare, at a city hospital surrounded by members of his family. Nothing more.

Browning's medical problems were substantial. Besides the brain damage sustained by both the crudely treated mastoid condition and years of acute alcoholism, he had cancer at the end. And most certainly, Browning was suffering from cirrhosis of the liver, another byproduct of his years of wild, unchecked and lethal drinking. (Some sources claim that Browning's death was due to paresis, the final stage of syphilis, in which the victim literally loses his mind. There is no firm medical evidence for this; however, it is known that Browning had a fondness for prostitutes, and he had the nickname to back it up—"Pietro *Red-light District* Distillery Interests Browning.")

The origin of Browning's drinking was well documented in the *Times* obituary under a subsection labeled "His Introduction to the Foams." According to the article, his drinking dated all the way back to his early amateur days.

> *"Old Pete" was never known to take a drink until he played a game in this city with an amateur nine. He was asked to fill in for one of the players. On third base, a keg of beer had been placed, and those who reached the foaming fountain were entitled to a glass of lager. Pete knocked so many three-baggers and home-runs that little beer was left for anyone else.*

On the surface, the tone was somewhat light, even humorous. Between the lines, however, lay a bone-chilling commentary on Browning's alcoholic abuse, which had begun when he was a teenager.

Funeral services were held the following afternoon, Tuesday, September 12, at 2:30 p.m. at the home of Browning's mother. From there, Browning was taken to Cave Hill Cemetery, the final resting place for many of Louisville's major-league ballplayers, as well as numerous nationally prominent local and state figures.

One of the more prominent major leaguers buried there was another Louisville batting champion, William "Chicken" Wolf, who died several years earlier in 1903 and whose end Browning mirrored exactly.

Both Wolf and Browning share distinguished company with Revolutionary War hero/explorer George Rogers (older brother of William Clark, part of the famed Lewis and Clark Expedition); seven-foot-eight Jim Porter, "the Kentucky Giant"; Meriwether Lewis Clark Jr., the creator of the Kentucky Derby and a grandson of explorer William Clark; J. Graham Brown, longtime owner of the Brown Hotel (whose house chef invented the nationally famed "Hot Brown" sandwich); Kentucky Fried Chicken king Harland Sanders; newspaper editor Henry Watterson, namesake of Louisville's Watterson Expressway; and hotel magnate Louis Seelbach, owner of one of the city's finest hotels, the Seelbach Hotel. Serving as Browning's pallbearers were John Dyler, his first manager, and a number of former teammates, including John Reccius and Tom McLaughlin.

And there Browning lay for years, his grave site marked by a simple granite gravestone. Then, on September 10, 1984, on the seventy-ninth anniversary of his death and during the centennial year of the Hillerich & Bradsby Company, the world's most famous bat maker joined with the City of Louisville to honor Browning with a new grave marker that correctly spelled his name and fully detailed his lifetime baseball achievements.

LOUISVILLE MAYOR HARVEY I. SLOANE
AND
HILLERICH & BRADSBY CO.
CORDIALLY INVITE YOU TO ATTEND
THE UNVEILING OF A NEW MEMORIAL FOR
PETE 'THE GLADIATOR' BROWNING,
LOUISVILLE'S FIRST BASEBALL STAR
WHO INSPIRED THE FIRST
LOUISVILLE SLUGGER BASEBALL BAT.
CAVE HILL CEMETERY
701 BAXTER AVENUE
11:00 A.M. MONDAY
SEPTEMBER 10, 1984

An official invitation to the September 10, 1984 dedication of Pete Browning's new marker. *Eclipse BBHR.*

A complex three-tiered figure, Browning endures to this day as a transcendental megastar known even to those with a cursory knowledge of the game, as one of American baseball's most colorful pieces of folklore and as a timeless, horrifying human tragedy.

All that's missing from the story is a plaque for Browning in Cooperstown.

## *Notable Quotes from Pete Browning*

Browning's stock and trade were the great hit—and the great quote. The following is a sampling of "Yogi-isms" from the original master of that baseball art form.

"If I should attempt to slide into a base, my legs would drop off." (*Louisville Courier-Journal*, July 27, 1887)

"You ask why I don't slide? Well, what is the use of sliding when you can get in standing up? There is no use soiling your clothes and increasing your laundry bills when you don't have to." (*Cincinnati Enquirer*, July 11, 1891)

On the early season difficulties he had seeing the ball: "It's my old trouble. I never could see 'em at this season of the year, but I'll climb towards the top yet." (*Louisville Courier-Journal*, May 30, 1888)

Browning once left a note for roommate Guy Hecker telling him that they were staying in room "aity ate." (*Louisville Diamonds*)

At a postseason testimonial dinner in 1887, the year Browning batted a career-best .402, he was presented a large gold watch. Surprised by the gift and facing a crowd that cried for a speech, he responded: "Where the hell's the gold chain?" The crowd exploded in laughter. (*American Gladiator*)

On June 20, 1886, an article appeared in the *Louisville Courier-Journal* headlined "Browning Can Write." It read: "A statement has been going the rounds to the effect that Pete Browning could not write. This caught the eye of the tall center fielder, and in refutation he has sent the following autograph, with his compliments to the baseball editor." His autograph was semilegible, and both of his names were misspelled. (*Louisville Diamonds*)

Pete Browning's new grave marker. *Eclipse BBHR.*

"I never ran across a fellow like [teammate Long John] Reilly. Every bat you pick up out there has got 'R' on it. He won't even let me carry one of his bats. There is only one stick that I want. Big Darby O'Brien [left fielder for the Brooklyn Bridegrooms] has got it. If Petie could make a trade with him, he would lead the league in hitting, you can gamble on that." (*Cincinnati Enquirer*, July 6, 1891)

"I can't hit the ball until I hit the bottle." (*Louisville Diamonds*)

"I have got 205 bats, if you want to know. I only use one of them, but I like to carry them around for other fellows." (*Cincinnati Enquirer*, July 6, 1891)

"Pete Browning has given up cigarette smoking. Pete says that since the formation of the Cigarette Trust, the smoke from the cigarettes has a tendency to grow warts on his lamps [eyes]." (*Cincinnati Enquirer*, June 11, 1892)

"Pete Browning could not play yesterday, owing to barnacles on his fingers." (*Cincinnati Enquirer*, October 11, 1892).

"For several days past, he [Browning] has had his eye on [right fielder Farmer] Weaver's 'stick,' and after the 'Farmer' had knocked out his two-bagger, Browning walked around slowly to the bat-stand, and, when Weaver was not looking, picked up the lucky piece of ash.

"Now, ballplayers like for no one else to use their bats, but Browning had slipped to the plate while Weaver's head was turned. It was then that he banged the ball into left center for three bases. He walked in after the last man had been put out and handed the bat to Weaver with a longing expression on his face.

"'Fine stick, fine stick,' said he, 'best I ever had in my hands. Want to buy it.' But Weaver would not sell, and about this time the remembrance of that long drive gladdened his heart, and he walked away smiling." (*Louisville Courier-Journal*, July 2, 1893)

"I am going to get out my old sash-weight bat tonight. I have been using a light stick. They're no good. No: you want to kill 'em when you got a light stick in your hands. You can't do none of these League pitchers on rising straight balls. They are pitching curves all the time, and you can't kill 'em. That's the reason I am going to get out my stick. It's a bird. I'll put on of that old oil Jerry Harrington's got out there at the clubhouse, and then I'll just meet 'em. No more light sticks for Petey." (*Cincinnati Enquirer*, July 15, 1891)

"I see that the Pittsburgh club has a bill against me. Well, you can just bet that Pete will never pay that. I can prove that I ordered them for the club. They didn't suit, and then the club tried to mark them on me. No, I never used $90 worth of bats last year [1892]. Oh, I keep a stick a few days, make a hit or two with it, and lay it away some place. The trouble with half of the bats made is that they are too light in the handle and won't go well." (*Cincinnati Enquirer*, April 27, 1892)

"I am not a lusher and never will be, and what is more, I want to deny all those ridiculous sayings that have been credited to me." (*Louisville Post*, June 17, 1891, pickup of a *New York Herald* story)

## Guy

The only pitcher in major-league history to win a batting title, Guy Hecker is also the only player in major-league history ever to win both a batting title and a pitching Triple Crown—substantial work when one considers that Hecker entered the majors in his midtwenties, set a number of records and then was gone after a brief but brilliant nine-year career (1882–90) as a pitcher and first baseman.

Born on April 3, 1856, in Youngsville, Pennsylvania, Hecker broke into organized baseball in 1879 as a first baseman with an Oil City, Pennsylvania team that also included future big-top star pitcher Tony Mullane. Several years later, the pair was reunited as teammates at Louisville, which had joined the newly formed major-league circuit, the American Association.

In the American Association's inaugural season, Louisville finished a strong third behind rookie batting champion Pete Browning and thirty-game winner Mullane. The former hit .378; the latter, in his only season with Louisville, ranked second in the new loop in wins with a 30-24 mark.

A rookie like Browning, Hecker played sixty-six games of Louisville's eighty-game schedule at first base and batted .276. He also went 6-6 with a wafer-thin 1.30 ERA. And early on, "The Blonde Guy," as Hecker was nicknamed because of his hair, gave a sign of greatness to come. On September 19, 1882, just eight days after Mullane had thrown the American Association's first no-hitter, Hecker followed with the league's second no-hitter.

In 1883, Louisville slipped to fifth place despite a pair of twenty-game winners in Hecker and Sam Weaver. That doesn't happen often, but in this case there was a good reason: the pair was the entire staff, and because of the resulting overload, both men were also twenty-game losers. Hecker checked in at 26-23, complemented by a dependable .273 batting average, while Weaver, in his only campaign in a Louisville uniform, filled out the balance with a 26-22 mark.

The 1884 season was Hecker's magnum opus as a pitcher, a brilliant Triple Crown year that included fifty-two wins, 385 Ks and a 1.80 ERA, plus league leaderships in innings (670.2), complete games (72) and lowest on-base percentage (.226). As usual, he produced excellent ancillary bat work (.297). And as usual, there was no pennant for Louisville.

The highest ever in American Association play, Hecker's fifty-two-win total currently ranks third on the all-time list. Without question, he is in imposing company. Just ahead of him are a pair of Cooperstown residents: "Old Hoss" Radbourne and John Clarkson. And in both cases, their career-high mound work produced flags. The all-time seasonal-wins champion, Radbourne drove Providence home to the 1884 National League flag with sixty triumphs (adding three more in the World Series sweep of the American Association champion New York Mets), while Clarkson gunned Chicago to the 1885 National League flag with fifty-three victories.

Unlike Radbourne and Clarkson, stars who shined for years afterward and eventually landed up in the Baseball Hall of Fame, Hecker was a brilliant nova who flared briefly and then was gone. Unknowingly, Louisville destroyed its ace in 1884, though it would take several years for that fact to become apparent. That season, however, Hecker appeared utterly invincible.

On July 4, 1884, he pitched both parts of a home double-header with Brooklyn and gave the overflow holiday crowd two complete-game wins. In the 5–4 opener, he struck out eight, scattered seven hits and overcame six errors. In the closer, he evenly displaced six hits and bypassed four errors en route to an 8–2 triumph.

In a losing cause later that summer, Hecker also showed fine colors, striking out seventeen batters in an error-plagued 4–3 loss to Columbus at

Louisville on August 26. Sandwiching the virtuoso performance were an eleven-strikeout, 6–1 victory over Toledo on August 24 and a ten-Ks, 5–3 win against Columbus on August 27.

In retrospect, it is a wonder that Hecker's arm did not fall off in 1884 considering the load that was placed on it. That pitching was as dangerous in that day as it is today, as evidenced by the following note, which appeared under the headline "The Pitcher for the Undertakers Broke His Arm" in the *Louisville Courier-Journal* on September 3, 1889. And mind you, this occurred not in a major-league game but in a routine amateur contest. Datelined Chicago, September 2, the note read:

> *A horrible accident occurred yesterday at a game of base ball between two nines that styled themselves the "Doctors" and the "Undertakers." In the seventh inning when the Undertakers were well in the lead, James McNerney, their pitcher, was delivering a swift in-shoot when his arm snapped a few inches from the shoulder, and he fell to the ground unconscious. An examination revealed the fact that his arm was broken, the bone almost protruding through the flesh. He was removed to his home.*

Though Louisville finished in a fifth-place tie with the Brooklyn Grays in 1885, Hecker remained topside with a strong 30-23 slate backed up by a workmanlike .273 average.

The following year, Hecker racked up twenty-six scores, his second twenty-win season (26-23). Despite the numbers, Hecker was in a gradual decline, though the drift, curiously enough, brought with it a quartet of major-league records that still stands today.

The first big-top mark came in the finale of an August 15, 1886 double-header against Baltimore when he scored seven times off a spectacular six-for-seven performance that saw him slug three home runs, drill three singles and reach base a seventh time via an error. And according to the *Louisville Courier-Journal* game account, there was nothing cheap about the homers, which "were all beautiful drives to the left-field fence, one ball going beneath the seats and losing itself amid the weeds and rubbish." Completing the scenario, Hecker picked up the win in the 22–5 rout that completed a double-header drubbing of Baltimore.

Today, Hecker still holds the major-league record for most runs scored in a game by a pitcher and a player. And he was the first pitcher in major-league history to homer three times in a game.

Guy Hecker. *National Baseball Hall of Fame Library, Cooperstown, New York.*

At the end of the 1886 season, Hecker claimed his second major-league record, becoming the first. last and only pitcher to date to take a big-top batting crown. It wasn't a cakewalk, though; Hecker was forced to go down to the last day of the season in order to secure his historic and record-setting batting title by a scant margin over teammate Pete Browning (.341 to .340). In light of the specialization of pitchers and the introduction of the "designated hitter," it seems unlikely that Hecker's feat will ever be duplicated.

(That batting title also produced his third major-league record: Hecker's unique batting title/pitching Triple Crown double, a standard that will never be matched.)

The next year, Hecker enjoyed his last productive season in the majors with an 18-12 record and a .319 batting average. This also marked the fourth and last of his prime major-league records, an unusual fielding mark obtained in a 2–0 loss to Cincinnati on closing day, October 9.

According to the *Sporting News* baseball record book, that afternoon Hecker became the first player to play eight innings at first base without accepting a chance. This is an important distinction to make since some sources say it was a full nine-inning contest. This is incorrect, and the boxscore for the game verifies that. As the visitors, Louisville had no ninth inning in the field after failing to at least knot the score in the team's final frame at bat. (For the statistically interested, Hecker had one putout and no assists in this odd record-setting game.)

Only in a very general sense does Hecker hold that particular "game" record. Yet, it can accurately be stated that if 1884 was his primo season as a pitcher, and 1886 was a record classic as a hitter, then his 1887 fielding handiwork marked the apex of a fine defensive career.

And that was it for the Blonde Guy.

Part of a terrible Louisville team that finished seventh in 1888, just a few games ahead of cellar-dweller Kansas City, Hecker posted an 8-17 mark, dipping below .500 for the first time in his career.

The next year, the Blonde Guy sought to both manage and play for Louisville. Though he lost the managership over a longstanding grudge, this proved fortuitous, as the club wandered through a nightmarish season that included a brief players' strike (one of the strikers was Hecker), arbitrary fines and pay dockings, an epic twenty-six-game losing streak, the sale of the club and the suspension of star Pete Browning for drunkenness for the final two months of the season. When all the dust had settled, Louisville lay in the cellar with an atrocious 27-111/.196 record. Hecker did not survive the season, though; he and his 5-13 record had been released by the club in mid-September.

His final big-league work came in 1890 as the playing manager of the Pittsburgh National League team, where he hit .226 and posted a 2-9 record for another last-place club while his old team went to the World Series—proof that timing and location are everything to a pitcher.

Retiring after the 1890 season with a career 173-146 record and a lifetime .283 batting average, Hecker managed in the minors for several years and then returned to Oil City, Pennsylvania, where it had all begun. There, he entered the oil business, and later opened a grocery store. In 1931, Hecker was involved in an automobile accident that left the old right-hander's pitching arm so damaged that he could not write except with a typewriter.

Issued a lifetime pass by the game in his final retirement years, Hecker later moved to Wooster, Ohio, where he died at age eighty-two on December 3, 1938. Survivors included his widow, Martha, and a son, Guy Clifford Hecker of New York.

## JIMMY

In the ten-year operation of the American Association, three different Louisville batsmen accounted for a quartet of American Association batting titles.

This singular domination was significant since the remaining six titlists were produced by five other teams. The lone duplication was Tip O'Neill of St. Louis, a back-to-back winner in 1887 and 1888. Other American Association batting title winners included Ed Swartwood (Pittsburgh/1883), Davey Orr (New York/1884), Tom Tucker (Baltimore/1889) and Dan Brouthers (Boston/1891).

The Louisville domination began with Pete Browning (1882 and 1885), continued with Guy Hecker (1886) and concluded with the eponymously named "Chicken" Wolf in 1890.

The American Association batting champion in 1890 off a league-leading .363 average and a circuit-topping 197 hits that led Louisville to its only major-league flag and World Series appearance, William Van Winkle "Chicken" Wolf is thought to be the only man to have competed in the American Association in all ten years that it operated.

Born in Louisville on May 12, 1862, and most popularly known as "Jimmy," he picked up his professional moniker—according to one story—in 1882 from teammate and fellow batting champion Pete Browning.

In a pregame lunch that year, the fleet, solid-fielding Wolf gorged himself on stewed chicken—contrary to his manager's orders to eat lightly. In the game that followed, Wolf made several uncharacteristic errors. Browning attributed them to the chicken Wolf had eaten and renamed him.

(For the record, there are several other versions of the origin of Wolf's moniker. Version two, reported in the August 6, 1891 issue of the *Louisville Courier-Journal*, says that Wolf got into a chicken-eating contest while dining with a baseball reporter in Cincinnati. Wolf was the runaway winner, and the next day the writer maliciously referred to him as "Chicken" Wolf in a game story. Version number three simply attributes the nickname to Wolf's love of poultry.)

Stripped of his vaunted speed toward the end of his eleven-year career (his last year being 1892 with St. Louis in the National League), Wolf joined the Louisville Fire Department after his retirement from baseball.

Tragedy marred Wolf's last years, however, and his untimely end eerily duplicated that of Pete Browning. The downward slide began with a terrible accident.

Driving an engine to a fire, Wolf hit a candy cart broadside as he turned a corner. The impact separated the engine from the team, and Wolf was hurled to the cobblestone street. He suffered a severe head injury that left him "mentally unbalanced," according to his *Louisville Courier-Journal* obituary.

Wolf worsened when one of his children died shortly thereafter, and he was finally committed to the state insane asylum at Lakeland in 1901. Released in March 1903, Wolf suffered a relapse several months later and died in the old City Hospital on May 16, 1903, just four days after his forty-first birthday.

Wolf was buried at Louisville's venerable Cave Hill Cemetery, one of a number of major leaguers interred there, including longtime teammate Pete

Browning, whose tragic final days two years later mirrored Wolf's. (Another teammate and well-known ballplayer, Philip Reccius, also traveled this same dark path after being violently struck in the temple by a batted ball.)

To those familiar with Wolf, his grave site is a lonely and bewildering sight, almost incomprehensible in its anguish, but he is not alone. Located high above the rest of the cemetery on an incline populated by American Holly trees, the graves of Jimmy Wolf and his son, Milton (1897–1901), are haunting reminders that when the furies of death clash with the energy of everyday life, it is often seemingly without reason and utterly without mercy.

Viewing the grave site of his young son, whose death was the final act that drove Wolf over the edge, one finds oneself almost speechless. If there were an epitaph to all of this, it could well be the words of screenwriters Irving Ravetch and Harriet Frank Jr. from their masterful film *The Cowboys*. Burying a young cowhand who had lost his life in a freak stampede while on a cattle drive, cattle boss Wil Anderson (John Wayne) eulogized the cowhand as follows:

> *Sometimes, it's hard to understand the drift of things. This was a good boy. He would've made a good man. He didn't get his chance. Death can come for you any place, any time. He's never welcome. But if you've done all you can do, and it's your best, in a way you're ready for him.*

Much the same can be said for Jimmy Wolf, long regarded as one of baseball's more amusing curiosities because of his off-beat baseball name, the archaic times in which he lived (virtually as unfathomable as Stonehenge) and the antique brand of major-league baseball that he played.

Wander beneath the surface, though, and Jimmy Wolf takes on a different shape—that of a fine ballplayer whose terrible lot in life it was to lose a treasured child, then his mind and finally his life. All the baseball stardom and accomplishments were no match for this dark end.

Jimmy Wolf. *National Baseball Hall of Fame Library, Cooperstown, New York.*

That Jimmy Wolf's life was infinitely more complicated and more complete is not surprising to those who understand the true nature of human experience: that it is the same, regardless of the time frame involved.

This is what we know today about Jimmy Wolf, and it stands as a monument to a good man and a well-lived life: Equal parts loving father, devoted husband, courageous civil servant and productive citizen, Jimmy Wolf was also a top-flight journeyman who, late in his career—freed at last from the shadow of Pete Browning—took center stage with his stick. Wielding it with force and purpose, he quietly drove his club first to a pennant and then to a World Series co-championship. Along the way, Jimmy Wolf picked up a little something for himself: superstardom for one brief, shining moment.

Few in their lives ever reach such heights, ever scale a mountain that large, ever revel in the magnificence of such a singular view or ever haul down this big of a prize. Jimmy Wolf was one of them.

## Reccius: The First Family of Louisville Baseball

Though long forgotten today, except by historians, the first family of Louisville baseball was the Reccius family. Oldest brother John William Reccius headed this Civil War–era family. The following is a look at this group—a major force in the beginnings of Louisville's baseball history.

### *(John) William Reccius*

Born: 1848, Germany
Died: January 25, 1911, Louisville
Born circa 1848 in Germany to John and Sophia Reccius, John William Reccius immigrated to the United States with his parents at age six. He was popularly known as William to avoid confusion with his younger brother John.

After attending public school in Louisville, he learned the machinist trade. In 1873, William Reccius opened a toy and sporting goods concern in Louisville on Third Avenue, between Market and Jefferson Streets. The store was a prominent business in Louisville in the 1880s and 1890s.

It was reported in a Wednesday, January 25, 1911 *Louisville Times* obituary that William Reccius was the first to buy a bill of goods from A.G. Spalding, the famed Chicago pitcher and future Hall of Famer who had just started his mammoth sporting goods establishment (1875).

By virtue of his age, William Reccius was the patriarch of Louisville's "first family of baseball" (circa 1875). The famed Reccius clan, a major piece in the foundation of Louisville amateur, semipro, minor-league and major-league baseball, included Frank, John and Philip, all professional players.

The Reccius family also included two other brothers—Michael (a local ballplayer) and Henry—and one married sister, Anna (Reccius) Dupre.

In 1875, William Reccius organized the Eclipse Baseball Club, which produced future major leaguers Pete Browning, Jimmy Wolf, Fred Pfeffer and his two younger brothers, John and Philip Reccius.

The original Louisville Eclipse, managed by William Reccius, had both an enormous local following and a national reputation as one of the country's top semipro teams and was the progenitor of Louisville's charter entry into the American Association in 1882. Its ballpark was the original Eclipse Ballpark at Twenty-eighth Street and Elliott Avenue, which William Reccius—according to his *Louisville Times* obituary—had established for the Louisville Eclipse semipro club (1875–81).

Along with local brewer J.H. Pank (of the Kentucky Malt Company), William Reccius co-owned the Louisville American Association major-league franchise from 1882 through 1884. His family was also the namesake of Reccius Park (at Twenty-eighth Street and Garland Avenue) and the Reccius Club. One of the most powerful clubs on Louisville's semipro scene, the Reccius outfit was well known via its rivalry with the Goss Bros. team. Another top local semipro club, the Goss Bros. team was piloted by brothers John and Mace Goss.

One of the city's most well-known lodge men, William Reccius belonged to the Knights of Pythias and the Kilwinning Lodge of Masons. He was also a member of the state guard for many years. In the early 1870s, according to his *Louisville Times* obituary, he was captain of the Waddell Grays, "a local company that established a splendid record for suppressing the feuds in Owen County [Kentucky]." (Hence, his nickname "Captain" Reccius. He was also identified by some sources of the era as J. William Reccius.)

William Reccius was married to Kate Wolf. At the time of his death, they resided at 2852 West Market Street. Besides his wife, he was survived by two sons and two daughters.

William Reccius is buried at historic Cave Hill Cemetery (section 8, lot 42, grave 2).

## *John Reccius*

(1859–1930)

For a long time, John Reccius was thought to be part of the first set of twins to play in the Major Leagues. However, cemetery records show that John Reccius was born in Louisville on October 29, 1859—not June 7, 1862, as reported. A major-league ballplayer for two years (a pitcher and outfielder with the 1882 and 1883 Louisville Eclipse of the American Association), he died in his native city on September 1, 1930, and is buried at old Cave Hill Cemetery (section 24, south half of lot 154).

## *Philip Reccius*

(1862–1903)

Philip Reccius's earliest documented organized baseball work came with the semipro Louisville Eclipse at first base on June 24, 1880. He logged two hits in a 9–1 win over Evansville. The following year, he saw action as a third baseman with the Louisville Eclipse in May and June.

When the Louisville Eclipse went major league in 1882, Philip Reccius—along with older brother John Reccius, Pete Browning and Joe Crotty—went to the big show. Also on the 1881 Louisville Eclipse was future major-league star Fred Pfeffer, considered one of the two greatest second baseman of the premodern era, who began his major-league career in 1882 with the Troy National League Trojans.

Principally a third baseman, Philip Reccius spent eight years (1882–90) in the majors—all in the American Association. He also saw action in the outfield and at shortstop and was 6-12 as a pitcher. His best offensive season was in 1885, when he had ninety-seven hits for a .241 average for the Louisvilles. As a pitcher, he had only one season of consequence, going 6-7 (2.71 ERA) with Louisville in 1884.

He played his career-best major-league game on Saturday, May 21, 1887, with the Cleveland Blues when he went three for six in his debut with that team. His work in the 15–12 win over the Philadelphia Athletics at Cleveland included two triples and one double.

Philip Reccius also had an extensive minor-league career, remaining active until 1901 as a player-manager with Evansville of the Three-I League. It was during this second career that he sustained the injury that led to his early institutionalization and death.

Philip Reccius is in the bottom row, far left, of this antique scorecard of the 1885 American Association Louisvilles, which finished in a tie for fifth place with the Brooklyn Grays. *Top row*: Amos Cross (C), Joe Miller (SS), John "Monk" Cline (3B/OF), Ed Whiting (C) and Norman Baker (P). *Middle row*: John Kerins (1B), Leech Maskrey (LF), Pete Browning (CF), Jimmy Wolf (RF) and William Geer (SS). *Bottom row*: Philip Reccius (3B-RHP), Guy Hecker (RHP), Jim Hart (Manager), Dan Sullivan (C) and Joe Crotty (C). *Bottom left*: Tom McLaughlin (2B). *Courtesy of Brace Photo, Chicago, Illinois.*

In 1892, he was pitching for Spokane of the Pacific Northwestern League when a Seattle batsman hit a head-high scorcher back through the box. Reccius was unable to avoid it. It struck him above the left temple and dropped him to the ground. (Although it is not precisely known whether he was a right-hander or southpaw, this information suggests the latter, based on the assumption that Philip Reccius was following through on his delivery when the ball hit him.)

Remarkably, his basic baseball instinct enabled him to throw the runner out at first before collapsing.

The head injury (a loose piece of bone, according to his *Louisville Courier-Journal* obituary) finally caught up with Philip Reccius, first causing his insanity and then his death. Born in Louisville on June 7, 1862, Philip Reccius died on February 15, 1903, and was buried at Louisville's venerable Cave Hill Cemetery (section 6, range 197, lot 8) on the city's east side. That cemetery is home to numerous Louisville baseball figures, including Browning, Wolf and brothers John and William Reccius.

Regarding the correct spelling of his first name (some sources have gone with the "double-l" version), the cemetery records and grave marker of Philip Reccius both read "Philip" with one "l."

## *Frank Reccius*

(1864-?)

A minor-league and semipro ballplayer, Frank (Whitey) Reccius was born in 1864. He was also a well-known baseball promoter.

## *Michael Reccius*

Little is known about Michael outside of the facts that he was a semipro and amateur ballplayer and was listed as a survivor of John Reccius in the latter's obituary.

The little information available about him includes two antique-era baseball listings. On the front page of the Wednesday, August 7, 1878 edition of the *Louisville Courier-Journal*, in an account of a local game of Tuesday, August 6, 1878, it was reported that Michael Reccius played first base for the Picked Nine in a game versus the Waddell Brown Stockings. Michael Reccius batted seventh in the 12–6 loss and got one hit. A member of his team was Pete Browning.

On Thursday, August 8, 1878, Michael Reccius again played first base in a 9–7 win by the Louisvilles over the Grays at Central Grounds. Batting eighth in the lineup, Michael Reccius got two hits. His teammates included his brother John (at second base) and Pete Browning.

# THE PHANTOM OF LOUISVILLE: THE LOST 1901 MINOR-LEAGUE SEASON

For whatever reason, Louisville's first true minor-league season (1901) has never been acknowledged as being a part of its baseball history. The minor-league history of Louisville has always started, for reasons as mercurial as the city's baseball history itself, with the 1902 campaign in the American Association—which is not correct. The 1902 season was Louisville's first full-time minor-league season. However, the 1901 Western Association season was the city's first minor-league season, period—a fact emphatically backed up by the record book.

The way to the 1901 Western Association membership was circuitous.

After battling for two years to regain its major-league status through various outlets (the National League, the American League and a reconstructed, but very short-lived, American Association), Louisville read the handwriting on the wall (i.e.: that it would never again be a major-league city, but it could be a minor-league city for as long as it wanted) and became one of the eight charter teams in the Western Association for the 1901 season.

Although its membership lasted only half the season before the Louisville franchise was transferred to Grand Rapids, Michigan, because of poor attendance, it was nonetheless Louisville's inaugural minor-league season, the predecessor of the city's fabulous minor-league history, which began full-time in 1902 and continues to this day.

The following is a highlighted look at Louisville's long-lost 1901 Western Association minor-league season (additional 1901 stats are in Part III).

Welcome home, guys.

## *Harvey Bailey: An Ace for All Time*

In action split between Louisville and Grand Rapids, southpaw Harvey Bailey (a former major-league pitcher) led the league in games (fifty-three), games started (forty-nine), complete games (forty-four), innings pitched (434), wins (thirty-five), win-loss percentage (.729), hits allowed (421) and bases on balls (118).

Broken down, his remarkable numbers—which were actually two separate seasons joined together to make one super season—looked like this:

| Club | G | GS | CG | IP | W | L | PCT. | H | BB | SO | R ShO |
|---|---|---|---|---|---|---|---|---|---|---|---|
| **Louisville** | 21 | 21 | 18 | 172 | 15 | 4 | .789 | 156 | 59 | 67 | 70 3 |
| **Grand Rapids** | 32 | 28 | 26 | 262 | 20 | 9 | .690 | 265 | 59 | 123 | 132 1 |
| **TOTAL** | 53 | 49 | 44 | 434 | 35 | 13 | .729 | 421 | 118 | 190 | 202 4 |

*Note: ERA statistics unavailable.

## *Gus Weyhing, Walt Wilmot and Germany Smith*

Other top-line stars on the team included former major-league stars Gus "Rubber-Winged Gus" Weyhing, Walt Wilmot and George "Germany" Smith.

One of three premodern Louisville major-leaguers who are legitimate Hall of Fame candidates (along with Pete Browning and Tony Mullane), Weyhing amassed a career 264-232 record in the majors, principally for second-division teams.

The much-loved Louisville native played in four big-top leagues between 1887 and 1901—the American Association, the National League, the Players League and the American League. During his career, the colorful right-hander turned out four thirty-win seasons, three twenty-victory campaigns and a no-hitter.

And along with Jouett Meekin, Weyhing—interestingly enough—is one of two players known to have played for Louisville on both the major-league and minor-league levels.

A Wisconsin native, Walter Robert Wilmot (1863–1929) spent ten years in the majors (1888–98), all in the National League, as an outfielder for the Washington Nationals, Chicago White Stockings and New York Giants.

His major career stats included a lifetime .276 batting average and 1,098 hits. His best offensive season was in 1894 with Chicago when he batted .330 and banged out 197 hits (including forty-five doubles and twelve triples).

In addition to being the playing manager of the team, Wilmot—who patrolled right field for Louisville—was also the owner of the club.

George J. Smith (1863–1924), who heralded from Pittsburgh, spent fifteen years in the majors (1884–98) for the Altoona Mountain Citys of the Union

Gus Weyhing. *National Baseball Hall of Fame Library, Cooperstown, New York.*

Association; the Cleveland Blues of the National League; the Brooklyn Grays/Bridegrooms of the American Association and the National League; the Cincinnati Reds in the National League; and the St. Louis Browns of the National League.

An accomplished shortstop, his career work included 1,592 hits and membership on two pennant-winning teams (the 1889 Brooklyn AA Bridegrooms and the 1890 Brooklyn National League Bridegrooms).

After leaving the majors, he played for the Minneapolis Millers of the Northwestern League in 1899 and 1900 before joining Louisville in 1901.

## *Harley Parker and the Vetter brothers*

Harley Parker (1872–1941) was a practicing physician in Chicago. He pitched for the Chicago White Stockings and Cincinnati Reds in 1893, 1895, 1896 and 1901.

George (RHP) and Phil Vetter (C) were brothers and well-known semipro stars on the Louisville baseball scene.

## *Louisville Major to Louisville Minor*

Louisville's transformation from a major-league city to a minor-league town, in which the 1901 Western Association membership was the next-to-last stop, was the result of a circuitous route.

On January 26, 1900, the *Louisville Courier-Journal* reported that Louisville would be dropped by the National League along with three other teams: Baltimore, Washington and Cleveland. This became official on March 8, 1900, when the National League jettisoned the aforementioned quartet and became an eight-club circuit.

On February 13, 1900, Louisville got its second lease on its major-league life when it earned a slot in the new eight-team American Association major-league circuit. President of the organization was future Hall of Famer Adrian "Cap" Anson. Also notably involved was another future Cooperstown resident, John McGraw, who headed the committee to find an eighth club to fill out the circuit, which included western clubs Chicago, Milwaukee, St. Louis and Louisville and three eastern teams—Boston, Philadelphia and Baltimore. However, by Thursday, February 15, 1900, the new American Association had folded.

But Louisville had not played all its cards.

In a desperate bid to maintain its major-league status, Louisville turned its attention toward getting a position in the new American League. This lobbying reached its strongest point on March 13, 1900, when American League president Ban Johnson extended an invitation to Louisville representatives to come to the American League meeting in Chicago on Friday, March 16, and join the new circuit.

It sounded too good to be true—and was.

Resolving some internal problems that left the circuit at eight clubs (without Louisville), Johnson, on Saturday, March 31, announced that Louisville would not be a part of the new American League, which, on March 20, had signed a peace agreement with the National League.

For the record, the inaugural 1900 American League lineup looked like this (in order of finish): Chicago, Milwaukee, Indianapolis, Detroit, Kansas City, Cleveland, Buffalo and Minneapolis. Interestingly enough, the major-league issue was still not solved.

According to a June 23, 1900 report in the *Louisville Courier-Journal*, Ban Johnson—for some reason—promised Louisville that it would get an entry in the American League for the 1901 season. This did not work out, even though the American League was totally revamped for the 1901 season (in order of finish, it looked like this: Chicago White Sox, Boston, Detroit, Philadelphia, Baltimore, Washington, Cleveland and Milwaukee). The next year, the American League dropped Milwaukee and added the St. Louis Browns in 1903, a roster that would last for a half century.

The major-league quest continued the next year.

On January 5, 1901, a new and yet another American Association major-league circuit was formed. That was followed by the sale of the Louisville franchise on Friday, January 25, 1901, to Colonel I.F. (Ike) Whiteside. A Jeffersonville, Indiana businessman, Whiteside bought the new Louisville American Association franchise from John Saunders.

Incorporated on Monday, February 5, records showed that Whiteside owned 80 of the 105 purchased shares. Total capitalization was $20,000 (400 shares at $50 each, 295 shares remaining to be bought).

The roster of teams included four western clubs (Louisville, Milwaukee, Indianapolis and Detroit) and four eastern teams (Boston, Washington, Philadelphia and Baltimore).

However, on Wednesday, February 27, 1901, the new league was declared off by W.H. Watkins, its chief promoter, and the new league's president, Charles Powers, who had left the presidency of the Interstate League to take over the reins of the new American Association.

On Tuesday, March 26, Louisville joined the Western Association, and on Monday, April 8, owner/player Walt Wilmot was given the keys to the ballpark. On Thursday, April 25, Louisville lost its seasonal opener 7–2 to Indianapolis, that loss beginning the city's epic minor-league history, which continues to this day.

## DIXIE: A LOUISVILLE STAR, AN AMERICAN BALLPLAYER

An ace with Louisville during World War I, Frank Talmadge "Dixie" Davis (1890–1944) was an American ballplayer in every way. Over the course of twenty-one seasons spent at every level conceivable, from the low minors to the big leagues, the crafty screwball pitcher fashioned a lifetime 261-216 win-loss record (.550) off an eleven-year 75-71 (.514) majors total and a fourteen-year minor-league account of 186-145 (.562)—a vivid contrast to his meager size (five feet, ten and a half inches/155 pounds).

As a minor leaguer, the wily right-hander was twice a twenty-game winner in the minors (in 1917 and again in 1919, both times with Louisville); denied ex-Louisville standout Grover Cleveland Lowdermilk (25-14, 250 Ks, 1.70 ERA) the 1917 AA pitching Triple Crown outright with a career-best twenty-five wins; and, in the twilight of his career, saved the 1929 Little World Series for the Kansas City Blues.

And he had his time in the majors, too.

After a decade in the minors, he hit his stride in 1920 with the St. Louis Browns, producing an 18-12 mark for the fourth-place Browns, their highest finish since 1908. The team was led by future Hall of Fame first-baseman

Dixie Davis. *Eclipse BBHR.*

George Sisler, who batted .407 off a major-league record 256 hits—a mark that stood until broken by Ichiro in 2004.

The 1920 work wasn't a fluke.

The following year, on August 9, 1921, Davis hurled a complete nineteen-inning game against the Washington Senators, with the Browns finally prevailing 8–6. It was an extraordinary game from beginning to finish. Davis hurled a no-hitter the final nine innings, and in the sixteenth inning, he apparently hit an inside-the-park home run but was called out for failing to touch first base.

On September 24, at Fenway Park, Davis pitched both ends of a double-header against the Boston Red Sox, losing the opener 2–1 (scattering nine hits) and then cruising in the closer 11–0, rewarding manager Lee Fohl's confidence in him.

The Browns finished third, recording their first winning season in five years with an 81-73 mark, Davis going 16-16.

In 1922, the Browns had their finest season ever with a record of 93-61, Davis going 11-6 for a team that revolved around three major stars. Sisler led the league again in batting (.420), as well as runs (134), hits (246) stolen bases (fifty-one) and triples (eighteen). Perennial staff ace, Urban Shocker, a right-hander, won twenty-four games, while outfielder Ken Williams took the home run and RBI titles (thirty-nine and 155, respectively). In addition, Williams ran second to Sisler in stolen bases (thirty-seven).

As a team, the Browns led the league in batting average (.313) and ERA (3.38) However, in their finest season, the Browns came up one game short at the end to the New York Yankees (94-60) following a tight pennant race. The Yankees subsequently lost the fall classic to the New York Giants for the second consecutive year.

In Davis's final four seasons with them, the Browns came in fifth, fourth, third and seventh before Davis returned to the minors for good in 1927. Ironically, their lone pennant and World Series play came in the year of his death. Battling the Detroit Tigers all season long, Davis's old club clinched the American League flag on the final day of the 1944 season with a home win over the Tigers. Their 89-65 record enabled them to win the AL flag by one game over the Tigers, ironically the same margin that had separated them and the champion Yankees in the 1922 AL pennant race. Pitted against their cross-town rival, the St. Louis Cardinals, the Browns then lost a seesaw 1944 World Series in six games.

Born on October 12, 1890, in Wilson Mills, North Carolina, Davis died of pneumonia in the ambulance that was taking him to a hospital on February 4, 1944, in Raleigh, North Carolina. At the time of his death, Davis was in the tobacco business at Oxford, North Carolina, and Virgilina, Virginia.

That's all we know about him, but it's more than enough. His life as a pitcher (and man) was rich and full, and he left his mark. For that, he deserves to be remembered.

## *Dixie Davis Career Statistics*

Davis, Frank Talmadge (Dixie)
Born: October 12, 1890, Wilson Mills, North Carolina
Died: February 4, 1944, Raleigh, North Carolina
Height: 5 feet, 10½ inches
Weight: 155 pounds
Batted and threw right
Specialty: screwball; considered crafty and shrewd
Home address (1919): 14 Park Boulevard, Winston-Salem, North Carolina
Notes: At the time of his death, Davis was in the tobacco business in Oxford, North Carolina, and Virgilina, Virginia. He was in the Major Leagues for eleven years: 75-71 (.514); and minor leagues for fourteen years: 186-145 (.562). His overall totals (twenty-one years) were: 261-216 (.550).

| Year | Club (Class) | League | G | CG | IP | W | L | Pct. | H | BB | SO | R | ER | ERA |
|---|---|---|---|---|---|---|---|---|---|---|---|---|---|---|
| **1911** | Knoxville (D) | APP. | 34 | NA | 257 | 17 | 11 | .606 | 189 | 76 | **181** | 76 | NA | NA |
| **1912**[a] | Knoxville (D) | APP. | 16 | NA | 131 | 13 | 3 | **.813** | 80 | 39 | 162 | 24 | NA | NA |
| **1912**[b] | Cincinnati | NL | 7 | 0 | 27 | 0 | 1 | .000 | 25 | 16 | 12 | 17 | 8 | 2.67 |
| **1912** | Columbus (AA) | AA | 6 | 2 | 44 | 5 | 1 | .833 | 22 | 31 | 28 | 13 | NA | NA |
| **1913** | Columbus (AA) | AA | 44 | NA | 273 | 17 | 16 | .515 | 247 | 134 | 96 | 109 | NA | NA |
| **1914** | Columbus (AA) | AA | 44 | NA | 246 | 15 | 10 | .600 | 252 | 127 | 107 | 125 | 100 | 3.65 |
| **1915** | Columbus (AA) | AA | 37 | NA | 254 | 16 | 14 | .533 | 226 | 157 | 116 | 125 | 84 | 2.98 |
| **1915**[c] | Chicago | AL | 2 | 0 | 3 | 0 | 0 | .000 | 2 | 2 | 2 | 0 | 0 | 0.00 |
| **1916**[d] | Columbus (AA) | AA | 42 | NA | 237 | 13 | 15 | .464 | 218 | 114 | 121 | NA | 86 | 3.27 |
| **1917**[e] | Louisville (AA) | AA | 44 | NA | 292 | **25** | 11 | **.694** | 238 | **131** | 136 | 107 | 76 | 2.34 |
| **1918**[f] | Philadelphia | NL | 17 | 1 | 47 | 0 | 2 | .000 | 43 | 30 | 18 | 25 | 16 | 3.06 |
| **1919**[g] | St. Louis | NL (traded to Louisville; no games played) | | | | | | | | | | | | |

| Year | Club (Class) | League | G | CG | IP | W | L | Pct. | H | BB | SO | R | ER | ERA |
|---|---|---|---|---|---|---|---|---|---|---|---|---|---|---|
| **1919**[h] | Louisville (AA) | AA | 48 | NA | 372 | 22 | 20 | .524 | 306 | **161** | **165** | 132 | 100 | 2.42 |
| **1920** | St. Louis | AL | 38 | 22 | 269 | 18 | 12 | .600 | 250 | 149 | 85 | 117 | 95 | 3.18 |
| **1921** | St. Louis | AL | 40 | 20 | 265 | 16 | 16 | .500 | 279 | 123 | 100 | 150 | 131 | 4.45 |
| **1922** | St. Louis | AL | 25 | 7 | 174 | 11 | 6 | .647 | 162 | 87 | 65 | 91 | 79 | 4.09 |
| **1923** | St. Louis | AL | 19 | 5 | 109 | 4 | 6 | .400 | 106 | 63 | 36 | 61 | 44 | 3.64 |
| **1924** | St. Louis | AL | 29 | 11 | 160 | 11 | 13 | .458 | 159 | 72 | 45 | 84 | 73 | 4.10 |
| **1925** | St. Louis | AL | 35 | 9 | 180 | 12 | 7 | .632 | 192 | 106 | 58 | 121 | 92 | 4.60 |
| **1926** | St. Louis | AL | 27 | 2 | 83 | 3 | 8 | .273 | 93 | 40 | 39 | 56 | 43 | 4.66 |
| **1926** | Kansas City (AA) AA | (no games played) | | | | | | | | | | | | |
| **1927** | Kansas City (AA) | AA | 22 | NA | 140 | 12 | 7 | .632 | 124 | 59 | 51 | 60 | 56 | 3.60 |
| **1928** | Kansas City (AA) | | 31 | NA | 141 | 8 | 6 | .571 | 158 | 74 | 55 | 84 | 81 | 5.17 |
| **1929** | Kansas City (AA) | AA | 21 | NA | 84 | 8 | 5 | .615 | 84 | 35 | 30 | 45 | 38 | 4.07 |
| **1930** | Kansas City (AA) | AA | 4 | 0 | 12 | 0 | 2 | .000 | 16 | 5 | 3 | 10 | 7 | 5.25 |

| Year | Club (Class) | League | G | CG | IP | W | L | Pct. | H | BB | SO | R | ER | ERA |
|---|---|---|---|---|---|---|---|---|---|---|---|---|---|---|
| | Chattanooga (A) | SA | 34 | NA | 175 | 8 | 16 | .333 | 210 | 97 | 78 | 120 | 94 | 4.84 |
| **1931** | Chatt./ Atlanta (A) | SA | 16 | NA | 80 | 4 | 6 | .400 | 77 | 39 | 33 | 44 | 40 | 4.50 |
| | Winston-Salem (C) | PDMT. | 8 | NA | 48 | 3 | 2 | .600 | 43 | 40 | 37 | NA | NA | NA |

NA: Not Available.
Bold font indicates league leadership.
Official record compiled by Ray Nemec and Philip Von Borries.

Legends
a: Sold August 23. Reported price, $650.
b: Transferred September 11 as part payment for Packard.
c: Selected but returned February 10.
d: Traded November 22 in the Barney, W.L. James and W. Killefer deal.
e: Drafted.
f: Exchanged with Stock and Dillhoefer for Packard, Stewart and Baird.
g: Traded to Louisville in the Clemons deal.
h: Transferred in player agreements.

Names and Records of Dixie Davis's Minor-League Teams

| | |
|---|---|
| **1911** | Knoxville Appalachians (2-6; 1½ games behind Johnson City Soldiers with 58-38/.604 record; third were the Asheville Moonshiners) |
| **1912** | Knoxville Reds (2-6; 2 games behind Bristol Boosters with 56-46/.549 record)<br>Columbus Senators (3-8; 7½ games behind Minneapolis Millers with 98-68/.590 record) |
| **1913** | Columbus Senators (4-8; 7 games behind Milwaukee Brewers with 93-74/.557 record) |
| **1914** | Columbus Senators (4-8; 10½ games behind Milwaukee Brewers with 86-77/.528 record) |
| **1915** | Columbus Senators (8-8; 33½ games behind Minneapolis Millers with 54-91/.372 record) |
| **1916** | Columbus Senators (7-8; 27 games behind Louisville Colonels with 71-90/.441 record) |
| **1917** | Louisville Colonels (2-8; 2½ games behind Indianapolis Indians with 88-66/.571 record) |
| **1919** | Louisville Colonels (3-8; 7½ games behind St. Paul Saints with 86-67/.562 record) |
| **1926** | Kansas City Blues (5-8; 17 games behind Louisville Colonels with 87-78/.527 record) |
| **1927** | Kansas City Blues (2-8; 2 games behind Toledo Mud Hens with 99-69/.589 record) |
| **1928** | Kansas City Blues (4-8; 11½ games behind Indianapolis Indians with 88-80/.524 record) |
| **1929** | Kansas City Blues (1-8; 8½ games ahead of runner-up St. Paul Saints with 111-56/.665 record). Won Junior World Series over International League champion Rochester Red Wings 5 games to 4, taking the concluding game 6-5 in 11 innings on October 13, 1929. |
| **1930** | Kansas City Blues (5-8; 18½ games behind Louisville Colonels with 75-79/.487 record)<br>Chattanooga Lookouts (6-8; 31½ games behind Memphis Chickasaws with 67-87/.435 record) |

| | |
|---|---|
| **1931** | Chattanooga Lookouts (4-8; 18½ games behind Birmingham Barons with 79-74/.516 record) |
| | Atlanta Crackers (6-8; 20 games behind Birmingham Barons with 78-76/.506 record) |
| | Winston-Salem Twins (6-8; 43½ games behind Charlotte Hornets with 55-79/.410 record) |

Leagues
AA: American Association
AL: American League
APP: Appalachian
NL: National League
PDMT: Piedmont
SA: Southern Association

## Death in the Afternoon

The early deaths of Louisville major-league stars Pete Browning, Chicken Wolf, Philip Reccius and Reddy Mack are well known and well documented. All were members of the 1885 and 1886 Louisville teams in the American Association; all died at an early age; and all were institutionalized or reported "insane" before their deaths.

Other Louisville major leaguers who died early were Denny Mack (born Dennis McGee), who spent three years at Villanova University and died at age thirty-seven in 1888 due to an internal hemorrhage and seizures related to a fall at home; pitcher Pete Dowling, who was hit by a train in 1905 (Dowling's death was believed to be a suicide by some, based on his history of mental instability); and left-hander Al Mays, who drowned at age thirty-nine in 1905.

Not so well known but perhaps even more haunting were the untimely or bizarre deaths of six top-line Louisville minor-league stars and a seventh who died before he got a chance to play for the Colonels.

The following is a look at that ill-fated septet.

## *William Johnston (Buffalo Bill) Hogg*

BORN: September 11, 1881, Port Huron, Michigan
DIED: December 8, 1909, New Orleans
MAJOR-LEAGUE DEBUT: April 25, 1905
MAJOR-LEAGUE FINALE: September 2, 1908
One of five double-digit winning pitchers for Louisville's first minor-league pennant-winning team (1909), William "Buffalo Bill" Hogg went 17-14 in his only year with the Colonels. A few months later, on December 8, 1909, he died of Bright's disease in New Orleans at the age of twenty-eight. Without stars like him, the Colonels plunged into the cellar the next year and did not win another American Association flag until 1916.

A six-foot, two-hundred-pound, right-handed switch-hitter, Hogg played four years in the majors (1905–08), all with the old New York Highlanders (now the Yankees) of the American League. His best marks included a 14-13 slate in 1906 and a 10-8 mark in 1907.

## *Dennis Lawrence (Dan) McGann*

BORN: July 15, 1871, Shelbyville, Kentucky
DIED: December 13, 1910, Louisville
MAJOR-LEAGUE DEBUT: August 8, 1896
MAJOR-LEAGUE FINALE: October 7, 1908
A twelve-year veteran of Major League Baseball, Dan McGann was slated to join the 1911 Louisville Colonels. However, on December 13, 1910, the despondent McGann—who was known to suffer from severe depression—committed suicide in room 32 of the Bosler Hotel at Second and Jefferson Streets in Louisville. He was thirty-nine.

The cause of his premature end was a .32-caliber bullet through his heart. One of the first people to arrive on the scene was his lone surviving brother, Joseph D. McGann, a businessman from nearby Shelbyville, Kentucky, birthplace of the deceased ballplayer.

The tragedy brought an end to a fine baseball career and denied the Louisville club significant talent.

A six-foot, 190-pound switch-hitting first baseman who threw right, McGann began his major-league career with a partial season in 1896 with the legendary Boston Beaneaters. The team included the likes of future Hall of Famers Kid Nichols, Billy Hamilton, Hugh Duffy, Jimmy Collins and

Frank Selee. (Dan McGann's major-league work also included some action at second base.)

One of baseball's earliest dynasties, the team took three straight National League pennants (1891–93) and then, after a three-year reign by another baseball dynasty, the Baltimore Orioles, the Beaneaters came back with a pair of back-to-back National League flags in 1897 and 1898.

Following his 1896 rookie season, McGann reappeared in the big leagues in 1898 with the Baltimore Orioles and then split the 1899 season between the eventual National League champion Brooklyn Superbas and the National League also-ran Washington Senators.

After spending the 1900 and 1901 seasons with the National League St. Louis Cardinals, he then split the 1902 season between the Baltimore Orioles' American League club and the New York National League Giants.

It was at the latter stop that he enjoyed his greatest success, playing on the 1904 and 1905 National League flag-winning teams of future Hall of Famer John McGraw. The latter team then took the 1905 World Series 4-1 from Connie Mack's Philadelphia Athletics, led by Giants ace and future charter Cooperstown member Christy Mathewson, who threw three shutouts. (Interestingly, all five games were shutouts.)

Traded to the Boston National League Doves (forerunner of the old Boston Braves), McGann's final baseball season was in 1910 with Milwaukee of the American Association.

His major-league career totals included a lifetime .284 batting average, four .300 seasons and nearly fifteen hundred hits.

Curiously, McGann's younger brother—given name, Daniel McGann—committed suicide in the same manner (a self-inflicted gun shot) in April of that same year. A station agent for the L&N Railroad, Daniel McGann was often confused with his older brother, Dennis Lawrence McGann, who was nicknamed "Dan."

Dennis Lawrence "Dan" McGann was buried at Grove Hill Cemetery in Shelbyville, Kentucky, just east of Louisville.

## *Edward Benninghaus Kenna*

Born: October 17, 1877, Charleston, West Virginia
Died: March 22, 1912, Grant, Florida
Major-league debut: May 5, 1902
Major-league finale: May 9, 1902

Aside from a brief stint with the Philadelphia American League Athletics in 1902, right-hander Ed Kenna spent his entire eight-year career (1900–07) in the minors.

Inaugurating his professional career in 1900 with a 0-2 mark for the Toledo Mud Hens (Interstate League), the well-traveled Kenna went 16-9 with the Wheeling Stogies (Western Association) in 1901.

In his lone major league action, Kenna opened the 1902 season with a 1-1 record for the 1902 Philadelphia Athletics. That year's American League pennant winner, the club finished five and a half games ahead of the runner-up, the St. Louis Browns. Managed by future Hall of Famer Connie Mack, the Athletics included three other future Hall of Famers: Rube Waddell, Eddie Plank and, briefly, Nap Lajoie (traded after one game because of a legal ruling).

Kenna finished the 1902 season with the Milwaukee Creams (Western League), going 17-6. All his action from 1902 onward came in A-rated loops, the highest level after the Major Leagues.

Hitting his stride, Kenna produced a pair of back-to-back twenty-victory seasons. After going a league-leading 28-9 (and a circuit-topping .757 win percentage) for the Western League pennant-winning Creams in 1903, Kenna posted a 21-12 mark in 1904 for the Denver Grizzlies of the Western League.

He spent his last three professional years with the Louisville Colonels in the American Association.

What the six-foot, 180-pounder might have accomplished on the major-league level, however, will never be known.

On Thursday, August 31, 1905, he was involved in a freak accident in Kansas City, Missouri, between a trolley car and the horse-drawn conveyance that was taking Kenna, six other players and the team secretary to catch a train.

The accident ended his solid season at 16-13 and, in retrospect, his career.

The most seriously injured of the group, the fully seasoned and major-league-ready Kenna suffered a left eye that was almost gouged out, a nose that was split and fractured, a dislocated forearm, a severely bruised face, an injured left knee and a slight concussion.

The following season, Kenna went 12-21 in over three hundred innings of work while batting .325 (he batted right), but the damage had been done.

After a 3-7 mark in 1907 for the Colonels, he left the game at age twenty-nine with a 113-79 minor-league record and an overall 114-80 professional slate.

A well-educated ballplayer (Mount St. Mary's College & Seminary and West Virginia University), he was also the product of a prominent family: both his father (John Edward Kenna) and uncle (W.E. Chilton) were U.S. senators.

After leaving baseball, Ed Kenna became an editor at the *Charleston Gazette*. His life's writing also included a published volume of poetry.

Nicknamed the "Poet Pitcher" by his baseball contemporaries, Kenna died of heart trouble in Grant, Florida, at age thirty-four on March 22, 1912.

## *John Lewis (Johnny) Dodge*

BORN: April 21, 1889, Bolivar, Tennessee
DIED: June 19, 1916, Mobile, Alabama
MAJOR-LEAGUE DEBUT: August 29, 1912
MAJOR-LEAGUE FINALE: October 5, 1913
A member of the 1914 Louisville Colonels, for whom he played eighty-two games at third base, Johnny Dodge was a slick gloveman whose weak stick denied the 165-pound right-handed defensive dynamo a long career in the majors.

His big-top work included stops with the Phillies in 1912 and 1913 and the Reds in 1913.

Dodge was playing for Mobile in the Southern Association when he was struck in the face by a pitch from Nashville's aptly named Tom "Shotgun" Rogers on June 18, 1916. Dodge died the following day without ever regaining consciousness.

## *Wayland Ogden Dean*

BORN: June 2, 1902, Richwood, West Virginia
DIED: April 11, 1930, Huntington, West Virginia
MAJOR-LEAGUE DEBUT: April 17, 1924
MAJOR-LEAGUE FINALE: July 13, 1927
The ace of the 1923 Louisville Colonels with a 21-8 record, Wayland Dean was sold for $50,000 to the New York Giants in January 1924, going 6-12 for them. The following year, Dean had his best major-league season with a 10-7 mark.

Wayland Dean. *National Baseball Hall of Fame Library, Cooperstown, New York.*

His work with the Giants also included one World Series appearance (no decisions), in 1924, which the Giants lost to the Senators in seven games.

Pitching for the Phillies in 1926 and 1927, the six-foot-one, 178-pound right-hander retired with the Cubs in 1927 when arm problems ended his career. He finished up with an overall 24-36 major-league career total.

A talented switch-hitter, Dean died of tuberculosis at age twenty-seven in 1930.

## *Clyde Melno Hatter*

BORN: August 7, 1908, Poplar Hills, Kentucky
DIED: October 16, 1937, Yosemite, Kentucky
MAJOR-LEAGUE DEBUT: April 23, 1935
MAJOR-LEAGUE FINALE: May 10, 1937
A left-handed pitcher, Clyde Hatter played two seasons each with the Louisville Colonels (1931 and 1937) and the Detroit Tigers (1935 and 1937).

Born in Poplar Hills, Kentucky, Hatter attended Eastern Kentucky University, where he threw a no-hitter against Kentucky Wesleyan on April 22, 1929. As a member of the Louisville Colonels in 1931, Hatter lost the top half of the closing-day double-header on Sunday, September 27, against Toledo 10–0. (Ken Penner evened things up with a 3–0 triumph in the second part of the twin bill.)

A rookie on the 1935 American League champion Detroit Tigers, the five-foot-eleven, 170-pound Hatter appeared in eight games, two as a starter, pitching thirty-three and a half innings with no decisions and a 7.56 ERA. A right-handed batter, Hatter did well in limited action, batting .300 (three hits in ten at-bats).

Hatter did not play in the 1935 World Series, which the Tigers won in six games over the Cubs. After spending the 1936 season in the minor leagues,

Hatter rejoined the Bruins in 1937, appearing in three games and compiling a 1-0 record and an 11.57 ERA.

Five months after playing his last major-league game, he died in Yosemite, Kentucky, at age twenty-nine.

According to the *Louisville Courier-Journal* account, he died in the backseat of his father's car while en route from Danville to Yosemite. The younger Hatter, who had complained of a stomach ailment, asked his father Claude to drive him to Danville so he could mail some telegrams. They left Danville at about 5:30 p.m. His father talked to him until about 6:00 p.m. and then thought his son had fallen asleep. When they got home at 6:30 p.m., his father was unable to wake him. A doctor was called and said Hatter had been dead for several minutes. He attributed Hatter's death to a heart attack.

Former Tigers teammate Marv Owen recalled Hatter's untimely death years later in much blunter terms.

Interviewed in the 1980s, Owen said that Hatter had missed several games, which led Owen to check Hatter's room. Hatter told Owen he had been sick, so Owen called the team doctor. The doctor concluded that Hatter was drunk and reported his findings to manager Mickey Cochrane. Hatter was then sent back to the minor leagues; the 1937 season with the Louisville Colonels proved to be Hatter's last in professional baseball.

Owen described Hatter's end just months later: "He went home that winter and they found him dead in the back of his father's car. From booze."

In retrospect, it seems likely that the fatal heart attack had been precipitated by Hatter's alcoholism.

## *Aristotle George "Harry" Agganis*

BORN: April 20, 1929, Lynn, Massachusetts
DIED: June 27, 1955, Cambridge, Massachusetts
MAJOR-LEAGUE DEBUT: April 13, 1954
MAJOR-LEAGUE FINALE: June 2, 1955
One of the most heralded athletes in New England history, Harry Agganis earned all-American quarterback honors at Boston University, where he also excelled in baseball.

Eschewing a lucrative offer from the Cleveland Browns, who envisioned him as the heir apparent to future pro football Hall of Famer Otto Graham, Agganis signed for a reported $35,000 with the Boston Red Sox. He proved to be well worth the investment.

Harry Agganis. *Courtesy Boston Red Sox.*

In his only season of minor-league baseball, he turned out a .281 average, twenty-three homers and 108 RBIs for the 1953 Louisville Colonels and lost the American Association MVP award to Don Zimmer by one vote.

Brought up to the big club in 1954, the six-foot-two, two-hundred-pound, left-handed first baseman hit .251 (109 hits on 343 at-bats) and clouted eleven homers in 132 games for the 1954 Bosox. The next season, the "Golden Greek," as he was called, was batting .313 after 25 games, and the future looked bright and limitless.

While recovering in a Boston hospital from a chest ailment, the enormously popular, gifted and modest Agganis died suddenly at age twenty-six of a pulmonary embolism on June 27, 1955.

## PEE WEE: MY CAPTAIN, OH MY CAPTAIN

I only met Pee Wee Reese once, but that was enough—more than enough—to fully explain why Jackie Robinson had made it to the big leagues; why a packed house at Ebbets Field one night long ago had lit candles in honor of Reese's birthday; why everyone respected Reese (once in a great white northern city, when the abuse had become intolerable, Reese went over to his beleaguered second baseman and draped his arm over his shoulder; it spoke volumes); why everyone liked Reese instantly (and most probably thought his given Christian name was Pee Wee); why Reese had been a champion at everything he had done (from marbles, where he had gotten his nickname, to baseball to life); why the Dodgers had retired his number; why Reese had made it to the Hall of Fame, finally, despite forfeiting three prime years to the World War II; and why Reese had been so complete a success in the complex and difficult art of life and living.

As a son, husband, father, ballplayer, broadcaster, business executive and, most importantly, a human being, Harold Herman "Pee Wee" Reese was in a class all by himself.

It was September 1984, and I was standing in Louisville's historic Cave Hill Cemetery, admiring the new marker just unveiled for Pete Browning (we had written the copy for the new marker and also contributed design ideas). It was the centennial of the Hillerich & Bradsby Company, and as part of the celebration, the world-renowned company had—in concert with the city and then-mayor Harvey I. Sloane—erected a new monument to Browning, the namesake of the bat.

I was part of a group of dignitaries and officials, an entourage that included Reese, who in due time was introduced to me. A brief question from Reese quickly led to a detailed response and then more questions and more answers.

All of a sudden, I realized I was doing all the talking, while he stood modestly in the background, taking in all that I had to say. Of course, this was exactly his intent—and his great gift—to effortlessly put people at ease and make them the center, the focus, of attention. Not himself.

But if ever Reese deserved to be in the spotlight, it was that year. He had just been elected to the Baseball Hall of Fame, the apex of a brilliant career and the symbol of an extraordinary life. I couldn't stand there much longer and ignore that fact.

And then, when hope seemed to be at its thinnest and almost gone, an idea struck.

"Pee Wee, I understand you're a baseball writer of sorts also," I said. He looked at me quizzically.

"Surely," I continued, "you haven't forgotten that baseball classic, *The Louisville Slugger Playmaking Guide*, by Pee Wee Reese. No legitimate baseball player should be without a copy."

We both smiled, and from there, it was off to the races for the both of us, an equal give and take. Just as it should have been.

The ceremonies over, Reese made way to take his leave. But not before he left me with this.

"Young man," he said in front of the powerful assemblage gathered around the marker, "you've done fine work here on this marker. When I go, I want you to do mine."

The opening-day infield for the 1947 Brooklyn Dodgers, the team that broke the color line once and for all. *Left to right*: John "Spider" Jorgensen (3B), Pee Wee Reese (SS), Eddie Stanky (2B) and Jackie Robinson (1B). *National Baseball Hall of Fame Library, Cooperstown, New York.*

I told him that that would be a long, long time. And it was.

Years passed—fifteen to be exact. Then, in mid-August 1999, Reese died at his home in Louisville at age eighty-one. When I heard the news, I immediately thought of that day at Cave Hill, his engaging manner and his final words to me.

I'm going to keep my word—only this will be my monument to him.

He was a man who quietly and effectively moved the world, without benefit of vulgar self-aggrandizement and self-seeking publicity. Rather, he did it with grace, style, dignity, noble purpose and quiet leadership. He was the essence of two of my father's cardinal rules of life: be a force for good in the world and don't be a showboat; rather, lead by example and deed.

So in the end, this pint-sized shortstop from an even smaller town in Kentucky who carried the heart of a lion made a difference, a big difference. In baseball terms, Pee Wee Reese was an "impact player" on all of humanity—and then some.

Yet on the surface, one could barely see a trace of what Reese had done. One had to probe a little deeper, because Pee Wee Reese wasn't the type of man who told you that "he was the straw who stirred the drink." Or some such similar drivel.

It was simply beneath him to talk about his accomplishments. And they were many. Pee Wee was the personification of the old adage: actions speak louder than words. This goes a long way in explaining why the Dodgers assigned him the number they did. Number one. It fit him like his glove.

Goodnight, my captain, but not goodbye. We'll see you on the other side.

## PART III

# Louisville Numbers and Facts

## Louisville's Major-League and Minor-League Statistics, 1876–2001

NOTE: 2001 was selected as the cutoff point for Louisville's minor-league statistics in this section because that marked the centennial of minor-league baseball in this country, and it was also Louisville's 125th mathematical baseball anniversary (1876–2001). Future editions of *The Louisville Baseball Almanac* will carry the post-2001 years.

### Louisville Seasonal Team Leaders

Major League: 1876–77; 1882–1899
(Pitching Wins and Batting Average)

1876 Jimmy Devlin (30-35; .315)
1877 Jimmy Devlin (35-25)
George Hall (.323)
1882 Tony Mullane (30-24)
Pete Browning (.378, league champion)
1883 Guy Hecker (28-25)
Pete Browning (.338)
1884 Guy Hecker (52-20, league champion)
Pete Browning (.336)

| | |
|---|---|
| 1885 | Guy Hecker (30-23) |
| | Pete Browning (.362, league champion) |
| 1886 | Toad Ramsey (38-27) |
| | Guy Hecker (.341, league champion) |
| 1887 | Toad Ramsey (37-27) |
| | Pete Browning (.402) |
| 1888 | Icebox Chamberlain (14-9) |
| | Pete Browning (.313) |
| 1889 | Red Ehret (10-29) |
| | Chicken Wolf, Red Ehret (both .291) |
| 1890 | Scott Stratton (34-14) |
| | Chicken Wolf (.363, league champion) |
| 1891 | John Fitzgerald (14-18) |
| | Patsy Donovan (.321) |
| 1892 | Scott Stratton (21-19) |
| | Harry Taylor (.260) |
| 1893 | George Hemming (18-17) |
| | Willard Brown (.304) |
| 1894 | George Hemming (13-19) |
| | Fred Pfeffer (.308) |
| 1895 | Bert Cunningham (11-16) |
| | Fred Clarke (.347) |
| 1896 | Chick Fraser (12-27) |
| | Tom McCreery (.351) |
| 1897 | Chick Fraser (15-19) |
| | Fred Clarke (.390) |
| 1898 | Bert Cunningham (28-15) |
| | Fred Clarke (.307) |
| 1899 | Deacon Phillippe (21-17) |
| | Fred Clarke (.342) |

# Louisville Numbers and Facts

MINOR LEAGUE: 1901–62; 1968–72; 1982–2001
(Pitching Wins and Batting Average)

1901 Harvey Bailey (15-4; overall 35-13, league champion in action split between Louisville and Grand Rapids, Michigan)
Gus Weyhing (15-6)
Walter Wilmot (.311)
1902 Babe Ganzel (.366, league champion)
Ed Dunkle (30-10, league champion))
1903 Billy Clymer (.350)
Tom Walker (26-7)
1904 Dan Kerwin (.310)
Bill Campbell (26-14)
1905 Dan Kerwin (.305)
Ed Dunkle (17-11)
1906 Billy Hallman (.342, league champion)
Ambrose Puttmann (18-17)
1907 Jesse Stovall (.307)
Ambrose Puttmann (21-20)
1908 Joe Stanley (.279)
Ambrose Puttmann (26-12)
1909 J.F. Dunleavy (.244)
Emery Olson (.239)
Orville Selby (20-13)
1910 John Hughes (.283)
John Halla (10-23)
1911 Moose Grimshaw (.263)
Irv Higginbotham (19-22)
1912 Jack Stansbury (.301)
Grover Cleveland Lowdermilk (17-16)
1913 Will Osborn(e) (.320)
Grover Cleveland Lowdermilk (20-14)
1914 Hank Severeid (.317)
Jake Northrop (26-10, tied for league leadership with Melvin "Bert" Gallia of Kansas City, also 26-10)
1915 Bert Daniels (.299)
Jake Northrop (25-15)
1916 Jay Kirke (.303)
John Middleton (21-9)

1917 Jay Kirke (.317)
Frank "Dixie" Davis (25-11; tied for league leadership with Grover Cleveland Lowdermilk of Columbus, 25-14)
1918 Jack Lelivelt (.325)
Dolf Luque (11-2)
1919 Tim Hendryx (.368, league champion)
Tom Long (23-13)
1920 Jay Kirke (.330)
Tommy Long (18-13)
1921 Jay Kirke (.386, league champion)
Ernie Koob (22-9)
1922 Jay Kirke (.355, league champion)
Ben Tincup (22-14)
1923 Earle Combs (.380)
Wayland Dean (21-8)
1924 Ned Shannon (.340)
Ben Tincup (24-17)
1925 Joe Guyon (.363, league champion)
Nick Cullop (22-8)
1926 Al DeVormer (.368)
Nick Cullop (20-8)
1927 Joe Guyon (.358)
Ben Tincup (16-15)
1928 Ed Sicking (.368)
Ben Tincup (14-10)
1929 Dud Branom (.334)
Guy Williams (15-9)
1930 Butch Simons (.371)
Joe DeBerry (19-10)
1931 Billy Herman (.350)
Ken Penner (17-8)
1932 James Adair (.320)
Claude Jonnard (18-15)
1933 Butch Simons (.324)
John Marcum (20-13)
1934 Ray Radcliff (.335)
Richard Bass (17-8)
1935 Butch Simons (.352)
Jack Tising (13-15)

1936 Butch Simons (.353)
Wayne LaMaster (13-10)
1937 Butch Simons (.316)
Buck Marrow (14-14)
1938 Danny Bell (.327)
Wes Flowers (11-11)
Rufus Meadows (11-11)
Jack Tising (11-16)
1939 Chet Morgan (.291)
James Weaver (14-8)
1940 Chet Morgan (.317)
Wes Flowers (13-6)
James Weaver (13-9)
1941 Johnny Pesky (.325)
Ossie Judd (13-5)
Bill Sayles (13-12)
1942 Andy Gilbert (.296)
Nelson Potter (18-8)
1943 Tom McBride (.308)
Norm Brown (16-11)
1944 Steve Barath (.329)
James Wilson (19-8)
1945 Ty LaForest (.353)
Dwight Simonds (13-5)
1946 James Gleeson (.306)
Al Widmar (12-9)
1947 Paul Campbell (.304)
Clem Dreiseward (18-7)
1948 Tom Wright (.307)
John Griffore (10-13)
1949 Tom Wright (.368, league champion)
Cot Deal (15-9)
1950 Taft Wright (.318)
Bob Alexander (12-10)
1951 Taft Wright (.335)
James Atkins (18-9)
1952 Taft Wright (.297)
Tom Herrin (10-12)

1953 Bob Broome (.306)
Bill Werle (13-8)
1954 Marty Keough (.292)
Ike Delock (17-10)
1955 Marty Keough (.393)
Jerry Casale (17-11)
1956 Neil Chrisley (.298)
Ted Abernathy (12-16)
1957 Clarence Moore (.298)
David Benedict (12-12)
1958 Willie Tasby (.322, league champion)
Fred Besana (11-11)
1959 Casey Wise (.302)
Georges Maranda (18-6)
1960 Mack Jones (.309)
Bob Hendley (16-9)
1961 Howie Bedell (.327)
Hank Fischer (11-9)
1962 Dutch Bolger (.319)
Connie Grob (14-10)
1968 George Thomas (.288)
Darrel (Bucky) Brandon (13-11)
1969 Hal King (.322)
Jerry Janeski (15-10)
1970 Bob Montgomery (.324)
Don Cook (9-4)
1971 Ben Ogilvie (.304)
Roger Moret (11-8)
1972 Chris Colletta (.319)
Craig Skok (15-7)
1982 Kelly Paris (.326)
Ralph Citarella (15-6)
1983 Andy Van Slyke (.368)
Jeff Keener (11-5)
1984 Gene Roof (.302)
Steve Baker and Kevin Hagan (both 10-9)
1985 Casey Parsons (.279)
Fred Martinez (10-7)
Kevin Hagan (10-9)
Rick Ownbey (10-9)

| | |
|---|---|
| 1986 | Casey Parsons (.289) |
| | Joe Magrane (9-6) |
| | Mike Dunne (9-12) |
| 1987 | Lance Johnson (.333, league champion) |
| | Paul Cherry (11-5) |
| 1988 | Craig Wilson (.256) |
| | John Martin (7-13) |
| 1989 | Todd Zeile (.289) |
| | Bob Tewksbury (13-5) |
| 1990 | Bernard Gilkey (.295) |
| | Cris Carpenter (10-8) |
| | Stan Clarke (10-9) |
| | Omar Olivares (10-11) |
| 1991 | Stan Royer (.254) |
| | Rheal Cormier (7-9) |
| 1992 | Lonnie Maclin (.324) |
| | Rene Arocha (12-7) |
| | Jeff Ballard (12-8) |
| 1993 | Keith Lockhart (.300) |
| | Tom Urbani (9-5) |
| | Bob Sebra (9-12) |
| 1994 | Allen Battle (.313) |
| | Rigo Beltran (11-11) |
| 1995 | Ray Giannelli (.295) |
| | T.J. Mathews (9-4) |
| 1996 | Dmitri Young (.333, league champion) |
| | Rigo Beltran (8-6) |
| | Sean Lowe (8-9) |
| 1997 | Tim Costo (.302) |
| | Brady Raggio (8-11) |
| 1998 | Ron Belliard (.321) |
| | Rod Henderson (11-5) |
| 1999 | Lyle Mouton (.357) |
| | Kyle Peterson (7-6) |
| | Rod Henderson (7-11) |
| 2000 | Brady Clark (.304) |
| | Steve Soderstrom (9-11) |
| 2001 | Marty Malloy (.309) |
| | Jared Fernandez (10-9) |

**LOUISVILLE MAJOR-LEAGUE OPENING-DAY AND CLOSING-DAY RESULTS**
(1876–1899)

| DAY/DATE | PITCHER | RESULT | OPPONENT | SITE-ATTENDANCE |
|---|---|---|---|---|
| Tu. 4.25.76[1] | Jimmy Devlin | Lost 4-0 | Chicago | H/6,000 |
| Th. 10.5.76 | Jim Clinton | Lost 11-2 | Hartford | H/NA |
| Th. 5.10.77 | Jimmy Devlin | Lost 15-9 | Cincinnati | H/NA |
| Sat. 10.6.77 | Jimmy Devlin | Lost 4-0 | Chicago | A/NA |
| Tu. 5.2.82 | Tony Mullane | Lost 9-7 | St. Louis | A/NA |
| Sun. 10.1.82 | Tony Mullane | Won 5-1 | St. Louis | A/NA |
| Tu. 5.1.83 | Guy Hecker | Won 6-5 | Columbus | A/1,500 |
| Sun. 9.30.83 | Guy Hecker | Won 10-5 | Philadelphia | H/NA |
| Th. 5.1.84 | Guy Hecker | Won 5-1 | Toledo | H/NA |
| Wed. 10.15.84 | Guy Hecker | Won 9-3 | Pittsburgh | A/NA |
| Sun. 4.19.85 | Guy Hecker | Lost 4-1 | Cincinnati | H/10,000 |
| Th. 10.1.85 | (3 pitchers)[2] | Lost 13-8 | Baltimore | A/NA |
| Sat. 4.17.86 | Guy Hecker | Won 5-1 | Cincinnati | A/5,000 |
| Sun. 10.10.86 | Guy Hecker | Lost 8-6 | Philadelphia | H/1,500 |
| Sat. 4.16.87 | Tom (Toad) Ramsey | Won 8-3 | St. Louis | H/3,000 |
| Sun. 10.9.87 | Tom (Toad) Ramsey | Lost 2-0 | Cincinnati | H/5,000 |
| Wed. 4.18.88 | Tom (Toad) Ramsey | Lost 8-0 | St. Louis | A/5,000 |
| Sun. 10.14.88[3] | Tom (Toad) Ramsey | Won 2-1 | Kansas City | H |
|  | Scott Stratton | Won 9-1 | Kansas City | H |
| Wed. 4.17.89 | John Ewing | Lost 7-4 | Kansas City | H/2,500 |
| Mon. 10.14.89 | John Ewing | Lost 7-5 | Kansas City | H/NA |
| Fri. 4.18.90 | Scott Stratton | Lost 11-8 | St. Louis | H/5,523 |

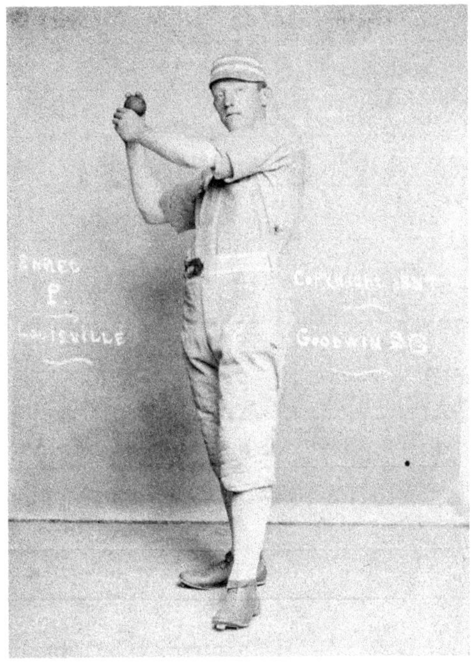

*Above, left*: Scott Stratton. The ace of the 1890 world co-champion Louisville Cyclones, Scott Stratton led his team to the American Association flag and that year's World Series against the National League champion Brooklyn Bridegrooms with a brilliant 34-14 mark. His fabulous work also included a long-lost sixteen-game winning streak, discovered in 1996. The mark, long erroneously reported as fifteen straight victories, equaled the American League standard (Walter Johnson, 1912, Senators; Joe Wood, 1912, Red Sox; Robert "Lefty" Grove, 1931, Athletics; and Lynnwood "Schoolboy" Rowe, 1934, Tigers) and was just three short of the all-time major-league mark held by National Leaguers Tim Keefe (1888) and Richard "Rube" Marquard (1912), both with the New York Giants. *National Baseball Hall of Fame Library, Cooperstown, New York.*

*Above, right*: Red Ehret. During the regular season, Philip "Red" Ehret backed up staff ace Scott Stratton with a sparkling 25-14 mark. In the 1890 World Series, though, he was the big gun, recording two wins, a save and a 1.35 ERA. (Stratton was 1-1-1 with a 2.37 ERA.) *National Baseball Hall of Fame Library, Cooperstown, New York.*

| DAY/DATE | PITCHER | RESULT | OPPONENT | SITE-ATTENDANCE |
|---|---|---|---|---|
| Tu. 10.14.90 | Philip (Red) Ehret | Won 13-1 | St. Louis | H/NA |
| Wed. 4.8.91 | Ed Daily | Won 7-6 | Columbus | H/5,000 |
| Sun. 10.4.91 | Jouett Meekin[4] | Lost 8-0 | St. Louis | A/ |
| | John Fitzgerald | Won 4-3 | St. Louis | A/[5] |
| Tu. 4.12.92 | Jouett Meekin | Won 5-2 | Cleveland | H/5,993 |
| Sat. 10.15.92 | Frederic Clausen | Lost 11-2 | Cleveland | A/300 |
| Th. 4.27.93 | Scott Stratton | Lost 4-2 | St. Louis | A/12,000 |
| Fri. 9.29.93[6] | Matty Kilroy | Won 6-0 | Baltimore | H/NA |
| Fri. 4.20.94 | John Menefee | Won 10-3 | Cleveland | H/4,000 |
| Sun. 9.30.94[7] | John Wadsworth | Won 10-8 | Brooklyn | H/NA |
| | Bert Inks | Lost 12-4 | Brooklyn | H/NA |
| Th. 4.18.95 | Bert Inks | Won 11-2 | Pittsburgh | H/8,000 |
| Sun. 9.29.95[8] | Tom McCreery | Won 13-8 | Cleveland | H/NA |
| Th. 4.16.96 | Charles Fraser | Lost 4-2 | Chicago | H/10,000 |
| Sat. 9.26.96 | Art Herman | Lost 3-2 | Cleveland | A/4,000 |
| Th. 4.22.97 | Charles Fraser | Won 3-1 | Cleveland | H/12,000 |
| Sun. 10.3.97 | Charles Fraser | Lost 9-7 | Cincinnati | H/5,000 |
| Fri. 4.15.98 | Bert Cunningham | Won 10-3 | Pittsburgh | H/10,000 |
| Sat. 10.15.98 | Bill Magee | Won 5-4 | Cleveland | H/NA |
| Fri. 4.14.99 | Bert Cunningham | Lost 15-1 | Chicago | H/10,000 |
| Sun. 10.15.99 | Deacon Phillippe | Won 9-5 | Chicago | A/NA |

NOTES

1. First shutout in National League history.
2. Guy Hecker (losing pitcher), Chicken Wolf and Philip Reccius. Game called after six innings on account of darkness.

3. Double-header; total attendance for both games listed as three thousand.
4. Lost to rookie Ted Breitenstein, who pitched a no-hitter in his first major-league start.
5. Double-header; total attendance for both games listed as five thousand.
6. Called after five innings on account of darkness.
7. Double-header; second game called after five innings on account of darkness.
8. Called after eight innings on account of darkness.

## Louisville Major-League Managers and Annual Records

### National League I

| Year | Manager | Won | Lost | Pct. | Finish | Pennant Winner |
|---|---|---|---|---|---|---|
| **1876** | Jack Chapman | 30 | 36 | .455 | 5-8 | Chicago White Stockings |
| **1877** | Jack Chapman | 35 | 25 | .583 | 2-6 | Boston Red Caps |

### American Association

| Year | Manager | Won | Lost | Pct. | Finish | Pennant Winner |
|---|---|---|---|---|---|---|
| **1882** | Denny Mack | 42 | 37 | .532 | 3-6 | Cincinnati Red Stockings |
| **1883** | Joe Gerhardt | 52 | 45 | .536 | 5-8 | Philadelphia Athletics |
| **1884** | Joe Gerhardt<br>Mike Walsh | 68 | 40 | .630 | 3-13 | New York Metropolitans |
| **1885** | Jim Hart | 53 | 59 | .473 | 5t-8* | St. Louis Browns |
| **1886** | Jim Hart | 66 | 70 | .485 | 4-8 | St. Louis Browns |
| **1887** | (Honest) John Kelly | 76 | 60 | .559 | 4-8 | St. Louis Browns |
| **1888** | (Honest) John Kelly<br>John Kerins<br>Mordecai Davidson | 48 | 87 | .356 | 7-8 | St. Louis Browns |

| YEAR | MANAGER | WON | LOST | PCT. | FINISH | PENNANT WINNER |
|---|---|---|---|---|---|---|
| **1889** | Dude Esterbrook | 27 | 111 | .196 | 8-8 | Brooklyn Bridegrooms |
| | Chicken Wolf | | | | | |
| | Dan Shannon | | | | | |
| | Jack Chapman | | | | | |
| **1890** | Jack Chapman | 88 | 44 | .667 | 1-8 | Louisville** |
| **1891** | Jack Chapman | 54 | 83 | .394 | 8-9 | Boston Reds |

* Tied for fifth with Brooklyn Grays.

** Runner-up: Columbus Solons.

## NATIONAL LEAGUE II

| YEAR | MANAGER | WON | LOST | PCT. | FINISH | PENNANT WINNER |
|---|---|---|---|---|---|---|
| **1892** | Jack Chapman | 63 | 89 | .414 | 9-12 | Boston Beaneaters |
| | Fred Pfeffer | | | | | |
| **1893** | Billy Barnie | 50 | 75 | .400 | 11-12 | Boston Beaneaters |
| **1894** | Billy Barnie | 36 | 94 | .277 | 12-12 | Baltimore Orioles |
| **1895** | John McCloskey | 35 | 96 | .267 | 12-12 | Baltimore Orioles |
| **1896** | John McCloskey | 38 | 93 | .290 | 12-12 | Baltimore Orioles |
| | Bill McGunnigle | | | | | |
| **1897** | Jim Rogers | 52 | 78 | .400 | 11-12 | Boston Beaneaters |
| | Fred Clarke | | | | | |
| **1898** | Fred Clarke | 70 | 81 | .464 | 9-12 | Boston Beaneaters |
| **1899** | Fred Clarke | 75 | 77 | .493 | 9-12 | Brooklyn Bridegrooms |

## Louisville Post-Season Major-League Results

1890: American Association pennant winner. Met National League flag winner Brooklyn Bridegrooms in World Series; declared co-champions when bad weather shut the series down after seven games, each team having won three games, lost three games and tied one game.

## Louisville Minor-League Opening-Day and Closing-Day Results
(1902–2001)

| Day/Date | Pitcher | Result | Opponent | Site/ Attendance |
|---|---|---|---|---|
| Wed. 4.23.1902 | Patsy Flaherty | Lost 16-6 | Kansas City | H/5,000 |
| Mon. 9.22.1902 | (Forfeit) | Won 9-0 | Minneapolis | A/NA |
| | Patsy Flaherty | Won 4-0 | Minneapolis | A/NA |
| | Patsy Flaherty | Won 4-3 | Minneapolis | A/NA |
| Wed. 4.22.1903 | Pat Bohannon | Lost 4-2 (10) | Indianapolis | H/5,000 |
| Sun. 9.20.1903 | Akers | Won 4-0 | Columbus | A/NA |
| Wed. 4.20.1904 | Campbell | Won 9-1 | Milwaukee | H/4,000 |
| Mon. 9.19.1904 | Campbell | Won 3-0 | Toledo | A/NA |
| Wed. 4.19.1905 | Ed Kenna | Won 10-3 | St. Paul | H/7,000+ |
| Mon. 9.18.1905 | Ed Dunkle | Lost 3-0 | Columbus | A/capacity crowd |
| Wed. 4.18.1906 | Ed Kenna | Won 11-7 | Minneapolis | H/10,000 |
| Sun. 9.16.1906 | Ambrose Puttmann | Lost 6-1 | Columbus | A/NA |
| | Ed Kenna | Lost 2-0 | Columbus | A/NA |
| Wed. 4.17.1907 | Bunton | Won 6-4 | Kansas City | H/NA |
| Sun. 9.15.1907 | Walter Frantz | Lost 10-4 | Columbus | A/2,000 |
| | James Durham | Won 10-2 | Columbus | A/2,000 |

| Day/Date | Pitcher | Result | Opponent | Site/ Attendance |
|---|---|---|---|---|
| Wed. 4.15.1908 | Ambrose Puttmann | Lost 2-1 | Milwaukee | H/5,000 |
| Mon. 9.14.1908 | Ed Poole | Lost 10-5 | Indianapolis | A/NA |
| Wed. 4.14.1909 | Jack Halla | Won 6-1 | Columbus | H/7,000 |
| Sun. 9.26.1909 | James Vaughn | Won 6-5 | Kansas City | H/8,000+ |
| | Clayton | Lost 5-3 | Kansas City | H/8,000+ |
| Wed. 4.13.1910 | Jack Halla | Won 6-0 | Columbus | A/10,000 |
| Sat. 9.24.1910 | Gus Richter | Lost 9-7 | Indianapolis | H/NA |
| Wed. 4.12.1911 | Gus Richter | Lost 4-3 | Kansas City | H/6,500 |
| Sun. 10.1.1911 | Bunn Hearn | Lost 5-4 | Indianapolis | A/NA |
| | E. Baker | Won 2-1 | Indianapolis | A/NA |
| Wed. 4.10.1912 | Grover Lowdermilk | Lost 6-4 | Minneapolis | H/10,000 |
| Sun. 9.22.1912 | Nick Maddox | Won 3-2 | Indianapolis | H/small crowd |
| | Robert Clemons | Lost 2-0 | Indianapolis | H/small crowd |
| Th. 4.10.1913 | Woodburn | Lost 11-7 | Kansas City | A/900 |
| Mon. 9.29.1913 | Jake Northrup | Won 5-2 | Milwaukee | H/NA |
| | White | Lost 9-2 | Milwaukee | H/NA |
| Wed. 4.15.1914 | Fred Toney | Won 7-2 | Columbus | H/5,000 |
| Sun. 9.27.1914 | Jake Northrup | Lost 6-3 | Cleveland | H/2,500 |
| | Scott (Rope) Perry | Won 7-5 | Cleveland | H/2,500 |
| Th. 4.15.1915 | Jake Northrup | Won 3-0 | Columbus | A/12,000 |
| Sun. 9.19.1915 | Jake Northrup | Lost 2-1 | Milwaukee | H/large crowd |
| | Dave Danforth | Tie 1-1 | Milwaukee | H/large crowd[1] |

| Day/Date | Pitcher | Result | Opponent | Site/ Attendance |
|---|---|---|---|---|
| Tu. 4.18.1916 | Jake Northrup | Lost 2-1 | Minneapolis | H/capacity crowd |
| Sun. 10.1.1916 | Dolf Luque | Won 3-1 | Toledo | H/NA |
| | William A. "Lefty" James | Lost 2-1 | Toledo | H/NA |
| Wed. 4.11.1917 | Ralph Comstock | Won 4-2 | Columbus | H/10,000 |
| Wed. 9.19.1917 | Frank (Dixie) Davis | Lost 4-2 | Kansas City | H/NA |
| Wed. 5.1.1918 | Fred Beebe | Lost 3-2 | Toledo | A/NA |
| Sun. 7.21.1918 | Bert Humphries | Lost 8-5 | Toledo | H/5,000 |
| | Dolf Luque | Won 6-1 | Toledo | H/5,000[2] |
| Wed. 4.23.1919 | Frank (Dixie) Davis | Won 14-2 | Milwaukee | H/large crowd |
| Sun. 9.28.1919 | Tom Long | Won 2-1 | Minneapolis | A/NA |
| | Emilio Palmero | Won 8-2 | Minneapolis | A/NA |
| Wed. 4.14.1920 | Ben Tincup | Lost 6-1 | Columbus | H/8,223 |
| Sun. 10.3.1920 | Ben Tincup | Won 15-4 | Milwaukee | H/NA |
| | Tom Long | Won 9-4 | Milwaukee | H/NA |
| Wed. 4.13.1921 | Wayne Wright | Won 5-4 | Toledo | H/8,737 |
| Sun. 10.2.1921 | Ben Tincup | Won 5-2 | Milwaukee | H/NA |
| | Roy Sanders | Lost 9-3 | Milwaukee | H/NA |
| Wed. 4.12.1922 | Tommy Estell | Lost 9-8 (12) | Minneapolis | H/8,177 |
| Sun. 10.1.1922 | Ed Holly | Lost 4-3 | St. Paul | A/NA |
| | Tommy Estell | Lost 10-1 | St. Paul | A/NA |
| Th. 4.19.1923 | Nick Cullop | Won 4-0 | Indianapolis | A/10,000 |

| DAY/DATE | PITCHER | RESULT | OPPONENT | SITE/ ATTENDANCE |
|---|---|---|---|---|
| Sun. 10.7.1923 | Wayland Dean | Lost 4-2 | St. Paul | H/NA |
| | Ben Tincup | Lost 7-3 | St. Paul | H/NA |
| Tu. 4.15.1924 | Nick Cullop | Won 6-4 | St. Paul | H/13,200 |
| Sun. 9.28.1924 | Ben Tincup | Won 14-5 | St. Paul | A/7,500 |
| | Marty Baylin | Lost 11-6 | St. Paul | A/7,500 |
| Tu. 4.14.1925 | Nick Cullop | Won 3-2 | Milwaukee | H/14,046 |
| Sun. 9.27.1925 | Holley | Lost 7-6 | Toledo | H/NA |
| | Joe Dawson | Lost 6-2 | Toledo | H/NA |
| Wed. 4.14.1926 | Nick Cullop | Won 10-5 | Milwaukee | A/6,000 |
| Sun. 9.26.1926 | Joe Dawson | Lost 3-1 | St. Paul | H/NA |
| | Otis Wicker | Lost 4-0 | St. Paul | H/NA |
| Tu. 4.12.1927 | Nick Cullop | Lost 1-0 (12) | Minneapolis | H/13,133 |
| Sun. 9.25.1927 | Malcolm Moss | Won 6-5 | Columbus | H/2,420 |
| | Leon Austin | Won 5-3 | Columbus | H/2,420 |
| Tu. 4.10.1928 | Roy Wilkinson | Lost 9-0/F | St. Paul | H/10,384[3] |
| Sun. 9.23.1928 | Earl Browne | Lost 12-8 | Columbus | H/2,022 |
| | Everett Henegar | Won 6-5 | Columbus | H/2,022 |
| Tu. 4.16.1929 | Ben Tincup | Lost 8-2 | Kansas City | H/8,789 |
| Sun. 9.30.1929 | Malcolm Moss | Lost 5-4 | Minneapolis | A/NA |
| | Guy Williams | Won 6-4 | Minneapolis | A/NA |
| Tu. 4.15.1930 | Roy Wilkinson | Won 11-2 | Milwaukee | H/11,036 |
| Sun. 9.21.1930 | John Marcum | Won 11-0 | Indianapolis | H/8,000 |
| Tu. 4.14.1931 | John Marcum | Lost 10-4 | Minneapolis | H/11,907 |

| Day/Date | Pitcher | Result | Opponent | Site/ Attendance |
|---|---|---|---|---|
| Sun. 9.27.1931 | Clyde Hatter | Lost 10-0 | Toledo | H/3,000 |
| | Ken Penner | Won 3-0 | Toledo | H/3,00 |
| Tu. 4.12.1932 | Ken Penner | Won 5-4 | St. Paul | H/6,366 |
| Sun. 9.25.1932 | Eldon McLean | Won 4-2 | Indianapolis | A/NA |
| | Dick Bass | Lost 3-1 | Indianapolis | A/NA |
| Wed. 4.12.1933 | Ken Penner | Lost 2-1 | Kansas City | H/3,218 |
| Sun. 9.10.1933 | Phil Weinert | Lost 4-3 | Indianapolis | A/NA |
| | Ken Penner | Won 5-4 | Indianapolis | A/NA |
| Tu. 4.17.1934 | Phil Weinert | Won 8-5 | Columbus | A/12,049 |
| Sun. 9.16.1934 | Dick Bass | Won 7-6 | Indianapolis | H/3,756 |
| | Jim Peterson | Won 13-0 | Indianapolis | H/3,756 |
| Tu. 4.16.1935 | Truett "Rip" Sewell | Won 3-2 | Toledo | A/1,877 |
| Sun. 9.15.1935 | Dick Bass | Lost 7-3 | Indianapolis | A/NA |
| | Delma Southard | Won 9-1 | Indianapolis | A/NA |
| Sun. 4.12.1936 | Wayne LaMaster | Won 6-1 | Milwaukee | H/10,550 |
| Mon. 9.7.1936 | Lancelot "Yank" Terry | Lost 12-4 | Indianapolis | A/NA |
| | Jack Tising | Won 5-4 | Indianapolis | A/NA |
| Fri. 4.16.1937 | Buck Marrow | Lost 11-0 | Toledo | H/5,886 |
| Sun. 9.12.1937 | Dick Bass | Lost 5-4 | Toledo | A/9,444 |
| Sun. 4.17.1938 | John Tising | Won 4-1 | St. Paul | H/8,516 |
| Sun. 9.11.1938 | Rufus Meadows | Lost 11-1 | Toledo | A/5,387 |
| Th. 4.13.1939 | Charley Wagner | Won 3-2 | Milwaukee | H/9,598 |

| Day/Date | Pitcher | Result | Opponent | Site/ Attendance |
|---|---|---|---|---|
| Sun. 9.10.1939 | Monte Weaver | Won 5-4 | Indianapolis | H/10,475 |
| | Fred Shaffer | Lost 8-7 | Indianapolis | H/10,475 |
| Th. 4.18.1940 | Wes Flowers | Won 8-7 | Minneapolis | H/8,861 |
| Sun. 9.15.1940 | Bud Parmelee | Won 13-2 | Toledo | H/5,905 |
| | Fred Shaffer | Lost 4-1 | Toledo | H/5,905 |
| Th. 4.17.1941 | Bill Butland | Won 3-1 | Kansas City | H/9,887 |
| Sun. 9.7.1941 | Bill Lefebvre | Won 5-4 | Columbus | A/6,238 |
| | Bill Sayles | Won 5-4 | Columbus | A/6,238 |
| Th. 4.16.1942 | Nelson Potter | Lost 4-1 | Toledo | H/9,105 |
| Mon. 9.7.1942 | Lou Lucier | Lost 6-3 | Indianapolis | H/2,315 |
| Th. 4.29.1943 | Emmett O'Neill | Lost 5-3 | Columbus | A/3,427 |
| Sun. 9.19.1943 | Vic Johnson | Won 8-2 | Indianapolis | H/2,618 |
| | Boogie Schupp | Won 6-2 | Indianapolis | H/2,618 |
| Wed. 4.19.1944 | Jim Wilson | Lost 2-1 | Columbus | H/6,751 |
| Sun. 9.10.1944 | George Diehl | Lost 10-6 | Toledo | A/NA |
| | Ray Patton | Won 8-1 | Toledo | A/NA |
| Wed. 4.18.1945 | Al Widmar | Won 4-2 | Toledo | A/8,808 |
| Sun. 9.9.1945 | Al Widmar | Won 10-3 | Columbus | H/7,145 |
| | Jake Lawson | Lost 3-2 | Columbus | H/7,145 |
| Wed. 4.17.1946 | Dwight Simonds | Lost 5-3 | Columbus | H/12,536 |
| Sun. 9.8.1946 | Emory Rudd | Lost 6-4 | Columbus | A/2,325 |
| | Deutsch | Lost 17-2 | Columbus | A/2,325 |
| Th. 4.17.1947 | Otie Clark | Lost 7-2 | Toledo | A/9,619 |
| Sun. 9.7.1947 | Wes Bailey | Won 4-3 | Toledo | H/NA |
| | Jungels | Lost 18-7 | Toledo | H/NA |
| Th. 4.15.1948 | Jack Griffore | Lost 4-1 | Minneapolis | H/13,403 |

| Day/Date | Pitcher | Result | Opponent | Site/ Attendance |
|---|---|---|---|---|
| Sun. 9.12.1948 | Jim Shea | Lost 6-4 | Toledo | A/NA |
| | Ellis Deal | Lost 16-5 | Toledo | A/NA |
| Wed. 4.19.1949 | Maurice McDermott[4] | Won 4-3 | Minneapolis | H/11,293 |
| Sun. 9.11.1949 | Bob Alexander | Won 5-3 | Columbus | H/3,121 |
| | John (Windy) McCall | Won 8-5 | Columbus | H/3,121 |
| Tu. 4.18.1950 | Bob Alexander | Won 8-6 | Toledo | A/6,451 |
| Sun. 9.10.1950 | Earl Johnson | Lost 5-1 | Toledo | A/NA |
| Tu. 4.17.1951 | Jim Hisner | Lost 3-0 | Kansas City | H/6,076 |
| Sun. 9.9.1951 | Don Asmonga | Won 3-1 | Indianapolis | H/3,691[5] |
| Wed. 4.16.1952 | Cliff Coggin | Lost 6-4 | Toledo | A/5,646 |
| Sun. 9.7.1952 | Bob Smith | Won 4-3 | Charleston | H/1,387 |
| | Ken Holcombe | Won 6-0 | Charleston | H/1,387 |
| Wed. 4.15.1953 | Bill Henry | Lost 11-7 | St. Paul | H/5,056 |
| Sun. 9.13.1953 | Russ Kemmerer | Lost 5-4 (10) | Minneapolis | A/1,744 |
| | George Uhaze | Won 6-4 (11) | Minneapolis | A/1,744 |
| Wed. 4.14.1954 | Hersh Freeman | Won 4-1 | Kansas City | H/7,714 |
| Sun. 9.12.1954 | Paul Foytack | Lost 4-2 | Columbus | H/1,955 |
| Th. 4.14.1955 | Bill Slack | Lost 6-4 | St. Paul | H/7,712 |
| Mon. 9.5.1955 | Truman Clevenger | Won 5-3 | Charleston | H/7,092 |
| | Duane Wilson | Lost 4-3 | Charleston | H/7,092 |
| Tu. 4.17.1956 | Tony Ponce | Won 3-2 | St. Paul | H/3,565 |
| Sun. 9.9.1956 | Dave Benedict | Won 5-3 | Wichita | A/832 |

| DAY/DATE | PITCHER | RESULT | OPPONENT | SITE/ ATTENDANCE |
|---|---|---|---|---|
| Th. 4.18.1957 | Harry Fisher | Lost 6-5 | Omaha | H/7,408[6] |
| Sun. 9.8.1957 | Don Rudolph | Won 5-1 | Charleston | A/978 |
| Tu. 4.15.1958 | Rex Jones | Lost 9-5 | Minneapolis | H/6,030 |
| Sun. 9.7.1958 | Rex Jones | Lost 7-2 | Wichita | A/3,100 |
| | Fred Besana | Lost 3-2 | Wichita | A/3,100 |
| Sun. 4.12.1959 | Ron Piche | Lost 6-5 | Indianapolis | H/7,605 |
| Wed. 9.9.1959 | Vic Rehm | Lost 1-0 | Fort Worth | A/607 |
| Sat. 4.16.1960 | Don Nottebart | Won 2-0 | St. Paul | H/4,298 |
| Sat. 9.10.1960 | Fred Olivo | Won 8-7 | Charleston | A/1,493[7] |
| Sat. 4.15.1961 | Cecil Butler | Lost 3-2 | Houston | A/3,750 |
| Th. 9.7.1961 | Winston Brown | Won 9-3 | Indianapolis | A/2,371 |
| Th. 4.19.1962 | Denny Lemaster | Lost 9-5 | Denver | H/1,900 |
| Fri. 9.7.1962 | Phil Niekro | Lost 12-10 | Omaha | A/650 |
| Sat. 4.21.1968 | Darrell Brandon | Won 2-1 | Toledo | H/10,193 |
| Sun. 9.8.1968 | Darrell Brandon | Won 2-1 | Richmond | H/5,442 |
| Sun. 4.20.1969 | John Thibdeau | Lost 11-3 | Buffalo | H/3,770 |
| | Garry Roggenburk | Won 5-4 | Buffalo | H/3,770 |
| Mon. 9.1.1969 | Jerry Janeski | Won 11-4 | Rochester | A/NA |
| Fri. 4.17.1970 | Charlie Pfeiffer | Lost 8-6 | Syracuse | H/8,750 |
| Th. 9.3.1970 | Mike Garman | Won 3-2 | Columbus | H/910 |
| Fri. 4.16.1971 | Jim Lonborg | Won 12-3 | Rochester | H/7,274 |
| Th. 9.2.1971 | Jose Santiago | Won 9-8 (12) | Winnipeg | H/1,340 |

| Day/Date | Pitcher | Result | Opponent | Site/ Attendance |
|---|---|---|---|---|
| Fri. 4.14.1972 | John Curtis | Lost 4-2 | Tidewater | A/2,021 |
| Mon. 9.4.1972 | Mike Nagy | Won 1-0 | Toledo | A/3,172[8] |
| Tu. 4.13.1982 | Jose Brito | Lost 5-2 | Evansville | A/2,734 |
| Sun. 8.29.1982 | Eric Rasmussen | Won 12-0 | Indianapolis | H/20,003 |
| Fri. 4.15.1983 | Ralph Citarella | Won 4-3 | Iowa | H/11,242 |
| Wed. 8.31.1983 | Rick Ownbey | Lost 6-4 | Indianapolis | A/2,535[9] |
| Fri. 4.6.1984 | Kevin Hagen | Lost 8-6 | Oklahoma City | A/9,213 |
| Tu. 9.4.1984 | Rick Ownbey | Won 3-0[10] | Wichita | H/2,405 |
| Fri. 4.12.1985 | Todd Worrell | Lost 4-0 | Indianapolis | H/29,787 |
| Mon. 9.2.1985 | John Martin | Won 8-7 (13) | Indianapolis | H/16,117 |
| Fri. 4.11.1986 | Greg Mathews | Lost 8-4 | Buffalo | H/29,428 |
| Mon. 9.1.1986 | Joe Magrane | Won 4-0 | Buffalo | H/8,477 |
| Fri. 4.10.1987 | Greg Bargar | Lost 10-8 | Iowa | H/14,450 |
| Th. 9.3.1987 | Ray Soff | Won 5-3 | Nashville | H/17,879 |
| Th. 4.7.1988 | Gibson Alba | Won 7-4 | Buffalo | H/6,704 |
| Wed. 9.1.1988 | Derek Botelho | Lost 4-1[11] | Indianapolis | H/18,261 |
| Wed. 4.5.1989 | Kenny Hill | Lost 8-3 | Buffalo | A/18,614 |
| Fri. 9.1.1989 | Bob Tewksbury | Won 9-4 | Buffalo | H/15,360 |
| Fri. 4.6.1990 | Omar Olivares | Won 5-0 | Oklahoma City | A/11,657 |
| Mon. 9.3.1990 | Ernie Camacho | Lost 7-6 | Nashville | H/8,282 |
| Wed. 4.10.1991 | Stan Clarke | Lost 4-1 | Iowa | H/5,118 |
| Tu. 9.3.1991 | Mike Loynd | Lost 6-3 | Nashville | H/4,490 |
| Th. 4.9.1992 | Mark Clark | Lost 4-3 | Iowa | H/12,292 |

| DAY/DATE | PITCHER | RESULT | OPPONENT | SITE/ ATTENDANCE |
|---|---|---|---|---|
| Mon. 9.7.1992 | Allen Watson | Won 6-2 | Indianapolis | H/12,135 |
| Th. 4.8.1993 | Allen Watson | Won 8-1 | Oklahoma City | H/7,176 |
| Tu. 9.6.1993 | Gary Buckels | Won 4-3 (12) | Indianapolis | H/11,091 |
| Th. 4.7.1994 | Brian Barber | Lost 5-3 | Iowa | A/5,111 |
| Sun. 9.4.1994 | Gary Buckels | Won 5-3 | Indianapolis | H/19,244 |
| Th. 4.6.1995 | Gary Buckels | Lost 4-3 | Indianapolis | H/13,581 |
| Mon. 9.4.1995 | Doug Creek | Lost 5-4 | Indianapolis | H/15,038 |
| Th. 4.4.1996 | Richard Batchelor | Won 5-4 | Indianapolis | H/4,696 |
| Mon. 9.2.1996 | Brian Maxcy | Won 3-2 (10) | Indianapolis | H/9,184 |
| Wed. 4.3.1997 | Sean Lowe | Won 10-3 | Indianapolis | H./16,705 |
| Mon. 9.1.1997 | Brian Barber | Lost 10-0 | Indianapolis | H/5,282 |
| Th. 4.9.1998 | Bobby Chouinard | Won 9-5 | Columbus | H/3,339 |
| Mon. 9.7.1998 | Robert Ellis | Lost 6-3 | Indianapolis | H/4,429 |
| Th. 4.8.1999 | Al Reyes | Lost 6-5 | Columbus | H/6,475 |
| Mon. 9.6.1999 | Allen Levrault | Lost 8-3[12] | Indianapolis | H/6,133 |
| Th. 4.6.2000 | Ted Rose | Won 12-10 | Norfolk | A/8,228 |
| Wed. 4.12.2000[13] | Neil Soderstrom | Lost 8-5 | Norfolk | H/13,242 |
| Mon. 9.4.2000 | Ed Yarnall | Lost 4-3 | Indianapolis | H/10,340 |
| Th. 4.5.2001 | Hector Merchado | Won 5-4 | Columbus | H/12,715 |
| Mon. 9.3.2001 | Larry Luebbers | Won 3-2 | Indianapolis | H/10,985 |

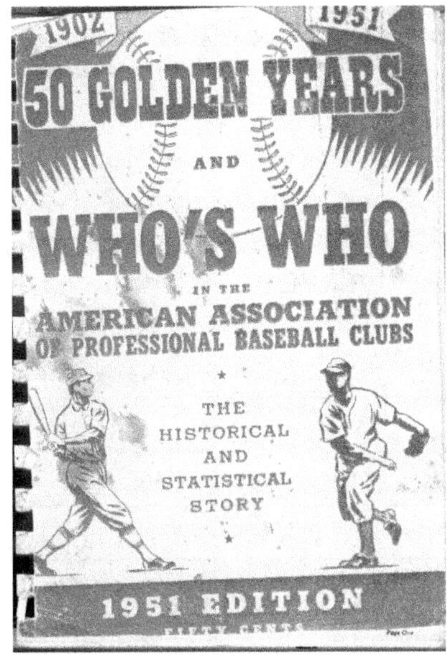


The *Fiftieth Anniversary Yearbook* of the American Association (1951), from 1902 through 1997 one of this country's top three minor-league circuits. *Eclipse BBHR.*

Notes

1. Called in the seventh due to darkness.
2. The league suspended play after July 21, 1918, due to World War I.
3. Tied 2-2 in twelfth; a dispute led to forfeit.
4. McDermott struck out seventeen, one short of the loop record set, interestingly enough, by two other Louisville southpaws. Those were Dave Danforth and Archie McKain. Danforth set his mark in a September 12, 1915 contest versus Kansas City. McKain equaled that standard in a June 19, 1934 nighttime tilt versus St. Paul. McDermott claimed the record outright on Tuesday, May 24, of the 1949 season in the second game of a double-header when he notched twenty strikeouts against St. Paul.
5. The 1951 season was the Golden Jubilee (fiftieth anniversary) season of minor-league baseball in Louisville. The club won its last fourteen games (and nineteen of its last twenty contests). That fourteen-game win skein tied Joe McCarthy's 1925 pennant winners (who took twenty-nine of thirty-one games in June of that year). Newspaper reports at the time of the 1951 work stated that there was uncertainty about whether those two streaks were the club's all-time records, since no records had been compiled before 1925.
6. The Tuesday, April 16 opener and Wednesday, April 17 opener makeup were rained out.
7. The attendance figure for the closer includes 311 children; 1,182 exclusive of children.
8. Pennant-clinching game.
9. On August 25, 1983, Louisville became the first minor-league franchise to draw one million fans in a season.
10. Louisville and Wichita ended the season at 78-76 each; Louisville won a 1-game playoff for outright fourth place and also postseason play.
11. Billy Lyons played all nine positions; he was the first Louisville player to do that since Jim Ryburn, a former Auburn football player, did it with the 1958 Louisville squad.
12. Last game played at Fairgrounds Stadium.
13. Inaugural game at Louisville Slugger Field.

## Louisville Minor-League Managers and Annual Team Records
1902–2001

American Association (1902–62)

| Year | Manager | W-L (%) | Rank | GB/GA | Pennant/ Divisional Winner |
|---|---|---|---|---|---|
| **1902** | Bill Clymer | 92-45 (.671) | 2-8 | -2 games | Indianapolis |
| **1903** | Bill Clymer | 87-54 (.617) | 2-8 | -4½ games | St. Paul |
| **1904** | George Tebeau | 77-70 (.524) | 5-8 | -18 games | St. Paul |
| **1905** | George Tebeau | 76-75 (.503) | 4-8 | -23½ games | Columbus |
| **1906** | Roy Brashear | 71-79 (.473) | 5-8 | -22 games | Columbus |
| **1907** | Dick Cooley | 77-77 (.500) | 5-8 | -13 games | Columbus |
| **1908** | Jimmy Burke | 88-65 (.575) | 2-8 | -4 games | Indianapolis |
| **1909** | Henry Peitz | 93-75 (.554) | 1-8 | +2½ games | Louisville[1] |
| **1910** | Del Howard | 60-103 (.363) | 8-8 | -44½ games | Minneapolis |
| **1911** | Del Howard | 67-101 (.339) | 8-8 | -33½ games | Minneapolis |
| **1912** | Jack Tighe | 66-101 (.395) | 7-8 | -40 games | Minneapolis |
| **1913** | Jack Hayden | 94-72 (.569) | 3-8 | -5½ games | Milwaukee |
| **1914** | Jack Hayden | 95-72 (.565) | 2-8 | -4 games | Milwaukee |
| **1915** | Jack Hayden | 78-72 (.520) | 4-8 | -12 games | Minneapolis |
| **1916** | Bill Clymer | 101-66 (.605) | 1-8 | +5½ games | Louisville[2] |
| **1917** | Bill Clymer | 88-66 (.571) | 2T-8 | -2½ games | Indianapolis[3] |
| **1918** | Bill Clymer | 41-36 (.532) | 4-8 | -4 games | Kansas City |
| **1919** | Joe McCarthy | 86-67 (.562) | 3-8 | -7½ games | St. Paul |
| **1920** | Joe McCarthy | 88-70 (.527) | 2-8 | -28½ games | St. Paul |
| **1921** | Joe McCarthy | 98-70 (.583) | 1-8 | +4½ games | Louisville[4] |
| **1922** | Joe McCarthy | 77-91 (.458) | 6-8 | -30½ games | St. Paul |
| **1923** | Joe McCarthy | 91-77 (.542) | 3-8 | -22 games | Kansas City |
| **1924** | Joe McCarthy | 91-76 (.545) | 3-8 | -5 games | St. Paul |

| Year | Manager | W-L (%) | Rank | GB/GA | Pennant/ Divisional Winner |
|---|---|---|---|---|---|
| **1925** | Joe McCarthy | 106-61 (.635) | 1-8 | +12½ games | Louisville[5] |
| **1926** | Bill Meyer | 105-62 (.629) | 1-8 | +11 games | Louisville[6] |
| **1927** | Bill Meyer | 65-103 (.387) | 7-8 | -36 games | Toledo |
| **1928** | Bill Meyer | 62-106 (.369) | 8-8 | -37½ games | Indianapolis |
| **1929** | Al Sothoron | 75-90 (.455) | 5-8 | -35 games | Kansas City |
| **1930** | Al Sothoron | 93-60 (.607) | 1-8 | +2½ games | Louisville[7] |
| **1931** | Al Sothoron | 74-94 (.440) | 7-8 | -30½ games | St. Paul |
| **1932** | Bruno Betzel | 67-101 (.399) | 8-8 | -33 games | Minneapolis |
| **1933** | Bruno Betzel | 70-83 (.458) | 6-8 | -31½ games | Columbus |
| **1934** | Bruno Betzel | 78-74 (.513) | 4-8 | -8½ games | Minneapolis |
| **1935** | Ken Penner | 52-97 (.349) | 8-8 | -36½ games | Minneapolis |
| **1936** | Burleigh Grimes | 63-91 (.409) | 7-8 | -27 games | Milwaukee |
| **1937** | Bert Niehoff | 62-91 (.405) | 8-8 | -27½ games | Columbus |
| **1938** | Bert Niehoff | 53-100 (.346) | 8-8 | -38 games | St. Paul |
| **1939** | Donnie Bush | 75-78 (.490) | 4-8 | -31½ games | Kansas City |
| | Bill Burwell | | | | |
| **1940** | Bill Burwell | 75-75 (.500) | 4-8 | -20 games | Kansas City |
| **1941** | Bill Burwell | 87-66 (.569) | 2-8 | -8 games | Columbus |
| **1942** | Bill Burwell | 78-76 (.506) | 5-8 | -6½ games | Kansas City |
| **1943** | Bill Burwell | 70-81 (.464) | 5-8 | -20 games | Minneapolis |
| **1944** | Nemo Leibold | 85-63 (.574) | 3-8 | -14½ games | Minneapolis |
| **1945** | Nemo Leibold | 84-70 (.545) | 3-8 | -10 games | Milwaukee |
| **1946** | Nemo Leibold | 92-61 (.601) | 1-8 | +4 games | Louisville[8] |
| **1947** | Nemo Leibold | 85-68 (.556) | 2-8 | -8 games | Kansas City |
| **1948** | Nemo Leibold | 56-98 (.364) | 8-8 | -44 games | Indianapolis |
| | Owen Scheetz | | | | |

| YEAR | MANAGER | W-L (%) | RANK | GB/GA | PENNANT/ DIVISIONAL WINNER |
|---|---|---|---|---|---|
| **1949** | Fred Walters | 70-83 (.458) | 6-8 | -23 games | St. Paul |
| | Mike Ryba[9] | | | | |
| **1950** | Mike Ryba | 82-71 (.536) | 5-8 | -7½ games | Minneapolis |
| **1951** | Mike Higgins | 80-73 (.523) | 4-8 | -15 games | Milwaukee |
| **1952** | Mike Higgins | 77-77 (.500) | 5-8 | -24 games | Milwaukee |
| **1953** | Mike Higgins | 84-70 (.545) | 3-8 | -6 games | Toledo |
| **1954** | Mike Higgins | 85-68 (.556) | 2-8 | -10½ games | Indianapolis |
| **1955** | John Marion | 83-71 (.539) | 4-8 | -9 games | Minneapolis |
| **1956** | John Marion | 60-93 (.392) | 8-8 | -31½ games | Indianapolis |
| | Max Carey | | | | |
| **1957** | Dutch Meyer | 49-105 (.318) | 8-8 | -44 games | Wichita |
| **1958** | Del Wilber | 56-95 (.371) | 8-8 | -33 games | Charleston |
| **1959** | Ben Geraghty | 97-65 (.599) | 1-5/ ED | +2 games | Louisville[10] |
| **1960** | Ben Geraghty | 85-68 (.556) | 2-8 | -2½ games | Denver |
| | Bill Adair | | | | |
| **1961** | Ben Geraghty | 80-70 (.533) | 2-6 | -6 games | Indianapolis |
| **1962** | Jack Tighe | 71-75 (.486) | 4-6 | -17½ games | Indianapolis |

NOTES

1. Milwaukee second with a 90-77 record.
2. Indianapolis second with a 95-71 record.
3. Tied for second with St. Paul.
4. Minneapolis second with a 92-73 record.
5. Indianapolis second with a 92-74 record.
6. Indianapolis second with a 94-71 record.
7. St. Paul second with a 91-63 record.
8. Indianapolis second with an 88-65 record.
9. Walters was 12-27 when Ryba took over on May 29; Ryba went 58-56.
10. Minneapolis second with a 95-67 record.

## International League (1968–72)

| Year | Manager | W-L (%) | Rank | GB/GA | Pennant/ Divisional Winner |
|---|---|---|---|---|---|
| **1968** | Eddie Kasko | 72-75 (.490) | 5T-8 | -11 games | Toledo* |
| **1969** | Eddie Kasko | 77-63 (.550) | 2-8 | -1½ games | Tidewater |
| **1970** | Billy Gardner | 69-71 (.493) | 6-8 | -15 games | Syracuse |
| **1971** | Darrell Johnson | 71-69 (.507) | 5-8 | -15 games | Rochester |
| **1972** | Darrell Johnson | 81-63 (.563) | 1-8 | +1 game | Louisville** |

* Tied with Syracuse Chiefs for fifth place.

** Charleston second with an 80-64 record.

## American Association (1982–97)

| Year | Manager | W-L (%) | Rank | GB/GA | Pennant/ Divisional Winner |
|---|---|---|---|---|---|
| **1982** | Joe Frazier | 73-62 (.541) | 2T-4/ ED | -1½ games | Indianapolis[1] |
| **1983** | Jim Fregosi | 78-57 (.578) | 1-4/ ED | +7½ games | Louisville[2] |
| **1984** | Jim Fregosi | 79-76 (.510) | 4-8 | -12½ games | Indianapolis[3] |
| **1985** | Jim Fregosi | 74-68 (.521) | 1-4/ ED | +2½ games | Louisville[4] |
| **1986** | Jim Fregosi | 64-78 (.451) | 4-4/ ED | -16 games | Indianapolis |
| | Dyar Miller | | | | |
| | Dave Bialas[5] | | | | |
| **1987** | Mike Jorgenson | 78-62 (.557) | 2-8 | -1 game | Denver |

| YEAR | MANAGER | W-L (%) | RANK | GB/GA | PENNANT/ DIVISIONAL WINNER |
|---|---|---|---|---|---|
| **1988** | Mike Jorgenson | 63-79 (.444) | 4-4/ ED | -26 games | Indianapolis |
| **1989** | Mike Jorgenson | 71-74 (.490) | 4-4/ ED | -15½ games | Indianapolis |
| **1990** | Gaylen Pitts | 74-72 (.507) | 3-4/ ED | -11 games | Nashville |
| **1991** | Mark DeJohn | 51-92 (.357) | 4-4/ ED | -30 games | Buffalo |
| **1992** | Jack Krol | 73-70 (.510) | 3-4/ ED | -13½ games | Buffalo |
| | Mark Riggins[6] | | | | |
| **1993** | Jack Krol | 68-76 (.472) | 3-4/ ED | -13½ games | Nashville |
| | Mark Riggins[7] | | | | |
| **1994** | Joe Pettini | 74-68 (.521) | 4-8 | -11½ games | Indianapolis |
| **1995** | Joe Pettini | 74-70 (.514) | 4-8 | -14 games | Indianapolis |
| **1996** | Joe Pettini | 60-84 (.417) | 4-4/ ED | -24 games | Buffalo |
| **1997** | Gaylen Pitts | 58-85 (.406) | 4-4/ ED | -28½ games | Buffalo |

NOTES

1. Tied for second with Iowa.
2. Iowa second with a 71-65 record.
3. Defeated Wichita in a one-game playoff for fourth place.
4. Nashville second with a 71-70 record.
5. Fregosi was 32-31 when he was hired to manage the Chicago White Sox on June 21, 1986; Miller was 0-5 as interim manager; Bialas was hired as Louisville manager on June 26, 1986, and went 32-42.
6. Riggins served briefly as interim manager and went 2-4.
7. Riggins served briefly as interim manager and went 3-6.

International League (1998–2001)

| Year | Manager | W-L (%) | Rank | GB/GA | Pennant/ Divisional Winner |
|---|---|---|---|---|---|
| 1998 | Gary Allenson | 77-67 (.535) | 1-4/WD | +½ game | Louisville* |
| 1999 | Gary Allenson | 63-81 (.438) | 3-4/WD | -21½ games | Columbus |
| 2000 | Dave Miley | 71-73 (.493) | 3-4/WD | -10 games | Indianapolis |
| 2001 | Dave Miley | 84-60 (.583) | 1-4/WD | +16½ games | Louisville** |

* Indianapolis Reds second with a 76-67 record.
**Columbus Clippers second with a 67-76 record.
*Manager notes*: Harry Leibold was known as Nemo Leibold; Mike Higgins was called "Pinky" Higgins; and John Marion was known as "Red" Marion.

**Louisville Minor-League Postseason Results**
(1902–2001)

| | |
|---|---|
| **1909** | American Association (AA) champion. Won AA pennant; Milwaukee Brewers were second. No postseason action held. |
| **1916** | AA champion. Won AA pennant; Indianapolis Indians were second. Defeated Single-A Western League champion Omaha Rourkes 4–1 in minor-league championship series. |
| **1921** | AA champion. Won AA pennant; Minneapolis Millers were second. Defeated International League champions Baltimore Orioles in Junior World Series. |
| **1925** | AA champion. Won AA pennant; Indianapolis Indians were second. Lost Junior World Series 5–3 to International League champion Baltimore Orioles. |
| **1926** | AA champion. Won AA pennant; Indianapolis Indians were second. Swept in Junior World Series 5–0 by International League (IL) titlist Toronto Maple Leafs. |
| **1930** | AA champion. Won AA pennant; St. Paul Saints were second. Lost Junior World Series to IL champion Rochester Red Wings. |

| | |
|---|---|
| **1939** | Overall AA champion. Won AA playoffs (4–1 over Minneapolis Millers in playoff opener; Indianapolis Indians 4–1 in AA playoff finals). Won Junior World Series 4–3 over IL rival Rochester Red Wings. |
| **1940** | Overall AA champion. Won AA playoffs (4–2 over Columbus Red Birds in playoff opener; 4–2 over regular season AA champion Kansas City Blues in AA finals). Lost Junior World Series 4–2 to IL foe Newark Bears. |
| **1941** | Won AA playoff opener versus Minneapolis Millers 4–2; lost AA finals to regular season AA champion Columbus Red Birds 4–1. |
| **1944** | Overall AA champions. Defeated AA regular season champion Milwaukee Brewers 4–2 in AA playoffs; swept St. Paul Saints 4–0 in AA finals. Lost Junior World Series 4-2 to IL champion Baltimore Orioles. |
| **1945** | Overall AA champions. Beat regular season AA flag winner Milwaukee Brewers 4-2 in AA playoff opener; won AA playoff finals 4–2 over St. Paul Saints. Defeated IL opponent Newark Bears 4–2 in Junior World Series. |
| **1946** | AA champion. Won AA pennant; Indianapolis Indians were second. Defeated St. Paul Saints 4–1 in AA playoffs; swept Indianapolis Indians 4–0 in AA finals. Lost Junior World Series 4–2 to IL champions Montreal Royals. |
| **1947** | Defeated Minneapolis Millers 4–3 in AA playoffs; lost to Milwaukee Brewers 4–3 in AA finals. |
| **1951** | Lost 4–1 to St. Paul Saints in opening round of AA playoffs. |
| **1953** | Lost to AA regular season champion Toledo Mud Hens 4–3 in opening round of AA playoffs. |
| **1954** | Overall AA champion. Defeated Columbus Red Birds 4–3 in opening playoffs; beat regular season AA champion Indianapolis Indians 4–1 in playoff finals. Won Junior World Series 4–2 over IL foe Syracuse Chiefs. |
| **1955** | Lost to Omaha Cardinals 4–3 in opening round of AA playoffs. |
| **1959** | Won Eastern Division of AA; Minneapolis Millers were second. Swept by Fort Worth Cats 4–0 in opening round of AA playoffs. |
| **1960** | Overall AA champion. Beat St. Paul Saints 4–2 in playoffs; defeated regular season AA champion Denver Bears 4-2 in finals. Beat IL titlist Toronto Maple Leafs 4–2 in Junior World Series. |

| | |
|---|---|
| **1961** | Overall AA champion. Beat Denver Bears in playoffs 4-3; defeated Houston Buffs 4–2 in AA playoff finals. Swept by IL foe Buffalo Bisons 4-0 in Junior World Series. (Regular season AA champions were the Indianapolis Indians.) |
| **1962** | Overall AA champion. Swept regular season AA champion Indianapolis Indians 3-0 in AA playoff opener. Defeated Denver Bears 4–2 in playoff finals. Lost Junior World Series to IL foe Atlanta Crackers, 4–3. |
| **1969** | Lost to Syracuse Chiefs 3–2 in opening round of IL playoffs. |
| **1972** | Regular season IL champion; Charleston Charlies finished second. Defeated Rochester Red Wings 2–1 in IL playoffs; lost to Tidewater Tides 3–2 in IL finals. |
| **1983** | Won Eastern Division of AA; Iowa Cubs were second. Defeated Oklahoma City 89ers 3–2 in AA playoff opener. Swept 4–0 by Western Division champion Denver Bears in AA playoff finals. |
| **1984** | Overall AA champion. Defeated Wichita Aeros in one-game playoff for fourth place. Beat AA regular season champion Indianapolis Indians 4–2 in playoff opener. Defeated Denver Bears 4–1 in playoff finals. |
| **1985** | Overall AA champion. Won Eastern Division; Nashville Sounds second. Won AA championship 4–1 over Western Division champion Oklahoma City 89ers. |
| **1987** | Lost to Indianapolis Indians 3–2 in opening round of AA playoffs. |
| **1994** | Swept by regular season champion Indianapolis Indians 3–0 in opening round of AA playoffs |
| **1995** | Overall AA champion. Swept regular season AA champion Indianapolis Indians 3–0 in playoff opener. Defeated Buffalo Bisons 3–2 in AA finals. |
| **1998** | Won Western Division in regular season; Indianapolis Indians second. Swept 3–0 by Durham Bulls in opening round of AA playoffs. |
| **2001** | IL champion. regular season Western Division titlist; Columbus Clippers were second. Defeated Southern Division champion Norfolk Tides 3–2 in opening IL playoffs; was leading Scranton/Wilkes-Barre Red Barons 1–0 in best-of-five Governor's Series when series was cancelled following the World Trade Center/Pentagon attacks on September 11, 2001. Louisville was declared IL champion. |

# Louisville Ownership, Historical Baseball Addresses and Burial Sites

## *Major League and Minor League (1876-present)*

### Louisville Major-League Ownership

National League I

| | |
|---|---|
| **1876–77** | Principal investors included Walter N. Haldeman (publisher of the *Louisville Courier-Journal*) and Charles E. Chase (a liquor company executive). John Haldeman, son of Walter Haldeman, owned one share—a gift from his father. |

American Association

| | |
|---|---|
| **1882** | J.H. Pank (brewer, Kentucky Malt Company) and William Reccius (sporting goods businessman) |
| **1883** | Pank, Reccius et al. |
| **1884** | After the 1884 season, the team was sold to a group of owners headed by brothers Zack and John Phelps. This new ownership group also included Will Jackson. The sale was prompted by the fact that even though the 1884 season was the American Association's most successful campaign, the Louisville club just broke even. |
| **1885** | Zack and John Phelps consortium |
| **1886** | Zack and John Phelps consortium |
| **1887** | Zack and John Phelps consortium |
| **1888** | Mordecai Davidson (furniture dealer) |
| **1889** | 1. Mordecai Davidson (minority stockholders included Zack Phelps)<br>2. Taken over by the American Association on July 2. |

| | |
|---|---|
| | 3. Sold to conglomerate of ten owners headed by George Rieger on July 3. (Group included Lawrence Parsons, elected president on July 11; it was recapitalized for the 1890 team for a figure reportedly between $10,000 and $15,000 on Wednesday, October 23, 1889.) |
| **1890** | Lawrence Parsons, principal owner |
| **1891** | Reorganized in March 1891 to satisfy mortgage held by Falls City Bank and also money advanced to the club by large stockholders (Lawrence Parsons, Major Thomas et al.) in 1890. Parsons resigned in early August (according to an August 6, 1891 *Louisville Courier-Journal* news story) and was succeeded by Dr. T. Hunt Stuckey as president. (One story says that Parsons fled the local baseball scene in May, when he suddenly vacated the presidency and turned the franchise over to local attorney Zack Phelps. That scenario, however, is not supported by the aforementioned August 6, 1891 *Louisville Courier-Journal* newspaper account. However, it is documented that Parsons's railroad boss cast a dim eye on his Louisville baseball ownership, feeling that the volatile baseball news coverage was injuring the name and business of the railroad company.)<br>The club was again put up for sale on November 16, 1891, at public auction to satisfy a bank mortgage. It was sold for $6,359.40 to a consortium headed by Larry Gatto. The five directors included Dr. T. Hunt Stuckey (also spelled "Stucky," president), a local physician; George Ruckstuhl (vice-president), an executive with the Frank Fehr Brewing Company; Thomas Batman (secretary/treasurer); Fred Drexler Jr. (director), businessman; and Larry Gatto (director), businessman. |

National League II

| | |
|---|---|
| **1892** | Fred Drexler Jr. bought the franchise from Dr. Stuckey. |
| **1897–99** | The franchise was sold to Barney Dreyfuss (majority owner) and Harry C. Pulliam. It moved to Pittsburgh after Louisville jettisoned from the National League following the 1899 season. |

## LOUISVILLE MAJOR-LEAGUE CLUB PRESIDENTS (1876–77; 1882–99)

| YEAR | LEAGUE | PRESIDENT |
|---|---|---|
| 1876–77 | NL | Walter N. Haldeman (newspaper publisher) |
| 1882–83 | AA | J.H. Pank (distillery executive) |
| 1884 | AA | William L. Jackson Jr. |
| 1885–87 | AA | Zack Phelps (lawyer) |
| 1888 | AA | W.L. Lyons (broker and city politician) |
| 1889 | AA | Mordecai H. Davidson (accountant and businessman) |
| | | Lawrence S. Parsons (railroad businessman) |
| 1890 | AA | Lawrence S. Parsons |
| 1891 | AA | Lawrence S. Parsons; Dr. T. Hunt Stuckey (erroneously reported by some sources as Julian B. Hart |
| 1892 | NL | Dr. T. Hunt Stuckey (physician) |
| 1893–96 | NL | Fred Drexler Jr. |
| 1897–99 | NL | Harry C. Pulliam (baseball executive) |
| 1899 | NL | Barney Dreyfuss (Hall of Fame baseball owner) |

NOTE: Presidents usually controlled the majority of the stock.

## LOUISVILLE MINOR-LEAGUE OWNERSHIP

### WESTERN ASSOCIATION

| | |
|---|---|
| 1901 | Walter Wilmot |

### AMERICAN ASSOCIATION

| | |
|---|---|
| 1902–09 | George Tebeau |
| 1909–12 | William Grayson |

| | |
|---|---|
| 1912–19 | Otto H. Wathan (distiller) |
| 1919–30 | William "Cap" Neal and Colonel Wathan Knebelkamp |
| 1930–39 | Colonel Wathan Knebelkamp |
| 1939–56 | Frank McKinney, Donnie Bush and Boston Red Sox owner Tom Yawkey (purchase price: $195,000) |
| 1956 | Cuban syndicate; went into bankruptcy |
| 1957–62 | Local ownership |

International League

| | |
|---|---|
| 1968 | Walter Dilbeck, an Evansville, Indiana real estate businessman, bought the Toronto Maple Leafs of the International League and moved them to Louisville. |
| 1969–72 | The team was bought in 1969 by Louisville attorney and shopping center magnate Bill Gardner, a nephew of longtime Red Sox owner Tom Yawkey. He operated it until 1972, when the city lost its minor-league baseball team for a decade after it was evicted from its stadium (Fairgrounds Stadium). This curious state of affairs occurred when the University of Louisville Cardinals' football program gained exclusive use of Fairgrounds Stadium, which it later renamed Cardinal Stadium. The Red Sox moved the Louisville franchise to Pawtucket. |

American Association

| | |
|---|---|
| 1982 | Louisville banker Dan Ulmer convinced A. Ray Smith—who had made a fortune in construction in Tulsa—to move his Springfield (Illinois) Redbirds club to Louisville. |
| 1986 | A consortium led by Louisville banker Dan Ulmer bought the team from A. Ray Smith for upwards of $4 million. Besides Ulmer, the group of local investors included Ed Glasscock, Jack Hillerich, Bob Stallings, Tom Musselman, Gene Gardner and Jim Morrissey. |

INTERNATIONAL LEAGUE

| | |
|---|---|
| 2008–present | Ownership comprised of Dan Ulmer, Ed Glasscock, Bob Stallings, Gary Ulmer, Ken Huber, Steve Trager and Mike Brown. (Robert Stallings passed away in 2010; the remaining owners bought his share.) |

## LOUISVILLE AND LOUISVILLE-AREA HISTORICAL BASEBALL ADDRESSES

SITES BY NAME

Baseball Alley (shortcut to Eclipse Minor-League Ballpark): 900 block of Fourth

Calvary Cemetery: 1600 Newburg Road

Cardinal Stadium (part of Fairgrounds Complex): just off Watterson Expressway, five minutes from Standiford Airport (alignment)

Cave Hill Cemetery: 701 Baxter Avenue

Central Grounds (August 8, 1878 *Louisville Courier-Journal* reference)

City Hospital (became General Hospital, now University Hospital)

Commercial Hotel: Harry Raymond's 1890 address

Deppen's Clothing Store: Fourth and Market, 1883; later, Market between Sixth and Seventh

Eclipse Park I (1875): Twenty-eighth and Elliott

Eclipse Park II: Twenty-eighth and Broadway (across the street from Eclipse Ballpark I; aka League Park)

Eclipse Ballpark (minor league): Seventh and Kentucky

Falls City Park: Sixteenth and Magnolia (intersection no longer exists)

Fourth Avenue/Fourth Street Park (August 9, 1891 reference)

Galt House: Second and Main, 1835–65 (burned); First and Main, 1865–21 (razed)

Gatto/Kolb Bar: 323 West Liberty (formerly Green Street)

Grove Hill Cemetery: Shelbyville, just east of Louisville (Dan McGann's grave)

Hecker Baseball Supply Company: 445 West Jefferson

J.F. Hillerich Co. (site where first Louisville Slugger bat, according to popular story, was made in 1884 for Pete Browning): First and Market

J.W. Reccius & Bros. Baseball Supplies (Reccius's Sporting Goods Store): 342 Third Avenue, between Market and Jefferson Streets; also at 408 West Market and 1728 West Market and 317 Fourth Avenue (April 27, 1902 reference)

Louisville Hotel (first, 1834–53; second, 1853–1920; razed, 1921): Main and Seventh
Louisville Slugger Field: downtown Louisville at 401 East Main Street
Louisville Slugger Museum: Eighth and Main
Nick & Jake's Place: 340 West Jefferson
Parkway Field: near University of Louisville (Eastern Parkway)
Phoenix Hotel: Scott Stratton's 1890 address
Reccius Park (July 2, 1900 reference): Twenty-eighth Street and Garland Avenue
Reccius Sporting Goods (see J.W. Reccius & Bros.)
Rhodes-Burfords (furniture store): downtown Louisville
Seelbach Hotel: Sixth and Main (circa 1889); later the Old Inn Hotel at Fourth and Walnut (1905)
St. Cloud Hotel: 1877 residence of Jimmy Devlin and William Hague
St. James Court (aka Baseball Park): just south of downtown Louisville (Magnolia, Fourth, Hill and Sixth; home plate at intersection of Hill/3B and Fourth/1B)
St. Louis Cemetery: adjacent to Calvary Cemetery
Waverly Hotel: Scott Stratton's 1892 address

NUMBERED SITES
289 Sixth: John Haldeman's 1877 address
506 Belgravia, St. James Court: Patsy Tebeau's 1902 residence (rented)
610 Myrtle: Chicken Wolf's 1890 address
1307 Willow Avenue: Bud Hillerich's final address (the word "willow" is old-time jargon for "bat")
1427 West Jefferson: Pete Browning's lifelong home
1510 East Broadway: Zack Phelps's final address
1908 West Walnut: Chicken Wolf's 1882 address
1920 West Market: Guy Hecker's 1886 address
1922 West Walnut: Chicken Wolf's final address
2065 Douglass Boulevard: Al Kolb's final address
2104 Logan: Red Ehret's 1890 address
2224 Grayson: known 1882–86 residence of John and Philip Reccius
2430 Grayson: Farmer Weaver's 1890 address
2524 Portland: Pfeffer family bar

## Louisville Burial Sites of Major Leaguers with Births and/or Deaths

*Players listed by position or affiliation: managers (M) , executives (E), owners (O), umpires (U), historical figures (HF) and hall of famers (HOF).

Calvary (1600 Newburg Road)

| Name | Location | Birth–Death | Position/ Affiliation |
|---|---|---|---|
| Bellman, John Hutchins | | 1864–1931 | P |
| Hulswitt, Rudolph Edward | Sec. 23, #462 | 1877–1950 | SS |
| Ludwig, William Lawrence | | 1882–1947 | C |
| McCloskey, John James | Sec. 24, lot 8; double-sided marker | 1862–1940 | M-E-HF |
| Monroe, Edward Oliver | | 1895–1969 | RHP |
| Weyhing, August | Sec.23, lot 64, grave 1 (shares site with wife; roadside marker) | 1866–1955 | RHP |

Note: Calvary handles records for itself and three other Louisville-area Catholic cemeteries: St. John's, St. Louis and St. Michael's.

Cave Hill (701 Baxter Avenue)

| Name | Location | Birth–Death | Position/ Affiliation |
|---|---|---|---|
| Boone, George Morris | Sec. O, lot 268 | 1871–1910 | P (RHP or LHP unknown) |
| Browning, Louis Rogers "Pete" | Sec. A, lot 549 | 1861–1905 | OF |

| Name | Location | Birth–Death | Position/ Affiliation |
|---|---|---|---|
| Camnitz, Samuel Howard "Howie" | | 1881–1960 | RHP |
| Cline, John P. | Northeast half, Sec. A, lot 585, no marker | 1858–1916 | OF |
| Collins, Hubert B. "Hub" | Northeast half, Sec. 5, lot 5; roadside marker | 1864–1892 | 2B-OF |
| Davidson, Mordecai | Sec. 18, range 375, lot 15; shares site with wife | 1846–1940 | O |
| Hach, Irwin William "Major" | Sec. 14, lot 114 | 1873–1936 | 2B-3B |
| Haldeman, John Avery | Sec. A, lot 113; roadside marker | 1855–1899 | 2B-HF |
| Hillerich, John Andrew "Bud" | Sec. 26, lots 89 and 90, family | 1866–1946 | HF |
| Kerins, John Nelson | Sec. 9, range 297, lot 48; no marker; to right of "M. Felde" | 1858–1919 | 1B-M |
| Koster, Frederick Charles | | 1905–1979 | OF |
| Langsford, Robert William (born Robert Hugo Lankswert) | Sec.8, range 216, lot 24 no marker, to right of "Vittitow" | 1865–1907 | SS |
| Pearce, Franklin Johnson | Sec. 28, lot 11; shares marker with Ella Jennings Pearce | 1860–1926 | P (RHP or LHP unknown) |
| Phelps, Zack A. | Sec. A, lot 390, roadside marker | 1857–1901 | E-HF |
| Pulliam, Harry C. | Sec. P, lot 85 | 1869–1909 | E-HF |

| NAME | LOCATION | BIRTH–DEATH | POSITION/ AFFILIATION |
|---|---|---|---|
| Reccius, John | Sec. 24, south half of lot 154; double-sided marker, "Bynum" on reverse | 1859–1930 | OF-P (believed to be LHP) |
| Reccius, John William | Sec. 8, lot 42, grave 2 | circa 1848–1911 | E-O-HF |
| Reccius, Philip | Sec. 6, range 197, lot 8 | 1862–1903 | 3B-LHP (believed to be a southpaw) |
| Reeder, Nicholas (born Nicholas Herchenroeder) | Sec, A, range 132, lot 41 | 1867–1894 | 3B |
| Schwenck, Rudolph | Sec. P, Lot 806 | 1884–1941 | P |
| Shreve, Leven Lawrence | | 1869–1942 | RHP |
| Wolf, William Van Winkle | Sec. 5, lot 186 | 1862–1903 | OF |

EASTERN (641 BAXTER AVENUE, NEXT TO CAVE HILL)

| NAME | BIRTH–DEATH | POSITION/AFFILIATION |
|---|---|---|
| Burnett, Hercules H. | 1869–1936 | OF-1B |
| Jacobs, Morris Elmore "Mike" | 1871–1949 | SS |
| Weyhing, John | 1869–1890 | LHP |

NOTE: Cemetery and adjoining crematorium are abandoned; cemetery records are in complete disarray.

Evergreen Cemetery (4623 Preston Highway)

| Name | Birth–Death | Position/Affiliation |
|---|---|---|
| Higbee, Mahlon | 1901–1968 | OF |
| Jeffries, Irvine Franklin | 1905–1982 | 3B-2B |

Portland Cemetery (3534 Pflanz Avenue)

| Name | Birth–Death | Position/Affiliation |
|---|---|---|
| Byers, Burley (born Christopher A. Bayer) | 1875–1933 | SS |
| Stultz, George Irvin | 1873–1955 | P (RHP or LHP unknown) |

Rest Haven Memorial (4400 Bardstown Road)

| Name | Birth–Death | Position/Affiliation |
|---|---|---|
| Long, James M. | 1862–1932 | OF |

St. John's Cemetery (1600 Newburg Road)

| Name | Birth–Death | Position/Affiliation |
|---|---|---|
| Terrell, John Thomas | 1867–1893 | C-LF |

St. Louis (1167 Barrett Avenue)

| Name | Location | Birth–Death | Position/ Affiliation |
|---|---|---|---|
| Dyler, John F. | | 1852–1916 | LF |
| Gatto, Lawrence "Larry" | Sec. C, lot 5, grave 3; roadside marker | 1856-1910 | HF |

| Name | Location | Birth–Death | Position/ Affiliation |
|---|---|---|---|
| Heinzman, John Peter | Sec. V, 146 western half | 1863–1914 | 1B |
| Richter, John Marcellus | | 1873–1927 | 3B |
| Smith, Rex (born Henry W. Schmidt) | | 1864–1895 | P (RHP or LHP unknown) |
| Walsh, Michael John | Sec. M, lot 59 | 1850–1929 | M-U |
| Wentz, John George (born John George Wernz) | | 1863–1907 | 2B |
| Zahner, Frederick Joseph | | 1870–1900 | C |

St. Michael's (1151 St. Charles Street)

| Name | Location | Birth–Death | Position/ Affiliation |
|---|---|---|---|
| McLaughlin, Thomas | Sec. H, lot 297; no grave number or grave marker | 1860-1921 | SS |
| Yantz, George Webb | | 1886–1967 | C |

Nearby Sites of Selected Louisville Major Leaguers (1876–1899)

| Name | Location | Birth–Death | Position/ Affiliation |
|---|---|---|---|
| Ehret, Phillip Sydney "Red" | Baltimore Pike Cemetery, Cincinnati, Ohio | 1868–1940 | RHP |
| Hecker, Guy Jackson | Wooster, Ohio Cemetery | 1856–1938 | RHP |

| | | | |
|---|---|---|---|
| Mack, Joseph "Reddy" (born Joseph McNamara) | St. Joseph Cemetery, Cincinnati, Ohio | 1866–1916 | 2B |
| Ramsey, Thomas A. "Toad" | Crown Hill Cemetery, Indianapolis, Indiana | 1864–1906 | LHP |
| Stratton, Chilton Scott | Valley Cemetery, Taylorsville, Kentucky | 1869–1939 | RHP |

Nearby Sites of Selected Louisville-Born Major Leaguers

| Name | Location | Birth–Death | Position/ Affiliation |
|---|---|---|---|
| Harry Leon "Kid" Keenan | St. Joseph Old Cemetery, Cincinnati, Ohio | 1875–1903 | RHP (made MLB debut at age sixteen) |
| Morrison, John Dewey "Jughandle Johnny" | Rosehill Cemetery, Owensboro, Kentucky | 1895–1966 | RHP |
| Sowders, John | Crown Hill Cemetery, Indianapolis, Indiana | 1866–1908 | LHP |

Nearby Sites of Selected Kentucky-Born Major-League Greats

| Name | Location | Birth–Death | Position/ Affiliation |
|---|---|---|---|
| Chandler, Albert B. "Happy" | Pisgah Presbyterian Church, Versailles, Kentucky | 1898–1991 | E-HF-HOF |
| Combs, Earle | Richmond Cemetery, Richmond, Kentucky | 1899–1976 | CF-HOF |

| NAME | LOCATION | BIRTH–DEATH | POSITION/ AFFILIATION |
|---|---|---|---|
| McGann, Dennis Lawrence "Dan" | Grove Hill Cemetery, Shelbyville, Kentucky | 1871–1910 | 1B |
| Reese, Harold Herman "Pee Wee" | Rest Haven Memorial Cemetery, Louisville, Kentucky | 1918–1999 | SS-HOF |

## PETE BROWNING'S 1886 TWENTY-FOUR-GAME HITTING STREAK

Pete Browning's 1886 hitting streak began on Saturday, May 15, with game twenty-two of the regular season, and continued through game forty-five of the regular season, played on Saturday, June 12. The streak stopped on Sunday, June 13, with game forty-six of the regular season. Because of questions about the length of the streak (various sources have listed it as being either thirty-one or thirty-four games), as well as the streak's proximity to the opening of the 1886 season, the following chart lists the first forty-six games of the regular season for the sake of verification and accuracy. However, as previously stated, the streak ran from regular season game twenty-two through regular season game forty-five and stopped in regular season game forty-six. Browning's streak is highlighted in bold.

| DAY/DATE | SCORE | OPP/PITCHER/SITE | BATTING | GAME (W-L) |
|---|---|---|---|---|
| Sat. 4.17 | Won 5-1 | Cin/Larry McKeon/A | 0-4 | 1 (1-0) |
| Sun. 4.18 | Won 4-3 | Cin/George Pechiney/H | 1-1 (double) | 2 (2-0) |
| Mon. 4.19 | OPEN DATE | | | |
| Tu. 4.20 | Lost 9-2 | Cin/Tony Mullane/H | 0-3 | 3 (2-1) |
| Wed. 4.21 | Won 12-1 | StL/Bob Caruthers/A | 3-5 (double) | 4 (3-1) |

| DAY/DATE | SCORE | OPP/PITCHER/SITE | BATTING | GAME (W-L) |
|---|---|---|---|---|
| Th. 4.22 | Won 6-5 (10) | StL/George "Jumbo" McGinnis/A | 2-5 | 5 (4-1) |
| Fri. 4.23 | OPEN DATE | | | |
| Sat. 4.24 | Lost 15-9 | StL/Nathaniel "Nat" Hudson/A | 1-5 | 6 (4-2) |
| Sun. 4.25 | Lost 16-10 | StL/Dave Foutz/A | 3-5 (double) | 7 (4-3) |
| Mon. 4.26 | Lost 8-3 | Pitt/Ed Morris/H | 2-4 (HR) | 8 (4-4) |
| Tu. 4.27 | Lost 8-3 | Pitt/James "Pud" Galvin/H | 1-4 | 9 (4-5) |
| Wed. 4.28 | Won 2-1 | Pitt/Ed Morris/H | 0-3 | 10 (5-5) |
| Th. 4.29 | RAINOUT W. PITTSBURGH | | | |
| Fri. 4.30 | Won 7-1 | Cin/Tony Mullane/A | 0-3 | 11 (6-5) |
| Sat. 5.1 | Won 8-1 | Cin/Larry McKeon/A | 1-4 | 12 (7-5) |
| Sun. 5.2 | Lost 10-5 | Cin/Tony Mullane/H | 0-4 | 13 (7-6) |
| Mon. 5.3 | OPEN DATE | | | |
| Tu. 5.4 | Lost 5-2 | Cin/Larry McKeon/A | 3-4 | 14 (7-7) |
| Wed. 5.5 | Won 6-5 | Cin/Tony Mullane/H | 3-4 | 15 (8-7) |
| Th. 5.6 | OPEN DATE | | | |
| Fri. 5.7 | Lost 8-1 | StL/Nathaniel "Nat" Hudson/H | 2-4 | 16 (8-8) |
| Sat. 5.8 | Lost 21-5 | StL/Dave Foutz/H | 3-5 (double) | 17 (8-9) |
| Sun. 5.9 | Won 5-4 | StL/George "Jumbo" McGinnis/H | 2-3 | 18 (9-9) |

| Day/Date | Score | OPP/Pitcher/Site | Batting | Game (W-L) |
|---|---|---|---|---|
| Mon. 5.10 | open date | | | |
| Tu. 5.11 | Lost 9-1 | StL/Dave Foutz/H | 1-4 | 19 (9-10) |
| Wed. 5.12 | open date | | | |
| Th. 5.13 | Lost 4-2 | Pitt/Ed Morris/A | 1-4 | 20 (9-11) |
| Fri. 5.14 | Won 4-1 | Pitt/John Hofford/A | 0-3 | 21 (10-11) |
| **Sat. 5.15** | **Won 6-4** | **Pitt/Ed Morris/A** | **2-4** | **22 (11-11)** |
| **Sun. 5.16** | **open date** | | | |
| **Mon. 5.17** | **Lost 5-3** | **Pitt/Ed Morris/A** | **1-4** | **23 (11-12)** |
| **Tu. 5.18** | **Lost 11-9** | **Phil/Al Atkinson/A** | **1-5** | **24 (11-13)** |
| **Wed. 5.19** | **Lost 6-3** | **Phil/Bobby Mathews** | **1-4** | **25 (11-14)** |
| **Th. 5.20** | **rainout w. Philadelphia** | | | |
| **Fri. 5.21** | **Lost 6-3** | **Phil/Ted Kennedy/A** | **1-3 (double)** | **26 (11-15)** |
| **Sat. 5.22** | **Won 2-1** | **Balt/Matty Kilroy/A** | **2-4 (double)** | **27 (12-15)** |
| **Sun. 5.23** | **open date** | | | |
| **Mon. 5.24** | **Won 6-5** | **Balt/Billy Taylor/A** | **2-4 (2 doubles)** | **28 (13-15)** |
| **Tu. 5.25** | **Won 6-1** | **Balt/Matty Kilroy/A** | **1-3 (double)** | **29 (14-15)** |
| **Wed. 5.26** | **Lost 10-9** | **Balt/Abner Powell/A** | **2-5** | **30 (14-16)** |
| **Th. 5.27** | **Won 5-1** | **NY/Jack Lynch/A** | **1-3** | **31 (15-16)** |
| **Fri. 5.28** | **Won 8-1** | **Phil/Al Atkinson/A** | **3-4** | **32 (16-16)** |
| **Sat. 5.29** | **Lost 4-0** | **Brk/Henry Porter/A** | **1-4** | **33 (16-17)** |
| **Sun. 5.30** | **Won 8-2** | **Brk/Henry Porter/A** | **1-3** | **34 (17-17)** |
| **Mon. 5.31** | **Lost 14-5** | **NY/Al Mays/A** | **2-4** | **35 (17-18)** |
| | **Lost 9-6** | **Brk/Henry Porter/A** | **1-3** | **36 (17-19)** |

| Day/Date | Score | OPP/Pitcher/Site | Batting | Game (W-L) |
|---|---|---|---|---|
| **Tu. 6.1** | OPEN DATE | | | |
| **Wed. 6.2** | **Lost 7-1** | **NY/Al Mays/A** | **2-4 (triple)** | **37 (17-20)** |
| **Th. 6.3** | **Lost 11-2** | **Brk/Henry Porter/A** | **3-4 (double)** | **38 (17-21)** |
| **Fri. 6.4** | **Won 7-3** | **NY/Al Mays/A** | **1-4** | **39 (18-21)** |
| **Sat. 6.5** | OPEN DATE | | | |
| **Sun. 6.6** | **Won 18-3** | **StL/Dave Foutz/H** | **1-6** | **40 (19-21)** |
| **Mon. 6.7** | **Won 6-4** | **StL/Bob Caruthers/H** | **2-5 (double)** | **41 (20-21)** |
| **Tu. 6.8** | **Lost 9-3** | **StL/Nathaniel "Nat" Hudson/H** | **2-4** | **42 (20-22)** |
| **Wed. 6.9** | **Won 16-7** | **StL/George "Jumbo" McGinnis/H** | **1-6 (double)** | **43 (21-22)** |
| **Th. 6.10** | **Won 3-2 (10)** | **StL/Bob Caruthers/H** | **2-4 (double)** | **44 (22-22)** |
| **Fri. 6.11** | OPEN DATE | | | |
| **Sat. 6.12** | **Won 3-1** | **StL/Dave Foutz/A** | **1-4** | **45 (23-22)** |
| Sun. 6.13 | Won 4-2 | Cin/George Pechiney/H | 0-4* (HBP) | 46 (23-23) |

*Browning's twenty-four-game hitting streak was stopped, oddly enough, by a Lexington, Kentucky native, George Pechiney. The *Louisville Courier-Journal* reported of the streak-ending game: "Browning hit the ball hard and often, but the fielders always managed to capture his long drives."

### 24-Game Hitting Streak Totals

| G | BA | AB | Hits | 2B | 3B | HR |
|---|---|---|---|---|---|---|
| 24 | .378 | 98 | 37 | 9 | 1 | 0 |

### Seasonal Batting Totals

| G | BA | AB | Hits | 2B | 3B | HR |
|---|---|---|---|---|---|---|
| 112 | .340 | 467 | 159 | 29 | 6 | 2 |

# JAY KIRKE'S RECORD 1921 SEASON

## APRIL

| DAY/DATE | GAME | RESULT/OPPONENT/SITE | SUMMARY | HITS |
|---|---|---|---|---|
| Wed. 4.13 | 1 | W 5-4/Toledo/H | 1-4 | 1 |
| Th. 4.14 | 2 | W 5-0/Toledo/H | 1-4 | 2 |
| Fri. 4.15 | 3 | W 6-5 (10)/Toledo/H | 1-5 | 3 |
| Sat. 4.16 | 4 | W12-2/Toledo/H | 3-5 | 4-6 |
| Mon. 4.18 | 5 | W 3-2 (11)/Columbus/H | 0-3 | (6) |
| Tu. 4.19 | 6 | W 4-1 /Columbus/H | 1-3 | 7 |
| Wed. 4.20 | 7 | L 5-4/Columbus/H | 2-4 | 8-9 |
| Sat. 4.23 | 8 | L 5-0/Columbus/A | 0-4 | (9) |
| Sun. 4.24 | 9 | L 6-5/Columbus/A | 2-4 | 10-11 |
| Mon. 4.25 | 10 | L 5-4 (10)/Toledo/A | 3-3 | 12-14 |
| Tu. 4.26 | 11 | L 5-0/Toledo/A | 1-4 | 15 |
| Wed. 4.27 | 12 | W 4-3 (11)/Toledo/A | 1-6 | 16 |
| Th. 4.28 | 13 | L 8-7/Toledo/A | 2-5 | 17-18 |
| Sat. 4.30 | 14 | L 5-4/Indianapolis/A | 4-4 | 19-22 |

*Overall Record: 7-7

## MAY

| DAY/DATE | GAME | RESULT/OPPONENT/SITE | SUMMARY | HITS |
|---|---|---|---|---|
| Sun. 5.1 | 15 | L 4-0/Indianapolis/A | 0-3 | (22) |
| Mon. 5.2 | 16 | W 15-3/Indianapolis/A | 4-6 | 23-26 |
| Wed. 5.4 | 17 | W 10-3/Indianapolis/H | 2-4 | 27-28 |
| Th. 5.5 | 18 | L 12-2/Indianapolis/H | 1-4 | 29 |
| Fri. 5.6 | 19 | W 6-2/Indianapolis/H | 1-4 | 30 |
| Sun. 5.8 | 20 | L 4-3/Indianapolis/H | 1-4 | 31 |

| Day/Date | Game | Result/Opponent/Site | Summary | Hits |
|---|---|---|---|---|
| Tu. 5.10 | 21 | W 4-3 (10)/Minneapolis/A | 4-5 | 32-35 |
| Wed. 5.11 | 22 | L 5-1/Minneapolis/A | 0-4 | (35) |
| Th. 5.12 | 23 | L 8-1/Minneapolis/A | 0-4 | (35) |
| Sat. 5.14 | 24 | W 6-3/St. Paul/A | 2-5 | 36-37 |
| Sun. 5.15 | 25 | L 9-7/St. Paul/A | 5-5 | 38-42 |
| Th. 5.19 | 26 | L 18-11/Kansas City/A | 2-6 | 43-44 |
| Fri. 5.20 | 27 | W 7-4 (13)/Kansas City/A | 0-6 | (44) |
| Sat. 5.21 | 28 | W 9-7/Kansas City/A | 2-5 | 45-46 |
| Sun. 5.22 | 29 | W 9-6/Kansas City/A | 3-6 | 47-49 |
| Mon. 5.23 | 30 | W 12-4/Milwaukee/A | 2-6 | 50-51 |
| Tu. 5.24 | 31 | L 6-4/Milwaukee/A | 1-4 | 52 |
| Wed. 5.25 | 32 | W 9-3/Milwaukee/A | 3-5 | 53-55 |
| Th. 5.26 | 33 | W 16-7/Milwaukee/A | 3-6 | 56-58 |
| Sat. 5.28 | DH 34-35 | L 5-4 (11)/Indianapolis/A | 0-5 | (58) |
| | | W 10-7/Indianapolis/A | 2-4 | 59-60 |
| Sun. 5.29 | 36 | L 4-3/Indianapolis/A | 2-4 | 61-62 |
| Mon. 5.30 | DH 37-38 | W 3-0/Indianapolis/A | 3-4 | 63-65 |
| | | L 10-9 (10)/Indianapolis/A | 4-5 | 66-69 |

*Overall Record: 20-18

## June

| Day/Date | Game | Result/Opponent/Site | Summary | Hits |
|---|---|---|---|---|
| Wed. 6.1 | 39 | L 8-4/Kansas City/H | 1-4 | 70 |
| Th. 6.2 | 40 | L 12-11 (10)/Kansas City/H | 3-6 | 71-73 |
| Fri. 6.3 | 41 | W 11-3/Kansas City/H | 1-5 | 74 |
| Sat. 6.5 | 42 | W 5-4/Kansas City/H | 0-5 | (74) |

| DAY/DATE | GAME | RESULT/OPPONENT/SITE | SUMMARY | HITS |
|---|---|---|---|---|
| Sun. 6.5 | 43 | W 10-7/Milwaukee/H | 5-5 | 75-79 |
| Mon. 6.6 | 44 | L 3-0/Milwaukee/H | 0-4 | (79) |
| Tu. 6.7 | 45 | L 2-1/Milwaukee/H | 1-2 | 80 |
| Wed. 6.8 | 46[1] | W 8-4 (8)/Milwaukee/H | 4-5 | 81-84 |
| Th. 6.9 | 47 | W 6-2/Minneapolis/H | 1-4 | 85 |
| Fri. 6.10 | 48 | W 5-4/Minneapolis/H | 1-4 | 86 |
| Sat. 6.11 | 49 | L 5-4 (14)/Minneapolis/H | 0-6 | (86) |
| Sun. 6.12 | 50 | W 9-3/Minneapolis/H | 2-5 | 87-88 |
| Tu. 6.14 | 51 | W3-2 (10)/St. Paul/H | 0-3 | (88) |
| Wed. 6.15 | DH 52-53 | L 6-2/St. Paul/H | 1-4 | 89 |
| | | W 10-9 (11)/St. Paul/H | 1-5 | 90 |
| Th. 6.16 | 54 | W 5-4 (12)/St. Paul/H | 1-5 | 91 |
| Fri. 6.17 | 55 | W 6-1/Toledo/H | 2-4 | 92-93 |
| Sat. 6.18 | 56 | W 14-8/Toledo/H | 4-5 | 94-97 |
| Sun. 6.19 | 57 | L 11-2/Toledo/H | 0-4 | (97) |
| Mon. 6.20 | 58 | W 7-2/Columbus/H | 2-4 | 98-99 |
| Tu. 6.21 | 59 | W 5-4/Columbus/H | 1-4 | 100 |
| Wed. 6.22 | DH 60-61 | W 13-4/Columbus/H | 3-5 | 101-03 |
| | | L 12-3/Columbus/H | 1-5 | 104 |
| Th. 6.23 | 62[2] | W 6-5 (7)/Columbus/H | 0-3 | (104) |
| Fri. 6.24 | 63 | L 7-3/Toledo/A | 0-3 | (104) |
| Sat. 6.25 | 64 | W 11-4 (10)/Toledo/A | 2-6 | 105-06 |
| Sun. 6.26 | 65 | W 3-2/Toledo/A | 1-4 | 107 |
| Mon. 6.27 | 66 | W 9-8/Toledo/A | 3-5 | 108-10 |
| Wed. 6.29 | DH 67-68 | W 8-2/Columbus/A | 3-5 | 111-13 |
| | | W 14-5/Columbus/A | 3-5 | 114-16 |
| Th. 6.30 | 69 | W 6-0/Columbus/A | 3-4 | 117-19 |

## Louisville Numbers and Facts

*Overall Record: 42-27

NOTES
1. Game called after eight complete to allow Milwaukee to catch train for next date.
2. Game called after seven complete to allow teams to catch trains for next dates.

### JULY

| DAY/DATE | GAME | RESULT/OPPONENT/SITE | SUMMARY | HITS |
|---|---|---|---|---|
| Fri. 7.1 | 70 | W 8-6/Columbus/A | 2-4 | 120-121 |
| | 71 | W 4-1 (11)/Columbus/A | 2-4 | 122-123 |
| Sat. 7.2 | 72 | W 12-4/Indianapolis/H | 3-5 | 124-126 |
| Sun. 7.3 | 73 | W 6-1/Indianapolis/H | 3-4 | 127-129 |
| Mon. 7.4 | DH 74-75 | W 13-7/Indianapolis/H | 3-5 | 130-132 |
| | | L 3-2 (10)/Indianapolis/H | 1-4 | 133 |
| Wed. 7.6 | DH 76-77 | L 2-0/St. Paul/A | 1-4 | 134 |
| | | L 6-4/St. Paul/A | 0-4 | (134) |
| Th. 7.7 | 78 | L 9-5/St. Paul/A | 0-5 | (134) |
| Fri. 7.8 | DH 79-80 | W 10-3/St. Paul/A | 2-5 | 135-136 |
| | | W 8-3/St Paul/A | 3-4 | 137-139 |
| Sat. 7.9 | 81 | L 5-1/St. Paul/A | 1-3 | 140 |
| Sun. 7.10 | 82 | L 5-4/Minneapolis/A | 0-4 | (140) |
| Mon. 7.11 | 83 | W 11-6/Minneapolis/A | 1-4 | 141 |
| Tu. 7.12 | DH 84-85 | W 13-9/Minneapolis/A | 3-4 | 142-144 |
| | | W 9-7/Minneapolis/A | 1-4 | 145 |
| Wed. 7.13 | 86 | W 4-3/Minneapolis/A | 2-4 | 146-147 |
| Th. 7.14 | 87 | W 16-6/Milwaukee/A | 2-6 | 148-149 |
| Fri. 7.15 | 88 | L 2-1/Milwaukee/A | 0-4 | (149) |
| Sat. 7.16 | 89 | L 6-5/Milwaukee/A | 2-5 | 150-151 |

| Day/Date | Game | Result/Opponent/Site | Summary | Hits |
|---|---|---|---|---|
| Sun. 7.17 | 90 | W 2-1/Milwaukee/A | 1-4 | 152 |
| Mon. 7.18 | 91 | L 7-6/Kansas City/A | 3-5 | 153-155 |
| Tu. 7.19 | 92 | W 5-0/Kansas City/A | 1-4 | 156 |
| Wed. 7.20 | 93 | L 19-10/Kansas City/A | 3-5 | 157-159 |
| Th. 7.21 | 94 | W 7-6 (10)/Kansas City/A | 1-5 | 160 |
| Sat. 7.23 | 95 | L 10-4/Kansas City/H | 0-4 | (160) |
| Sun. 7.24 | DH 96-97 | L 11-7/Kansas City/H | 2-5 | 161-162 |
| | | L 7-4/Kansas City/H | 0-4 | (162) |
| Mon. 7.25 | 98 | L 8-6 (15)/Kansas City/H | 3-8 | 163-165 |
| Tu. 7.26 | 99 | W 8-2/Milwaukee/H | 2-5 | 166-167 |
| Wed. 7.27 | 100 | L 4-2/Milwaukee/H | 1-3 | 168 |
| Th. 7.28 | 101 | L 9-7/Milwaukee/H | 1-3 | 169 |
| Fri. 7.29 | 102 | W 9-3/Milwaukee/H | 4-4 | 170-173 |
| Sat. 7.30 | 103 | L 2-1/St. Paul/H | 1-3 | 174 |
| Sun. 7.31 | 104 | W 11-4/St. Paul/H | 3-5 | 175-177 |

*Overall Record: 60-44

## August

| Day/Date | Game | Result/Opponent/Site | Summary | Hits |
|---|---|---|---|---|
| Mon. 8.1 | 105 | L 8-4/St. Paul/H | 3-5 | 178-180 |
| Tu. 8.2 | 106 | L 15-9/St. Paul/H | 3-4 | 181-183 |
| Wed. 8.3 | 107 | W 9-5/Minneapolis/H | 2-4 | 184-185 |
| Th. 8.4 | 108 | L 13-8 (12)/Minneapolis/H | 3-5 | 186-188 |
| Fri. 8.5 | 109 | L 9-6/Minneapolis/H | 1-5 | 189 |
| Sat. 8.6 | 110 | W 5-4/Minneapolis/H | 4-5 | 190-193 |
| Sun. 8.7 | 111 | W 5-3/Minneapolis/H | 1-3 | 194 |
| Mon. 8.8 | 112 | L 8-7/Toledo/H | 1-5 | 195 |

| Day/Date | Game | Result/Opponent/Site | Summary | Hits |
|---|---|---|---|---|
| Tu. 8.9 | DH 113-114 | W 15-1/Toledo/H | 2-3 | 196-197 |
| | | W 10-8/Toledo/H | 3-5 | 198-200 |
| Wed. 8.10 | 115 | W 7-6/Toledo/H | 3-5 | 201-203 |
| Fri. 8.12 | 116 | W 4-2/Columbus/H | 2-3 | 204-205 |
| Sat. 8.13 | 117 | W 9-5/Columbus/H | 1-5 | 206 |
| Sun. 8.14 | DH 118-119 | L 4-2/Columbus | 0-4 | (206) |
| | | W 2-1/Columbus/H | 0-2 | (206) |
| Wed. 8.17 | 120 | W 8-1/Milwaukee/A | 2-5 | 207-208 |
| Th. 8.18 | 121 | W 5-3/Milwaukee/A | 2-4 | 209-210 |
| Fri. 8.19 | 122 | W 6-3/Milwaukee/A | 3-4 | 211-213 |
| Sat. 8.20 | 123 | L 4-3 (12)/Milwaukee/A | 1-5 | 214 |
| Sun. 8.21 | 124 | L 11-8/Kansas City/A | 2-5 | 215-216 |
| Mon. 8.22 | 125 | W 14-9/Kansas City/A | 3-5 | 217-219 |
| Tu. 8.23 | 126 | L 11-10/Kansas City/A | 2-5 | 220-221 |
| Wed. 8.24 | 127 | W 7-5/Kansas City/A | 2-5 | 222-223 |
| Fri. 8.26 | 128 | W 2-1/St. Paul/A | 0-4 | (223) |
| Sat. 8.27 | 129 | W 7-4/St. Paul/A | 2-5 | 224-225 |
| Sun. 8.28 | DH 130-131 | L 13-3/St. Paul/A | 1-4 | 226 |
| | | W 3-1/St. Paul/A | 0-3 | (226) |
| Mon. 8.29 | 132 | L 12-8/Minneapolis/A | 1-4 | 227 |
| Tu. 8.30 | 133 | L 10-9 (10)/Minneapolis/A | 2-5 | 228-229 |
| Wed. 8.31 | 134 | W 15-1/Minneapolis/A | 2-4 | 230-231 |

*Overall Record: 78-56

SEPTEMBER

| DAY/DATE | GAME | RESULT/OPPONENT/SITE | SUMMARY | HITS |
|---|---|---|---|---|
| Th. 9.1 | 135 | W 5-4/Minneapolis/A | 1-4 | 232 |
| Sat. 9.3 | 136 | W 6-5/Indianapolis/A | 0-4 | (232) |
| Sun. 9.4 | 137 | W 6-1/Indianapolis/A | 2-5 | 233-234 |
| Mon. 9.5 | DH 138-139 | L 8-1/Indianapolis/A | 0-3 | (234) |
| | | L 7-3/Indianapolis/A | 2-4 | 235-236 |
| Wed. 9.7 | 140 | W 6-4/Toledo/A | 2-5 | 237-238 |
| Th. 9.8 | 141 | L 7-5/Toledo/A | 4-5 | 239-242 |
| Fri. 9.9 | 142 | L 8-3/Toledo/A | 1-4 | 243 |
| Sat. 9.10 | DH 143-144 | L 8-7 (10)/Toledo/A | 1-4 | 244 |
| | | W 6-4 (8)*/Toledo/A | 1-4 | 245 |
| Sun. 9.11 | DH 145-146 | L 3-1/Columbus/A | 1-4 | 246 |
| | | W 3-2/Columbus/A | 2-4 | 247-248 |
| Mon. 9.12 | 147 | W 6-4/Columbus/A | 0-4 | (248) |
| Tu. 9.13 | 148 | W 10-3/Columbus/A | 1-4 | 249 |
| Wed. 9.14 | 149 | W 4-3/Columbus/A | 1-4 | 250 |
| Th. 9.15 | 150 | W 7-1/Indianapolis/H | 2-4 | 251-252 |
| Fri. 9.16 | 151 | W 6-4/Indianapolis/H | 1-4 | 253 |
| Sun. 9.18 | DH 152-153 | L 7-6/Indianapolis/H | 3-4 | 254-256 |
| | | W 6-0/Indianapolis/H | 0-4 | (256) |
| Tu. 9.20 | 154 | W 7-6/Minneapolis/H | 2-4 | 257-258 |
| Wed. 9.21 | 155 | W 9-1/Minneapolis/H | 1-2 | 259 |

| Day/Date | Game | Result/Opponent/Site | Summary | Hits |
|---|---|---|---|---|
| Th. 9.22 | 156 | L 13-8/Minneapolis/H | 2-4 | 260-261 |
| Fri. 9.23 | 157 | L 7-5 (10)/St. Paul/H | 2-5 | 262-263 |
| Sat. 9.24 | 158 | W 9-1/St. Paul/H | 1-4 | 264 |
| Sun. 9.25 | DH 159-160 | W 7-3/St. Paul/H | 1-4 | 265 |
| | | W 3-2/St. Paul/H | 1-3 | 266 |
| Tu. 9.27 | 161 | L 13-1/Kansas City/H | 2-4 | 267-268 |
| Wed. 9.28 | DH 162-163 | W 7-3/Kansas City/H | 2-4 | 269-270 |
| | | W 13-9/Kansas City/H | 3-5 | 271-273 |
| Th. 9.29 | 164 | L 8-3/Kansas City/H | 2-4 | 274-275 |
| Fri. 9.30 | 165 | L 9-1/Milwaukee/H | 1-4 | 276 |

* darkness

** Overall Record: 97-68

## October

| Day/Date | Game | Result/Opponent/Site | Summary | Hits |
|---|---|---|---|---|
| Sat. 10.1 | 166 | Lost 6–1/Milwaukee/H | 3-4 | 277-279 |
| Sun. 10.2 | 167 | W 5–2/Milwaukee/H | 2-4 | 280-281 |
| | 168 | L 9–3/Milwaukee/H | 1-2 | 282 |

*Final record: 98-70

## Jay Kirke's Final 1921 Statistics

| G | BA | SA | AB | H | 2B | 3B | HR | TB | R | RBI | BB | SO | SB |
|---|---|---|---|---|---|---|---|---|---|---|---|---|---|
| 168 | .386 | .578 | 730 | 282 | 43 | 17 | 21 | 422 | 125 | 157 | NA | NA | NA |

Kirke ranks fifth on the all-time seasonal hits list. The first four spots are held by Pacific Coast League stars. Kirke's work included two twenty-game hitting streaks: from July 25, 1921, to August 13, 1921; and from September 13, 1921, to October 2, 1921.

| | | | | |
|---|---|---|---|---|
| Paul Strand | 325 | Salt Lake City | PCL | 1923 |
| Ike Boone | 323 | Mission | PCL | 1929 |
| Oscar Eckhardt | 315 | Mission | PCL | 1933 |
| Smead Jolley | 314 | San Francisco | PCL | 1929 |
| Jay Kirke | 282 | Louisville | AA | 1921 |

Louisville was 98-70 (.583) in regular season play. Its original home schedule called for twelve Saturdays, twelve Sundays and the July 4 holiday. Louisville finished four and a half games ahead of runner-up Minneapolis (92-73) to take the American Association pennant and then defeated International League champion Baltimore five games to three in the 1921 Little World Series. This triumph is still considered the greatest upset in the history of the Little World Series (the Minor League World Series, which was also called the Junior World Series). Kirke batted cleanup (fourth) and played first base.

## 1901 LOUISVILLE MINOR-LEAGUE STATISTICS

### 1901 LOUISVILLE SEASONAL RESULTS (INCLUDES PRE- AND POST-TRANSFER RESULTS)

THURSDAY, APRIL 25, 1901, TO FRIDAY, JUNE 28, 1901, AS LOUISVILLE (BEFORE TRANSFER); SATURDAY, JUNE 29, 1901, TO SUNDAY, SEPTEMBER 22, 1901, AS GRAND RAPIDS (AFTER TRANSFER).

| DATE | PITCHER | RESULT | OPPONENT | SITE/ ATT. | G | LOU. RECORD |
|---|---|---|---|---|---|---|
| Th. 4.25 | Gus Weyhing | Lost 7-2 | Indianapolis | H/ 3,500 | 1 | 0-1 |
| Fri. 4.26 | Harvey Bailey | Lost 13-0 | Indianapolis | H/ NA | 2 | 0-2 |

| DATE | PITCHER | RESULT | OPPONENT | SITE/ ATT. | G | LOU. RECORD |
|---|---|---|---|---|---|---|
| Sat. 4.27 | Sam McMackin | Lost 8-7 | Indianapolis | H/ NA | 3 | 0-3 |
| Sun. 4.28 | Gus Weyhing | Won 9-7 | Indianapolis | H/ 3,500 | 4 | 1-3 |
| Tu. 4.30 | Harvey Bailey | Won 4-3 | Columbus | A/ 1,700 | 5 | 2-3 |
| Wed. 5.01 | Jouett Meekin | Lost 6-4 | Columbus | A/ 500 | 6 | 2-4 |
| Th. 5.02 | Sam McMackin | Won 14-2 | Columbus | A/ 500 | 7 | 3-4 |
| Fri. 5.03 | Gus Weyhing | Won 8-5 | Columbus | A/ 200 | 8 | 4-4 |
| Sat. 5.04 | Sam McMackin[1] | Lost 7-4 | Dayton | A/ 500 | 9 | 4-5 |
| Sun. 5.05 | Gus Weyhing | Lost 5-2 | Dayton | A/ 2,200 | 10 | 4-6 |
| Mon. 5.06 | Harvey Bailey | Won 8-3 | Dayton | A/ 300 | 11 | 5-6 |
| Tu. 5.07 | Sam McMackin | Lost 7-3 | Dayton | A/ NA | 12 | 5-7 |
| Th. 5.09 | Gus Weyhing | Won 6-1 | Fort Wayne | A/ 400 | 13 | 6-7 |
| Sat. 5.11 | Sam McMackin[2] | Lost 8-5 | Fort Wayne | A/ 500 | 14 | 7-7 |
| Sun. 5.12 | Gus Weyhing | Won 13-1 | Fort Wayne | A/ 2,500 | 15 | 7-8 |
| Sun. 5.12[3] | Harvey Bailey | Won 10-1(7) | Fort Wayne | A/ 2,500 | 16 | 8-8 |
| Mon. 5.13 | Sam McMackin | Won 9-3 | Marion | A/ 500 | 17 | 9-8 |
| Tu. 5.14 | Harvey Bailey | Won 6-4 | Marion | A/ 500 | 18 | 10-8 |
| Wed. 5.15 | Gus Weyhing | Lost 4-2 | Marion | A/ 600 | 19 | 10-9 |
| Th. 5.16 | Harvey Bailey | Won 4-3 | Marion | A/ 500 | 20 | 11-9 |
| Fri. 5.17 | Jouett Meekin | Lost 11-2 | Toledo | A/ 1,500 | 21 | 11-10 |

| DATE | PITCHER | RESULT | OPPONENT | SITE/ ATT. | G | LOU. RECORD |
|---|---|---|---|---|---|---|
| Sat. 5.18 | Gus Weyhing | Won 2-1 | Toledo | A/ 1,500 | 22 | 12-10 |
| Sun. 5.19 | Harvey Bailey | Won 7-0 | Toledo | A/ 2,000 | 23 | 13-10 |
| Mon. 5.20 | Harley Parker | Lost 4-2 | Toledo | A/ 300 | 24 | 13-11 |
| Wed. 5.22 | Gus Weyhing | Won 10-4 | Grand Rapids | A/ 800 | 25 | 14-11 |
| Th. 5.23 | Harvey Bailey | Won 12-4 | Grand Rapids | A/ 600 | 26 | 15-11 |
| Fri. 5.24 | Harley Parker | Lost 5-4 | Grand Rapids | A/ 500 | 27 | 15-12 |
| Sat. 5.25[4] | Gus Weyhing | Won 6-1 (8) | Columbus | H/ 150 | 28 | 16-12 |
| Sun. 5.26 | Harvey Bailey | Won 10-1 | Columbus | H/ NA[5] | 29 | 17-12 |
| Mon. 5.27 | Harley Parker | Won 7-4 | Columbus | H/ NA | 30 | 18-12 |
| Tu. 5.28 | Gus Weyhing | Won 7-1 | Columbus | H/ NA | 31 | 19-12 |
| Th. 5.30 | Harvey Bailey | Won 2-0 | Indianapolis | A/ 6,000 | 32 | 20-12 |
|  | Harley Parker | Lost 5-2 | Indianapolis | A/ 6,000 | 33 | 20-13 |
| Fri. 5.31 | Gus Weyhing | Lost 2-1 | Indianapolis | A/ 1,000 | 34 | 20-14 |
| Sat. 6.01 | Harvey Bailey | Won 6-5 | Indianapolis | A/ 1,150 | 35 | 21-14 |
| Sun. 6.02 | Jouett Meekin | Lost 4-3 (10) | Dayton | H/ 2,500 | 36 | 21-15 |
| Mon. 6.03 | Gus Weyhing | Lost 7-5 | Dayton | H/ NA | 37 | 21-16 |
| Tu. 6.04 | Harvey Bailey | Won 3-1 | Dayton | H/ NA | 38 | 22-16 |
| Wed. 6.05 | Jouett Meekin | Lost 3-2 | Dayton | H/ 200 | 39 | 22-17 |
| Fri. 6.07 | Gus Weyhing | Won 7-3 | Wheeling | H/ NA | 40 | 23-17 |

| Date | Pitcher | Result | Opponent | Site/ Att. | G | Lou. Record |
|---|---|---|---|---|---|---|
| Sat. 6.08 | Jouett Meekin | Lost 9-5[6] | Wheeling | H/ 400 | 41 | 23-18 |
| Sun. 6.09 | George Vetter | Won 8-2 | Wheeling | H/ 4,000 | 42 | 24-18 |
| | Gus Weyhing | Won 5-4 | Wheeling | H/ 4,000 | 43 | 25-18 |
| Mon. 6.10 | Jack Burns | Won 21-4 | Seymour (IND) | A/ 2,000 | (Exhibition) | |
| Tu. 6.11 | Gus Weyhing | Won 4-1 | Fort Wayne | H/ NA | 44 | 26-18 |
| Th. 6.13 | Harvey Bailey | Won 12-6 | Fort Wayne | H/ NA | 45 | 27-18 |
| Fri. 6.14 | Jack Burns[7] | Won 8-7 | Fort Wayne | H/ NA | 46 | 28-18 |
| Sat. 6.15 | Harvey Bailey | Won 6-1 | Toledo | H/ 1,000 | 47 | 29-18 |
| Sun. 6.16 | Gus Weyhing | Lost 11-0 | Toledo | H/ 2,500 | 48 | 29-19 |
| Mon. 6.17 | Jack Burns | Won 5-4 | Toledo | H/ NA | 49 | 30-19 |
| Tu. 6.18 | Harvey Bailey | Lost 9-4[8] | Toledo | H/ NA | 50 | 30-20 |
| Wed. 6.19 | Gus Weyhing | Won 7-3 | Marion | H/ NA | 51 | 31-20 |
| Th. 6.20 | James McKenna | Lost 4-0 | Marion | H/ "very small crowd" | 52 | 31-21 |
| Sat. 6.22 | Harvey Bailey | Won 6-4 | Marion | H/ "good crowd" | 53 | 32-21 |
| | Jack Burns | Lost 5-2 | Marion | H/ "good crowd" | 54 | 32-22 |

| DATE | PITCHER | RESULT | OPPONENT | SITE/ ATT. | G | LOU. RECORD |
|---|---|---|---|---|---|---|
| Sun. 6.23 | Gus Weyhing | Won 10-4 | Columbus | H/ 1,000 | 55 | 33-22 |
| | Harvey Bailey | Won 5-0 | Columbus | H/ 1,000 | 56 | 34-22 |
| Mon. 6.24 | James McKenna | Lost 11-0 | Columbus | H/ NA | 57 | 34-23 |
| Wed. 6.26 | Gus Weyhing | Won 3-1 | Dayton | A/ 400 | 58 | 35-23 |
| Th. 6.27 | Harvey Bailey | Lost 3-2 | Dayton | A/ 300 | 59 | 35-24 |
| Fri. 6.28 | Jack Burns | Lost 7-5 | Dayton | A/ NA | 60 | 35-25 |
| Sat. 6.29[9] | Gus Weyhing | Won 4-2 | Columbus | A/ 834 | 61 | 36-25 |
| Sun. 6.30 | Harvey Bailey | Won 7-5 | Columbus | A/ 1,806 | 62 | 37-25 |
| Mon. 7.01 | Harvey Bailey[10] | Won 6-5 | Columbus | A/ 449 | 63 | 38-25 |
| Wed. 7.03 | Harvey Bailey | Won 6-0 | Indianapolis | H/ 800 | 64 | 39-25 |
| Th. 7.04 | Harvey Bailey[11] | Lost 8-7 | Indianapolis | H/ 3,500 | 65 | 39-26 |
| | Harvey Bailey | Won 7-5 | Indianapolis | H/ 3,000 | 66 | 40-26 |
| Fri. 7.05 | Chappel | Lost 5-4 | Dayton | H/ NA | 67 | 40-27 |
| Sat. 7.06 | Fred Luther | Won 3-2 | Dayton | H/ 1,800 | 68 | 41-27 |
| Sun. 7.07 | Harvey Bailey | Lost 6-3 | Dayton | H/ 3,000 | 69 | 41-28 |
| Tu. 7.09 | Fred Luther | Lost 3-0 | Indianapolis | A/ 526 | 70 | 41-29 |
| Wed. 7.10 | Harvey Bailey | Won 10-4 | Indianapolis | A/ 501 | 71 | 42-29 |
| Th. 7.11 | Fred Luther | Lost 4-2[12] | Indianapolis | A/ 533 | 72 | 42-30 |

| DATE | PITCHER | RESULT | OPPONENT | SITE/ ATT. | G | LOU. RECORD |
|---|---|---|---|---|---|---|
| Fri. 7.12 | Harvey Bailey | Lost 6-0 | Wheeling | A/ NA | 73 | 42-31 |
| Sat. 7.13 | Fred Luther | Won 3-1 | Wheeling | A/ NA | 74 | 43-31 |
| Mon. 7.15 | Harvey Bailey | Won 9-5 | Wheeling | A/ NA | 75 | 44-31 |
| Tu. 7.16 | Harvey Bailey | Lost 6-4 | Toledo | A/ NA | 76 | 44-32 |
| Wed. 7.17 | Jack Burns | Lost 10-3 | Toledo | A/ NA | 77 | 44-33 |
| Th. 7.18[13] | Harvey Bailey | Tied 2-2 (16) | Toledo | A/ NA | | |
| Fri. 7.19 | Fred Luther | Won 6-5 (12) | Marion | A/ 400 | 78 | 45-33 |
| Sat. 7.20 | Jack Burns | Won 6-5 | Marion | A/ 500 | 79 | 46-33 |
| Sun. 7.21 | Fred Luther | Lost 6-4 | Marion | A/ 1,800 | 80 | 46-34 |
| Mon. 7.22 | Harvey Bailey | Won 8-2[14] | Fort Wayne | A/ 300 | 81 | 47-34 |
| Tu. 7.23 | Jack Burns | Lost 8-5 | Fort Wayne | A/ 200 | 82 | 47-35 |
| Wed. 7.24 | Fred Luther | Won 7-5[15] | Fort Wayne | A/ 200 | 83 | 48-35 |
| Th. 7.25 | Harvey Bailey | Won 3-2 (10) | Fort Wayne | H/ 200 | 84 | 49-35 |
| Fri. 7.26 | Jack Burns | Lost 5-4 | Fort Wayne | H/ 400 | 85 | 49-36 |
| Sat. 7.27 | Jack Burns | Won 8-6 | Fort Wayne | H/ 1,200 | 86 | 50-36 |
| | Harvey Bailey | Lost 10-9 | Fort Wayne | H/ 1,200 | 87 | 50-37 |
| Sun. 7.28 | Harvey Bailey | Won 8-2 | Wheeling | H/ 3,000 | 88 | 51-37 |
| Mon. 7.29 | Fred Luther | Lost 9-0 | Wheeling | H/ NA | 89 | 51-38 |

| Date | Pitcher | Result | Opponent | Site/ Att. | G | Lou. Record |
|---|---|---|---|---|---|---|
| Tu. 7.30 | Jack Burns | Won 18-3 | Wheeling | H/ NA | 90 | 52-38 |
| Th. 8.01 | Harvey Bailey | Won 9-5 | Marion | H/ NA | 91 | 53-38 |
| Fri. 8.02 | Jack Burns | Won 3-1 | Marion | H/ NA | 92 | 54-38 |
| Sat. 8.03 | Harvey Bailey[16] | Won 4-3 | Marion | H/ 650 | 93 | 55-38 |
| Sun. 8.04 | Fred Luther | Lost 3-2 | Toledo | H/ 3,000 | 94 | 55-39 |
| Mon. 8.05 | Jack Burns | Lost 10-0 | Toledo[17] | H/ NA | 95 | 55-40 |
| Tu. 8.06 | Harvey Bailey | Lost 7-1 | Toledo | H/ NA | 96 | 55-41 |
| Fri. 8.09 | Harvey Bailey | Won 4-2 | Fort Wayne | A/ 400 | 97 | 56-41 |
| Sat. 8.10 | Jack Burns | Won 5-1 | Fort Wayne | A/ 300 | 98 | 57-41 |
| Sun. 8.11 | Harvey Bailey[18] | Won 11-10 | Fort Wayne | A/ 1,200 | 99 | 58-41 |
| Mon. 8.12 | Jack Burns | Won 6-2 | Marion | A/ 350 | 100 | 59-41 |
| Tu. 8.13 | Alberts | Lost 7-1 | Marion | A/ NA | 101 | 59-42 |
| Wed. 8.14 | Jack Burns | Won 6-4 | Marion | A/ NA | 102 | 60-42 |
| Th. 8.15 | Harvey Bailey | Won 10-9 | Toledo (12) | A/ NA | 103 | 61-42 |
| Fri. 8.16 | Jack Burns | Lost 10-3 | Toledo | A/ NA | 104 | 61-43 |
| Sat. 8.17[19] | Alberts | Lost 13-3 | Toledo | A/ NA | 105 | 61-44 |
|  | Hoff | Lost 11-6 | Toledo | A/ NA | 106 | 61-45 |

| Date | Pitcher | Result | Opponent | Site/ Att. | G | Lou. Record |
|---|---|---|---|---|---|---|
| Mon. 8.19 | Alberts | Lost 1-0 | Wheeling | A/ NA | 107 | 61-46 |
| Tu. 8.20 | Jack Burns | Won 8-3 | Wheeling | A/ 300 | 108 | 62-46 |
| Wed. 8.21 | Alberts | Lost 10-1 | Wheeling | A/ NA | 109 | 62-47 |
| Fri. 8.23 | Jack Burns | Lost 6-1 | Matthews | H/ NA | 110 | 62-48 |
| Sat. 8.24 | Fred Luther | Won 9-2 | Matthews | H/ NA | 111 | 63-48 |
| Sun. 8.25 | Jack Burns | Won 1-0[20] | Matthews | H/ 2,000 | 112 | 64-48 |
| Mon. 8.26 | Fred Luther | Lost 2-1 | Dayton | H/ NA | 113 | 64-49 |
| Tu. 8.27 | Jack Burns | Won 11-6 | Dayton | H/ 300 | 114 | 65-49[21] |
| Wed. 8.28 | Lunborn | Won 5-0 | Dayton | H/ NA | 115 | 66-49 |
| Th. 8.29[22] | Fred Luther | Won 10-0 | Columbus | H/ NA | 116 | 67-49 |
| Fri. 8.30 | Harvey Bailey | Won 6-5 | Columbus | H/ 900 | 117 | 68-49 |
| Sat. 8.31 | Fred Luther | Won 7-3 | Columbus | H/ NA | 118 | 69-49 |
| Sun. 9.01 | Jack Burns | Won 10-7 | Matthews | H/ 3,000 | 119 | 70-49 |
| | Harvey Bailey | Won 6-3 | Matthews | H/ 3,000 | 120 | 71-49 |
| Mon. 9.02 | Lunborn | Won 10-0 | Matthews | H/ 3,500 | 121 | 72-49 |
| | Fred Luther | Won 14-1 | Matthews[23] | H/ 3,500 | 122 | 73-49 |
| Wed. 9.04 | Harvey Bailey | Lost 2-0 | Dayton | A/ 400 | 123 | 73-50 |
| Th. 9.05 | Fred Luther | Lost 5-1 | Dayton | A/ 450 | 124 | 73-51 |
| Fri. 9.06 | Jack Burns[24] | Lost 8-7 | Dayton | A/ 700 | 125 | 73-52 |

| Date | Pitcher | Result | Opponent | Site/ Att. | G | Lou. Record |
|---|---|---|---|---|---|---|
| Sat. 9.07 | Harvey Bailey | Lost 7-3 | Columbus | A/ 379 | 126 | 73-53 |
| Sun. 9.08 | Fred Luther | Lost 4-0 | Columbus | A/ 2,200 | 127 | 73-54 |
| | Jack Burns | Lost 6-2 | Columbus | A/ 2,200 | 128 | 73-55 |
| Wed. 9.11 | Harvey Bailey | Won 10-4[25] | Wheeling | H/ NA | 129 | 74-55 |
| Th. 9.12 | Fred Luther | Won 5-3 (7) | Wheeling | H/ NA | 130 | 75-55 |
| Fri. 9.13 | (NA) | Won 10-3 | Fort Wayne | H/ NA | 131 | 76-55 |
| Sat. 9.14 | Fred Luther[26] | Won 8-6 | Fort Wayne | H/ NA | 132 | 77-55 |
| Sun. 9.15 | Harvey Bailey | Won 6-4 | Fort Wayne | H/ 1,600 | 133 | 78-55 |
| Tu. 9.17 | Harvey Bailey | Won 9-3[27] | Toledo | H/ NA | 134 | 79-55 |
| Wed. 9.18 | Fred Luther | Won 5-4 | Toledo | H/ NA | 135 | 80-55 |
| | (Forfeit) | Won 9-0 | Toledo | H/ NA | 136 | 81-55 |
| Sat. 9.21 | Harvey Bailey | Won 10-7 | Marion | H/ NA | 137 | 82-55 |
| Sun. 9.22 | Jack Burns | Won 18-8 | Marion | H/ NA | 138 | 83-55 |
| | Fred Luther | Won 7-1 | Marion | H/ NA | 139 | 84-55 |

Total: 84-55-1

Notes

1. Seven innings of relief for Harvey Bailey.
2. McMackin relieved Bailey in the fourth inning; under the rules of the time, he received the loss, not Bailey.

3. Game was called after seven innings on account of darkness and cold weather.
4. Game was called after eighth inning because of rain.
5. Exact attendance unlisted; crowd was described as "very small."
6. Jack Burns was relieved in the fifth inning after Meekin had given up seven runs. Burns pitched scoreless relief.
7. In relief of Jouett Meekin, who gave up five runs in the fourth inning.
8. Toledo's starting pitcher was ill-fated and eventual Hall of Famer Addie Joss.
9. First listing as Grand Rapids.
10. In relief of Burns.
11. In relief of Burns.
12. Quit game at the end of the seventh inning to catch a train.
13. Game called after sixteen innings due to darkness.
14. Went into first place, replacing Muncie.
15. Regained first place.
16. Save; win went to Fred Luther.
17. Winning pitcher: Addie Joss.
18. In relief of Alberts.
19. Went into second place; Toledo went into first place.
20. Reported as a no-hitter.
21. LCJ mistake starts here; reported W-L total as 65-50.
22. Went back into first.
23. Game called after six innings due to darkness
24. In relief of Harvey Bailey.
25. Game called after seven innings due to rain.
26. In relief of Harvey Bailey.
27. Went back into first place.

## 1901 Western Association Standings

There are three main sources for Western Association minor-league standings. They are listed below.

*The Minor League Baseball Encyclopedia*, edited by Lloyd Johnson and Miles Wolff (Durham, NC: Baseball America, 1993)

| Standings | W | L | Pct. | GB | Manager |
|---|---|---|---|---|---|
| Louisville Colonels/ Grand Rapids (MI) #2 | 84 | 54 | .609 | | Walter Wilmot |
| Dayton (OH) Old Soldiers | 84 | 55 | .604 | ½ | William Armour |
| Toledo (OH) Mud Hens | 78 | 61 | .564 | 6½ | Charles Strobel |

| | | | | | |
|---|---|---|---|---|---|
| Grand Rapids Woodworkers#1/Wheeling (WVA) Stogies | 70 | 64 | .522 | 12 | George Ellis/ Bill White |
| Fort Wayne Railroaders | 74 | 68 | .521 | 12 | George Miller |
| Indianapolis Hoosiers/ Matthews | 57 | 79 | .419 | 26 | Bill Watkins |
| Columbus (OH) Senators | 55 | 86 | .390 | 30½ | Frank Metz/ Jimmy Gardner/Ed Zinram |
| Marion (IND) Glass Blowers | 53 | 88 | .376 | 32½ | Pat Wright |

NEWSPAPER STANDINGS

| | |
|---|---|
| Grand Rapids #2 /Louisville | 84-54 |
| Dayton | 83-55 |
| Toledo | 77-60 |
| Fort Wayne | 75-66 |
| Wheeling /Grand Rapids #1 | 71-70 |
| Indianapolis/Matthews | 57-74 |
| Columbus | 53-87 |
| Marion | 53-88 |

STANDINGS COMPILED BY RAYMOND NEMEC, AMERICA'S LEADING MINOR-LEAGUE EXPERT

| | |
|---|---|
| Dayton | 85-55 |
| Louisville/Grand Rapids#2 | 84-55-1 |
| Toledo | 78-65-3 |
| Grand Rapids #1/Wheeling | 76-64 |
| Fort Wayne | 74-68 |
| Indianapolis/Matthews | 57-81-4 |
| Columbus | 55-96-1 |
| Marion | 53-87-1 |

**1901 Louisville Western Association Minor-League Starters Roster**
(Louisville Statistics Only)

| | |
|---|---|
| Pitchers (Co-Aces) | LHP Harvey Bailey (15-4) |
| | RHP Gus Weyhing (15-6) |
| Catcher | John Zalusky (60 games, .236) |
| First base | Jack Grim (1b, 55 games, .255) |
| Second Base | William Evans (61 games, .232) |
| Shortstop | George Smith (61 games, .246) |
| Third base | Elmo Jacobs (61 games, .284) |
| Left Field | Jack Lally (60 games, .293) |
| Center Field | Claude McFarland (53 games, .300) |
| Right Field | Walt Wilmot (59 games, .311) |

**Principal Roster: 1901 Louisville Western Association Minor-League Team**
(Louisville Statistics Only)

Bailey, Harvey (LHP, 21 games, 15-4, .250)
Blake, Harry (OF, .000, 1 game)
Burns, Jack "Farmer" (OF-RHP; 16 games, 2-2, .233)
Evans, William (2B, 61 games, .232)
Grim, Jack (1B, 55 games, .255)
Jacobs, Elmo (3B, 61 games, .284)
Lally, Daniel J. "Jack" (OF, 60 games, .293)
McFarland, Claude (OF; 53 games; .300; also spelled McFarlan)
McKenna, James W. (RHP; 2 games, 0-2, .000)
McMackin, Sam (LHP; 6 games, 2-3, .350; frequently identified as "McMahon")
Meekin, Jouett (RHP-1B-OF; 12 games, 0-5, .122)
Parker, Harley P. (RHP; 4 games, 1-3, .286)
Smith, George "Germany" (SS, 61 games, .246)
Vetter, George (RHP; 1 game, 1-0, .250)
Vetter, Philip (C, 1 game, .000)
Weyhing, Gus (RHP, 21 games, 15-6, .197)
Wilmot, Walter (OF/Manager, 59 games, .311)
Zalusky, John F. (C, 60 games, .236)

# A Statistical Look at a Minor-League "Lifer": Nick Polly

| Year | Club | League | Pos | G | AB | R | H | TB | 2B | 3B | HR | RBI | SB | BA |
|---|---|---|---|---|---|---|---|---|---|---|---|---|---|---|
| 1935 | Davenport | Western | 1B-3B | 115 | 425 | 66 | 129 | 169 | 27 | 5 | 1 | 46 | 10 | .304 |
| 1936 | Davenport | Western | 3B | 114 | 437 | 82 | 121 | 173 | 26 | 7 | 4 | 52 | 4 | .277 |
| 1937 | Elmira | NY-PA | 3B | 3 | 5 | 0 | 0 | 0 | 0 | 0 | 0 | 0 | 0 | .000 |
|  | Dayton | Mid-Atl | 3B | 92 | 334 | 81 | 114 | 181 | 21 | 5 | 12 | 87 | 8 | .341 |
|  | Brooklyn | National | 3B | 10 | 18 | 2 | 4 | 4 | 0 | 0 | 0 | 2 | 0 | .222 |
| 1938 | Dallas/ OK City/ Fort Worth | Texas | 3B-2B | 83 | 248 | 22 | 60 | 73 | 8 | 1 | 1 | 27 | 1 | .242 |
| 1939 | (Out of organized baseball) |  |  |  |  |  |  |  |  |  |  |  |  |  |
| 1940 | Columbia | South Atl | 3B | 49 | 161 | 26 | 48 | 73 | 11 | 1 | 4 | 29 | 0 | .298 |
| 1941 | Columbia | South Atl | 3B | 133 | 480 | 81 | 145 | 215 | 20 | 4 | 14 | 84 | 5 | .302 |
| 1942 | B'ham | South Assn. | 3B-2B | 153 | 544 | 111 | 146 | 208 | 30 | 7 | 6 | 78 | 8 | .268 |
| 1943 | B'ham | South Assn. | 3B | 121 | 411 | 90 | 125 | 194 | 34 | 4 | 9 | 71 | 3 | .304 |
| 1944 | L'ville | Amer Assn. | 3B | 149 | 486 | 110 | 141 | 243 | 24 | 9 | 20 | **120** | 9 | .290 |
| 1945 | Boston | American | 3B | 4 | 7 | 0 | 1 | 1 | 0 | 0 | 0 | 1 | 0 | .143 |
|  | L'ville/ Toledo | Amer Assn. | 3B-OF | 118 | 379 | 65 | 119 | 169 | 23 | 0 | 9 | 65 | 5 | .314 |

* Bold font indicates led or tied for league leadership in that category.

Polly, Nicholas Joseph (Nick)
SURNAME AT BIRTH: Polachanin
BORN: April 18, 1917, Chicago, Illinois
DIED: January 17, 1993, Chicago, Illinois
HEIGHT: 5 feet, 11 inches
WEIGHT: 190 pounds
GRADUATED: Lane Tech High School, 1934
HOME ADDRESS (1945): 2331 North Leavitt Street, Chicago, Illinois
Batted and threw right
NOTES: Played semipro baseball for the Chicago Mills team in 1934.

Statistics courtesy of Ray Nemec.

## LOUISVILLE'S ALL-TIME MAJOR-LEAGUE TEAM AND MINOR-LEAGUE TEAMS

MAJOR-LEAGUE (1876–1899)

PITCHERS: Jimmy Devlin, Guy Hecker, Toad Ramsey, Deacon Phillippe
CATCHER: Pop Snyder
FIRST BASE: Dan Brouthers
SECOND BASE: Hub Collins
SHORTSTOP: Honus Wagner
THIRD BASE: Jimmy Collins
OUTFIELD: Pete Browning, Chicken Wolf, Dummy Hoy, Fred Clarke
MANAGERS: John McCloskey and Fred Clarke*
*Playing Manager

MINOR-LEAGUE (1902–2001)
(List restricted to minor-league "lifers" or high-impact major-league players.)

PITCHERS: RH Frank "Dixie" Davis, Grover Cleveland Lowdermilk, Dolf Luque, Jake Northrop, Ken Penner, Ben Tincup, Todd Worrell (reliever); LH Nick Cullop, Mickey McDermott, Ambrose Puttmann
CATCHER: Carlton Fisk, Todd Zeile, Billy Meyer
FIRST BASE: Jay Kirke

SECOND BASE: Billy Herman
SHORTSTOP: Harold "Pee Wee" Reese
THIRD BASE: Frank Malzone
OUTFIELD: Earle Combs, Joe Guyon, Merito Acosta, Jimmy Piersall, George Whiteman, Vince Coleman, Adam Dunn
MANAGERS: Joe McCarthy, Jim Fregosi
RESERVES: 2B Bruno Betzel, 1B-OF-2B Anthony Vincent "Bunny" Brief, 1B Edgar Dudley "Dud" Branom, 1B Cecil Cooper, OF Dwight Evans, OF Herman Layne, OF Willie McGee, SS Johnny Pesky, 3B Nick Polly, OF Melbern "Butch" Simons, OF Willie Tasby, OF Taft Wright, OF Dmitri Young (note new alignment)

## KENTUCKY-BORN HALL OF FAMERS

James Paul David "Jim" Bunning (b. October 23, 1931/Southgate)
Albert Benjamin "Happy" Chandler (b. July 14, 1898/Corydon; d. June 15,1991/ Versailles, Kentucky)
Earle Bryan Combs (b. May 14, 1899/Pebworth; d. July 21, 1976/ Richmond, Kentucky)
Harold Herman "Pee Wee" Reese (b. July 23, 1918/Ekron; d. August 14, 1999/Louisville)

# Bibliography

Alexander, Charles C. *Our Game: An American Baseball History*. New York: Henry Holt and Company, 1991. *The Baseball Encyclopedia*. New York: Macmillan Publishing Company, 1996.

Cohen, Richard, and David S. Neft. *The World Series: Complete Play-by-Play of Every Game, 1903–1985*. New York: Collier Books, 1986.

Creamer, Robert W. *Babe: The Legend Comes to Life*. New York: Simon & Schuster, 2005.

Dewey, Donald, and Nicholas Acoccela. *The Encyclopedia of Major League Baseball Teams*. New York: HarperCollins, 1993.

Johnson, Lloyd, ed. *The Minor League Register*. Durham, NC: Baseball America, Inc., 1994.

Johnson, Lloyd, and Miles Wolff, eds. *The Minor League Baseball Encyclopedia*. Durham, NC: Baseball America, Inc., 1994.

Kleber, John. *The Encyclopedia of Louisville*. Lexington: University Press of Kentucky, 2001.

———. *The Kentucky Encyclopedia*. Lexington: University Press of Kentucky, 1992.

Neft, David S., Richard M. Cohen and Michael L. Neft. *The Sports Encyclopedia: Baseball 2000*. New York: St. Martin's Griffin, 2002.

Nemec, David. *The Beer and Whiskey League*. New York: Lyons & Burford, 1995.

———. *The Great American Baseball Team Book*. New York: Signet, 1993.

———. *The Great Encyclopedia of 19th-Century Major League Baseball*. New York: Donald I. Fine Books, 1997.

———. *The Ultimate Baseball Book*. Edited by Harris Lewine and Daniel Okrent. Boston: Houghton-Mifflin, 1991.

O'Neal, Bill. *The American Association: A Baseball History, 1902–1991*. Austin, TX: Eakin Press, 1991.

Seymour, Harold. *Baseball: The Early Years*. New York: Oxford University Press, 1960.

Solomon, Burt. *The Baseball Timeline*. New York: DK Publishing, 2001.

Sullivan, Neil J. *The Minors*. New York: St. Martin's Press, 1990.

Von Borries, Philip. *American Gladiator: The Life and Times of Pete Browning*. Bangor, ME: Booklocker Publishing Company, 2007.

———. *Ameridi (American Diamonds): An American Baseball Reader*. Bangor, ME: Booklocker Publishing Company, 2008.

———. *Louisville Diamonds*. Paducah, KY: Turner Publishing Co., 1997.

## Special Sources

*King of Sports* (pamphlet by the Thoroughbred Racing Associations)

*Louisville Courier-Journal*

*Louisville Evening Post*

*Louisville Times*

Ray Nemec (American minor league baseball statistics)

# Index

## M



## N

## X



## Y



## Z

# About the Author

Philip Von Borries is the author of four other baseball books: *Louisville Diamonds*; *American Gladiator: The Life and Times of Pete Browning*; *Ameridi: An American Baseball Reader*; and *Legends of Louisville*. His baseball bylines have appeared in the *Boston Red Sox Program Magazine*, *Oakland Athletics Magazine*, the *Chicago Cubs Program Magazine*, the *Washington Times*, *Sports Collectors Digest* and *Oldtyme Baseball News*.

His baseball background also includes historical work on Pete Browning's new grave marker, dedicated in 1984 during the centennial anniversary of the Louisville Slugger bat. Most recently, he was a contributor to David Nemec's landmark baseball book, *Baseball Bios: The Early Years, 1871–1900*.

One of the few turfwriters to have won both the Eclipse Award (thoroughbred racing) and the John Hervey Award (harness racing), Von Borries has written for numerous American, Canadian and European publications, among them the *Thoroughbred Record*, the *Kentucky Derby Magazine*, the *European Racehorse*, the *Thoroughbred Times*, the *Blood-Horse*, the *Daily Racing Form*, *Turf & Sport Digest*, *Hoofbeats* and the *Standardbred*.

The author of *Racelines*, a horse racing anthology, he has done extensive publicity for the Arlington Million and the Kentucky Derby and television production work on the latter for ABC-TV. He also appeared as an extra in three horse racing movies—*Sylvester*, *Seabiscuit* and *Dreamer*.

In addition to baseball and horse racing, Von Borries has also written on a variety of other topics, including film, photography, art, science fiction and true crime. His fiction includes one published short story, "Savior" (original title, "Smokeout").

Philip Von Borries can be reached at his website: www.eclipse-bbhr.com.